The 1st Volunteer Cavalry Regiment, perhaps the shortest-lived yet most legendary of American army units, at parade drill shortly before being mustered out at Montauk, Long Island. The commander of these "Rough Riders," Colonel Theodore Roosevelt, wearing a light khaki uniform, is leading the group of mounted officers at right.

Theodore Roosevelt Collection, Harvard College Library

BIRTH OF THE
AMERICAN CENTURY

CENTENNIAL HISTORY

SPANISH~
AMERICAN WAR

By Ron Ziel

"THE RESULTS OF THIS WAR HAVE BEEN MORE FAR-REACHING THAN THOSE OF ANY OTHER WAR IN MODERN TIMES. WE HAVE AWAKENED TO FIND OURSELVES ONE OF THE GREAT POWERS OF THE WORLD."

-Nelson A. Miles, Major General, **Commanding United States Army, 1898**

Commodore George Dewey's flagship, *USS Olympia* had just been repainted in combat gray while moored at Hong Kong with the U.S. Navy Asiatic Squadron in April, 1898. Within days the Spanish-American War began and this ship led the attack which would become the most complete naval victory in history.

U.S. Naval Historical Center

BIRTH OF THE AMERICAN CENTURY

CENTENNIAL HISTORY OF THE SPANISH-AMERICAN WAR

By Ron Ziel   Edited by Jedidiah Clauss

AMEREON HOUSE
Mattituck, New York, U.S.A.

SUNRISE SPECIAL LTD.
Bridgehampton, New York, U.S.A.

Dedication

To my young nephews, Paul, Aaron, and Brian Ziel, hoping that they and their generation will acquire a renewed interest in American history, this book is dedicated.

Other Books Written by the Author

THE TWILIGHT OF STEAM LOCOMOTIVES

THE STORY OF STEAMTOWN AND EDAVILLE

STEEL RAILS TO THE SUNRISE
(with George H. Foster)

STEAM IN THE SIXTIES (with George H. Foster)

STEEL RAILS TO VICTORY

SOUTHERN STEAM SPECIALS (with Mike Eagleson)

THE TWILIGHT OF WORLD STEAM
(with Mike Eagleson)

LONG ISLAND HERITAGE, THE G-5

THE PENNSY ERA ON LONG ISLAND

ELECTRIC HERITAGE OF THE L.I.R.R.
(With John Krause)

VICTORIAN RAILROAD STATIONS OF LONG ISLAND (with Richard B. Wettereau)

THE L.I.R.R. IN EARLY PHOTOGRAPHS

MAINLINE STEAM REVIVAL

AMERICAN LOCOMOTIVES IN HISTORIC PHOTOGRAPHS

STEAM BENEATH THE RED STAR
(with Nils Huxtable)

Acknowledgments

There were many helpful individuals who assisted the author in various institutions credited in this book; some and other notable ones are named below. Dr. John Allen Gable, Executive Director, Theodore Roosevelt Association, who wrote the Introduction, read the manuscript, and advised and encouraged the author. Edwin C. Finney, Jr., of the U.S. Naval Historical Center, spent hours locating photographs and information and in long telephone conversations, as well as editing the Naval half of the book. Paul Eugene Camp of the Tampa Campus Library, University of South Florida, not only supplied information, but shot good-quality copy negatives of important 1898 photographs. Anthony T. Rosalia, a Spanish-American, one of whose ancestors, a Spanish officer, fought the U.S., assisted in important ways, including reading the manuscript and telephoning the Biblioteca Nacional in Madrid. Isabel Ortega, head of the photographic section of Biblioteca Nacional, expedited matters the best she could during a national photographers' strike! Margaret Vining of the Smithsonian Institution who made the Charles Johnson Post paintings available. Eric Fellows, who provided information and photographs concerning the *USS Oregon*. Wallace Finley Dailey, curator of the Theodore Roosevelt Collection, Harvard University's Houghton Library. Sandor B. Cohen, Assistant Director of the National Museum of American Jewish Military History. The Center for Cuban Studies in New York. Julie M. Pavri, Archivist of the Foundation of the New York State Nurses Association. Arthur J. Huneke, who supplied the newspapers of the *USS Maine* affair. Vincent F. Seyfried furnished Philippine Insurrection information. The Army-Navy Club, Washington, D.C. Typeset by Overnight Type, Cutchogue, N.Y.

Art direction, design, and paste-up work by Ron Ziel.
Translation of Spanish language documents by Anthony T. Rosalia.

Manufactured in the United States of America

International Standard Book Number 0-8488-1735-4

Table Of Contents

National Archives

American soldiers manning a sandbag road checkpoint on Luzon, Philippine Islands, 1899.

INTRODUCTION

To mark the centennial of the Spanish-American War, Ron Ziel, the noted and respected author of some 15 books on railroads, decided to write a comprehensive narrative history of the war of 1898. This book is intended for the general reader, and emphasizes the military history and the day-to-day events of the brief but important 1898 war. Ziel's attention to detail will make this book a useful reference, and such a work is needed as we consider the significance of this war. Ziel is doubtless correct in seeing the war as a turning point in world history.

The Spanish-American War ended Spanish rule over Cuba, Puerto Rico, and the Philippines, and established the United States as a major world power. For Cuba the Spanish-American War meant the successful conclusion of the island's long and bloody struggle for independence. For the Philippines, however, the war was only a step forward on what would be a long and tortured road that eventually led to independence in 1946, when the United States ended control of its largest possession. For Puerto Rico the war of 1898 marked the beginning of a career as a territory of the U.S., a relationship which a century later shows no signs of ending. While the war brought a conclusion to the Spanish empire in the Americas and the Pacific dating back to the days of Columbus, the conflict ushered in U.S. imperialism in the same regions. It is the question of American imperialism above all that makes the Spanish-American War one of the most controversial conflicts in U.S. history. But American imperialism was not the most important result of the war. The American empire was to be limited, and was always small potatoes compared with the empires of other powers. It was the rise of the U.S. to the status of world power that was in the long run the most important consequence of the war. The century that followed was most turbulent, and the role of the U.S. was crucial in deciding two world wars and the long Cold War. As we approach the centennial of the Spanish-American War, the world is relatively calm, a phase in world history seems to have ended, and Americans and others are afforded the opportunity to look back to 1898 and the rise of the U.S. as a world power. Ziel's work will help with this look at the start of what has been called the "American Century."

Not the least of the consequences of the war of 1898 was the elevation of George Dewey and Theodore Roosevelt to the role of popular heroes of the American people. While Admiral Dewey's part in the war was, of course, far more important than that of Colonel Roosevelt from a military standpoint, it was T.R. who would soon become Commander in Chief. Admiral Dewey won respect and honor for the U.S. Navy, and is a symbol of the competence, professionalism and importance of the American Navy in the years after 1898. For Colonel Roosevelt, his brief career as a Rough Rider won him first the governorship of New York in the fall of 1898 when he returned from Cuba, and then the vice presidency and the White House. T.R.'s popularity as a war hero was a weapon the Rough Rider could use against the conservatives in his Republican Party who had sought to destroy him at every turn since his election to the New York State Assembly in 1881. There was no stopping T.R. after the Cuban campaign.

Theodore Roosevelt's image as a cavalry colonel completed the persona of the outdoor man of action first seen by the public in the 1880's when Roosevelt was for a time a rancher in the Dakota Badlands; and, indeed, the idea for the 1st Volunteer Cavalry Regiment grew out of Roosevelt's experiences in the wild west. The Rough Rider image helped offset three facts about T.R. that were decidedly not political assets: T.R. was an Eastern aristocrat, he was an intellectual who wrote books, and he was by profession a politician and government bureaucrat. It is perhaps only poetic justice that the image of the Rough Rider would later hurt Roosevelt's historical reputation.

The Spanish-American War had other heroes, as BIRTH OF THE AMERICAN CENTURY shows, some neglected at the time, like the brave African-American "buffalo soldiers," the embattled Cuban insurgents, and others, like Richmond P. Hobson, old Joe Wheeler, Winfield S. Schley and Leonard Wood, who were famous at the time but are largely unknown by the American public today. Ziel's narrative helps to bring alive all these men who played such important parts in a war that is the most decisive and complete victory of any war in American history. There was incompetence both in Washington and among the top military commanders, as Ziel notes. But the vast majority of Americans in the war did the job their country asked them to do with bravery and distinction; and it was not an easy job. The Spanish-American War, as one veteran later put it, was no "tinfoil" affair. Ziel's book helps recapture the color, drama, and immediacy of this action-packed but brief war.

Humans are timekeepers, and clock and calendar watchers who try to capture, codify, and comprehend reality by numbers, dates, and anniversaries, which particularly centennials and their multiples, have a special significance for us. These centennials provide us with the occasions to look back, revisit, and reconsider the past. The centennial of the Spanish-American War of 1898 gives us the opportunity to go back to the beginnings of the era of American global involvement, and BIRTH OF THE AMERICAN CENTURY can be an important part of efforts to understand those beginnings.

It was a "splendid little war," said Secretary of State John Hay of the Spanish-American War. Today most of us understandably recoil at the use of the word "splendid" in connection with war. But in rejecting Hay's characterization, it is in turn our responsibility to decide or suggest what should be the bottom-line assessment of that war. That is our proper assignment collectively as Americans as we mark the centennial of 1898.

John Allen Gable
Executive Director
Theodore Roosevelt Association
Oyster Bay, New York, U.S.A.

Immediately after consolidating their position on San Juan Hill, a troop of Rough Riders posed triumphantly with their colonel. Roosevelt was particularly pleased with the big Navy revolver on his hip; it had been salvaged from the wreckage of the *USS Maine,* and during the heavy fighting on July 1, he used it to kill a Spaniard who was taking aim at him just a few yards away. Long after T.R.'s death, his self-saving revolver was stolen.

7

This painting, by Spanish naval surgeon Alfonso Saenz, embodies the spirit and action of the Battle of Santiago Bay, July 3, 1898. Dr. Saenz, whose ship went down under U.S. Navy gunfire, shows the American blockade squadron off the south Cuban coast closing with the emerging Spanish fleet. Commodore Winfield Scott Schley's flagship *USS Brooklyn* is prominent in the foreground. All painters of such naval battles have to employ ar-

tistic license, showing the combatant ships much too close — the vessels of each flotilla were actually spaced much further apart, as well as there being two to four miles distance between the two fleets, rather than just a thousand yards, as shown here. Had Saenz been accurate, only the *Brooklyn* would have been prominent, with the other American ships much smaller and the Spanish vessels mere specks on the horizon.

Ron Ziel photo; courtesy of Army-Navy Club

FOREWORD

There are, in the course of the development of great nations, certain pivotal events that are remembered by generations unborn — even centuries into the future — and are well-known to every school pupil. The French defeat of the Saracens at Tours in 732 A.D. halted the advance of Islam into Western Europe, curtailing the greatest threat to Christian civilization. The defeat of the Spanish Armada in 1588, cleared the seas for Great Britain to eventually become the world's premier naval power. The expedition of American Admiral Matthew Perry to Japan in the early 1850s opened that insular nation to world trade, culture and eventual great power status. By sending Vladimir I. Lenin to St. Petersburg disguised as a railway locomotive fireman in 1917, the Germans inadvertently cleared the way for the Russian Bolshevik Revolution to expand into the international Communist tide which would threaten the world during the last half of the 20th century.

Then there was the Spanish-American War of 1898. "The Spanish-American War?" the average turn-of-the-21st Century American may ask, straining at recall, "Oh, isn't that when Teddy Roosevelt charged up San Juan Hill in Cuba?" Well, yes it was. It was also when Commodore George Dewey scored the greatest one-sided naval victory of all time when his squadron destroyed the Spanish fleet in Manila Bay. Most important, it was the War with Spain that thrust the United States of America from its status as a strong — but merely regional — country to one of the six major world powers. What had taken most European nations a century or longer, hundreds of thousands of casualties, and billions of dollars to accomplish, the United States had achieved in four months, less than 1,000 combat dead, and 300 million dollars! Only England, France, Germany, Russia, and Japan rivaled the U.S. which had seized control of the Caribbean Sea, much of the North Atlantic Ocean, and a 10,000-mile arc across the Pacific Ocean, from the coast of Alaska to Mexico, westward past Hawaii, all the way to the Philippine archipelago, at a longitude running through China to the north and Australia to the south. The brief, inexpensive, nearly forgotten, and universally misunderstood Spanish-American War was — in many salient respects — the second most important war in American history. Only the Revolutionary War, which resulted in the U.S. becoming an independent country, was of greater significance than the conflict of 1898 which had overnight altered the world balance of power and had laid the groundwork for the great catastrophic events of the 20th century. Other wars in America's development have been far more costly in terms of human suffering, fortune, and material — the Civil War, the World Wars, and the Korean War — but all they accomplished was to restore the *status quo*, and the Vietnam War which was a reversal. Because of America's total victory over Spain, at the birth of the American century only England dominated a larger share of the surface of the Earth.

Politically, economically, and militarily, the U.S. had matured in the year 1898, ensuring its preeminence in the new century, a little over two years before its debut. The conquests and the enormous prestige gained by the U.S. in the war with Spain allowed America to set the agenda of world politics for much of the next 100 years. Aided by the fact that Colonel Theodore Roosevelt, one of the heroes of the war, became president just three years later, the U.S. began to immediately *behave* like a great world power, although far more benevolently than virtually all of the others. President Roosevelt, who had been the McKinley Administration's first Assistant Secretary of the Navy, continued to build up the fleet while actively encouraging the development of the submarine and envisioning the aircraft carrier. He dug the Panama Canal, keeping it under American control, asserted his bold "Big Stick" foreign policy by sending "The Great White Fleet" around the world, and did not hesitate to threaten the German Kaiser with war for interfering in the Western Hemisphere. Contrary to the fears of many political leaders at home and abroad, that T.R. was a hip-shooting war-monger, he became the first American to win the Nobel Peace Prize for mediating the end of the 1904-05 Russo-Japanese War. His strong aggressive leadership became the foundation of American policies that would be emulated by all succeeding U.S. Presidents. The benignly imperialistic strategy that was the hallmark of Theodore Roosevelt was firmly rooted in his Spanish-American War experience.

With large American expeditionary ground and naval forces having been sent to points 9,000 miles apart so suddenly and simultaneously then returning totally victorious, the isolationism that along with the Civil War and the closing of the frontier had focused the perspective of Americans inward was mostly — but not entirely — jettisoned. America had accomplished her transcontinental "Manifest Destiny" by 1890, and the nation was prosperous and proud — but restless. For the first time, U.S. forces had accomplished what Europe's major countries were well accustomed to — projecting power over oceanic expanses, an exercise that would be repeated so often, right into the next millennium. Had it not been for the "splendid little war" of 1898, it is doubtful that the U.S. would have been of a temperament to become involved in World War I. America's sudden projection of power westward, all the way across the Pacific Ocean just as the Japanese Empire was expanding south and east, also ensured the inevitability of the conflict with Japan, a little more than four decades later. Indeed, long before the First World War, Theodore Roosevelt had warned that, while Germany was of immediate danger, the long-term threat to American security would be emanating from Japan.

The Spanish conquests and their cruel excesses over four centuries of harsh colonial rule, was the grist that the "Yellow Journalists" in America — particularly William Randolph Hearst and Joseph Pulitzer — used to whip the American population into a war frenzy. These and other factors leading up to the conflict will be covered; the main thrust of this volume will refer to the immediate causes, preparations, and combat operations of 1898 and the ensuing Philippine Insurrection on sea and land. Finally, an epilogue will summarize how the outcome of the Spanish-American War influenced major events of the 20th century and beyond. That was the importance and the legacy of the almost forgotten — yet so significant — four-month war of 1898.

Ron Ziel
Water Mill, New York, U.S.A.

With improved typesetting techniques made possible by the new Linotype machine, high-speed printing presses and the halftone reproducing of photographs and artwork, plus overseas telegraphic cable connections providing instant intercontinental communications, the modern mass-circulation urban daily newspaper was a reality just before the outbreak of the Spanish-American War. The leading American publishers and most unrelenting competitors in the biggest market of all — New York City — were Joseph Pulitzer and his *New York World* and William Randolph Hearst, owner of the *New York Journal.* It was also the time of the birth of the newspaper comic strip, the most popular early one being "The Yellow Kid," which ran in the *World,* until Hearst hired its creator to produce it for the *Journal.* Pulitzer immediately retained another cartoonist to do a rival "Yellow Kid" — a battle which thoroughly entertained the reading public, for the first time turning comic strips into news stories. Sensational newspaper coverage became known as "Yellow Journalism" because of the squabble over the "Yellow Kid." A contemporary cartoon shows Hearst wearing the frock of his pilfered "Kid," labeled "war circulation" on the hem and the legend "Hully gee, Spain tried to use de Joynal" scrawled across his belly.

A contemporary drawing shows the 16th century Spaniards in action, massacring the inhabitants of a native village in one of their Caribbean island conquests. Men, women, children, and babies all fell before the swords, pikes, muskets, and flames of the ruthless New World genocide so furiously practiced by the invaders. While mass violence was the most abhorrent cause of the extermination of the native populations, diseases carried by the conquerors also spread among the natives, at times resulting in epidemics which accounted for tens of thousands of lives and made the Spaniards' agenda simpler to carry out. Most of the mass atrocities were systematically committed in little over a half-century following the voyages of Columbus — a murderous record never exceeded in human history, not even by the bloodthirsty 20th century tyrants in Germany, the Soviet Union, Cambodia, China, and Bosnia.

Saint James (Santiago), a patron saint of Spain (numerous locations throughout the Spanish Empire were named Santiago in his honor) was often credited by the Spaniards for intervening against their enemies on their behalf. In an illustration by the renowned Spanish artist Francisco de Herrera (1576-1656), Iago charges out of heaven to lead a Spanish attack in the West Indies.

Spanish Colonialism

The voyages of Christopher Columbus in the last decade of the 15th century which resulted in the discovery and early exploration of the land masses of the Western Hemisphere — appropriately called "The New World" by Europeans, launched a half millennium of overseas colonization by every nation that was to acquire oceanic naval capabilities. Within 50 years it became evident that the fact that the great navigator's patrons had been King Ferdinand and Queen Isabella of Spain, rather than the rulers of virtually any other power, had set in motion one of the greatest human tragedies in history. Even as Columbus reported back to the royal court in Madrid that the natives of the Caribbean Islands he had explored were invariably friendly and hospitable. Indeed, they were docile and awed at the appearance of Columbus and his men — who some even worshipped as "children of the sun;" the *conquistadores* who followed were developing an agenda of maniacal genocide.

Soon the red and yellow flag of Spain came to be known as the herald of blood and gold, and the Spanish explorers shed rivers of the former to steal shiploads of the latter. The duplicity and treachery of the *conquistadores* against the Aztec and Inca empires is well known today, but there were few surviving witnesses to the horrible carnage against the hapless natives of the West Indies. Once colonial governments were established, the repressive tyrannical regimes were often able to keep the details of their travesties secret for generations — in many instances forever. Still, enough had emerged by the late 19th century to enrage and disgust the civilized world, especially the United States, whose close proximity to Cuba, where legalized barbarity was flourishing as nowhere else under European colonial dominion, riveted the attention of the appalled American public. Fanned by atrocities against American citizens and the sensationalism of the "yellow journalists" in the United States (although it seems unlikely that even William Randolph Hearst could exaggerate the reporting of Spanish excesses), war sentiment had been rising since the end of the Civil War, a third-century prior to the Spanish-American conflict.

Bereft of the science of modern psychology available a century later, civilized peoples of the late 1800s were at a loss to explain why Spanish authority had behaved so terribly for the past 400 years. In the enlightened eve of the third millennium it was deemed politically incorrect to ascribe certain unique characteristics — especially undesirable ones — to national, ethnic, or religious groupings. But what can explain how the Spaniards systematically used the cruelest methods of torture, slave labor and mass extermination to totally annihilate millions of peaceful and unthreatening natives of the islands and the North and South American continents, wherever their adventurers and gold seekers saw fit to conquer? The Caribbean island of Hispaniola was estimated in 1898 to have had a population of one million when Columbus arrived. Within a mere 10 years after it was subjugated by Spain, 94 percent of the natives — 940,000! — had been killed, including tens of thousands who had committed suicide after mercy killing their wives and children to escape the Spaniards and their dogs which were trained to tear their victims to pieces and eat them!

Many Spaniards of the late Middle Ages had become absolute religious fanatics and fancied themselves the chief defenders of the Roman Catholic Church. In a cynical warped fashion, even as they considered themselves superior to all others and reacted with absolute barbarism to any questioning of their authority or the slightest affront to their dignity, they invoked the name of God and the Catholic Church to justify their crimes against humanity. Whether it was the Inquisition on the European continent or in its overseas conquests, God sailed with the *conquistadores* and since He was at their side with legions of saints, any means they used to spread the Gospel (and not, incidentally, Spanish power and authority) were justified. In violation of all that Jesus Christ and His Gospel taught, the Spaniards would convert native chiefs to Christianity, then torture them to learn where their treasures were hidden. Once the information was given, the dogs were loosed upon the new "Christian brothers!" Do the Spaniards have an inherent national penchant for cruelty? A visit to that beautiful land and its hospitable people today would seem to belie such a theory, but the cruel sport of bullfighting is still the national pastime. Similarly, while Nazi genocide in Germany lasted but 12 years and most of Communism's murderous rampages ended after less than 75 years, that of Spain went on for centuries.

Even in the United States today, vestiges of the religious fervor of colonial Spain are found in such weirdly named places as Corpus Christi (Body of Christ), Texas and the Sangre de Cristo (Blood of Christ) Mountains in Colorado and New Mexico. Even at the grizzliest of the native mass murders, a Spanish monk would wave a crucifix in front of the victims and preach redemption, very strongly implying that the heinous crimes were sanctioned by the Heavenly Father and His Church! In 1808, Bishop Coke expressed the view that "Spain has had the honor of discovering the New World and the disgrace of murdering its inhabitants. The former of these deeds she effected through the genius of a daring and enlightened foreigner, but the latter through her own native spirit, trammelled by intellectual fetters and accustomed to blood."

As early as 1552, the Spanish author Bartolomé de Las Casas wrote a book entitled *The Destruction of the Indies,* which was published in Seville. He detailed the tyrannical crime wave which the *conquistadores* had loosed in the Western Hemisphere. By the end of the 16th century, the French translator Miggrode estimated that *40 million* natives had been killed by the Spaniards; a figure which, in light of 20th century research, seems to be astronomical by a figure of at least five-fold. But even if Miggrode was so far off in his calculations, the number still was of Hitlerian proportions or much worse, considering the overall population a half-millennium ago. That religion, politics and the quest for national riches are a potion of unspeakable barbarity is exemplified in some of the few detailed incidents to be recorded at the time. In plotting the murder of 13 tribal leaders, the Spaniards decided to crucify them in remembrance of Jesus and His 12 apostles; a particularly blasphemous warping of Christianity. In 1511, Spanish forces on Cuba captured a respected Indian chief named Hatuey and prepared to burn him at the stake. As the bundled wood faggots were stacked about Hatuey, a Franciscan monk told him of his final opportunity for salvation and eternal life in heaven. "Do Spaniards go to heaven?" Chief Hatuey enquired. "Yes, all who are good," was the earnest reply of the monk. Immediately the chief said that he would rather go to hell, so as not to be forever in a place where the accursed race of Spaniards were admitted, and so that he may never again set eyes on such cruel people.

Apparently, the population of Spain felt no remorse concerning the atrocities of their countrymen, for there seems to have been little indignation over such printed reports like the following, which were circulated at home: "…the skulls of the natives are so hard that the Spaniards often break their swords in twain when they attempt to cut open their heads." The inhuman policies made as little economic as moral sense, for the sugar and tobacco plantations required thousands of laborers, as did mining and manufacturing, loading and unloading ships and fishing and food production. One malevolent, sadistic policy was to round up native workers in groups of 300 and turn them over to planters and foremen as slave labor. So demoniac were the conditions under which the slaves were forced to work, that within three months, 90 percent may be dead, so the Spanish slave driver just sent armed men out to capture 300 more! The French encyclopedist Pierre Larousse reported that "The Indian race was not yet quite extinct in Cuba when Spain was already consulting to replace it by demanding of the uncultured countries of Africa new idolators to gain to the cause of Christ; that is, new victims to subject to the bondage of servile and enforced labor. God only knows to how many millions of victims amounts today the frightful figure of this abominable trade." The economic "bottom line" was that since the Spaniards had so callously murdered and worked their victims to death, they had to indulge in the enormously expensive slave trade from Africa. Perhaps they had learned a sordid lesson from the native

genocide, for although they grossly mistreated the African slaves, they apparently managed to control their more lethal impulses and did not quite kill the bondsmen.

In the late 19th century, as the situation in the remaining colonial empire of Spain (she had lost most of her Western Hemisphere possessions by the 1820s) continued to inflame opinion in most civilized societies, it was the ambivalence of the European powers that helped to maintain the status quo. On the one hand, the Americans were becoming increasingly bellicose in their outrage over Cuba, so it seemed that a war could erupt between the United States and Spain. The Europeans, although disgusted with the Spanish record, were not too happy at the prospect that America might just win and vastly extend its strength and influence in the process, even though few had any conflicts of interest with Spain. On the other hand, virtually all of the European governments totally underestimated the United States, its power and its idealism, and they did not relish the prospect of a Spanish victory, which could hurt their lucrative American trade and jeopardize the lives of millions of their countrymen who had emigrated to North America.

It was interesting to note how the Monroe Doctrine came into play concerning the Cuban crisis; some American imperialists argued that its opposition to European interference in Western Hemispheric affairs was applicable. Like most such broadly interpreted policies, the Monroe Doctrine could be construed either way, but President James Monroe's message to Congress on December 2, 1823, was prompted by a different set of circumstances than that which prevailed in the Caribbean 75 years later. After Simon Bolívar and José de San Martín led the revolutions which freed South America from Spanish rule, other European powers began to indicate an interest in acquiring some of the newly-independent republics, prompting the less than half-century-old U.S. government to venture into its first big aggressive foreign policy declaration. Also instigating Monroe's concern was the attempt of the Czarist government to exclude all but Russian ships from the Northwest coast of North America above the 51st parallel. Secretary of State John Quincy Adams formulated a principle that no new colonies could be established in the Western Hemisphere by foreign powers, prompting Monroe to convey the brash new policy to Congress almost exactly as Adams had presented it to the President: "The American continents, by the free and independent condition which they have assumed and maintained, are henceforth not to be considered as subjects for future colonization by any European powers."

Monroe's Doctrine, however, made no mention of *existing* colonies, only that the United States would oppose the seizure of *new* colonies by any foreign nation, so the colonies which Spain still retained after 1823 did not come under the aegis of Monroe's policy. (Indeed, in the 1960s, after Fidel Castro established a Communist dictatorship in

Cuba, some frustrated American leaders complained that the Monroe Doctrine had been violated, claiming that the Soviet Union had really taken charge.) Monroe's strongly-asserted policy was, at first, regarded with contempt and cynicism by the targets of its declaration, for the Europeans apparently had not intended to intervene in South America. For decades after its issuance, Monroe's policy was largely forgotten and the Americans even tolerated minor assaults on it, such as British moves in Central America and the taking by the United Kingdom of the Falkland Islands. In 1845, President James K. Polk revived the Monroe Doctrine when France and Great Britain objected to the U.S. annexation of Texas and regarding the Anglo-American dispute over Oregon. Continuing into the 1850s, American Presidents invoked the Doctrine in reference to various questions involving European meddling in Latin America. During the American Civil War, the Europeans took advantage of the internal battle for survival in the United States to challenge the Monroe Doctrine, the most flagrant being when France established the rule by Archduke Maximilian in Mexico. U.S. enforcement of the Doctrine during the Venezuelan Dispute with England during Grover Cleveland's administration could have led to a third Anglo-American conflict in little over a century, but it was settled peacefully, due largely to the mutual interests of the two ascending powers.

Although the weak attempts to apply the Monroe Doctrine to ending Spanish rule of Cuba did not gain much support, the growing influence of the policy and the high regard in which it was held by the American people helped to link the whole process of events and decisions by the American government leading up to the start of the Spanish-American War. So what if Spain possessed Cuba centuries before Monroe, many would argue; the sheer brutality of Spanish colonial oppression demanded that the spirit of his policy be invoked, if not the actual Doctrine itself.

In the first 300 years of colonizing the Western Hemisphere, Spain had committed indignities and atrocities against British, Dutch, French and other European governments; they had not done much marauding against them in the 1800s. With much heavier American commerce and influence in the Caribbean, it seemed almost inevitable that serious incidents would involve U.S. interests. The Spaniards, more than most Europeans, looked down contemptuously on Americans, considering them to be nothing more than money-mad cowboys, uncultured — and they were *Protestants!* Although there was awareness among Americans of the excesses of Spanish misrule in Puerto Rico, the Philippines and other possessions, it was to be Cuba, just 90 miles away, that would spark the conflict.

Spaniards enjoying the spectacle as their dogs tear the natives to pieces.

The Cuban Powder Keg

With Cuba being in such close proximity to the United States, escaping refugees often headed for American gulf ports, where they brought first-hand stories of the abysmal conditions they had just left behind (a circumstance that was to be repeated beginning in 1959, after the establishment of a Communist dictatorship by Fidel Castro) on the unfortunate island. Americans had cheered the revolutions that freed much of South America from Spanish rule in the 1820s, and once their own Civil War and the Indian Wars were over or in their twilight stages, they began actively aiding — indeed, sometimes participating in large numbers and with heavy equipment — the revolutionary activities in Cuba. That the United States vigorously enforced its neutrality laws, often intercepting shiploads of Cuban filibusterers (irregular military personnel engaging in unlawful revolutionary expeditions to a foreign country) further angered the American people. It may be that the Spanish authorities had the legal right to execute the Cuban revolutionaries and the Americans who assisted them, but the policy of extreme retribution and killing anyone even *suspected* of revolu-

tionary sympathies after being tried by "drumhead courts" — the "kangaroo courts" of the 19th century — was roundly condemned in the United States and Europe.

Incidents involving American citizens date back to pre-Civil War times. Narcisco López, a Venezuelan and former Spanish army officer, began attempting to liberate Cuba in 1848. He failed and fled to New York, where he raised sympathy and money for the cause of Cuban freedom. On August 12, 1851, López returned to Cuba with an armed force of 450 men, including Americans of which Colonel W.S. Crittenden of Kentucky, a Mexican War veteran, was a senior officer. With the 130 men under his command, Crittenden was attacked by a force of 500 Spaniards whom he routed, killing General Enna, the commander. Later overwhelmed by vastly superior forces, the López expedition scattered; Crittenden, attempting to reach New Orleans, was captured at sea and shot, along with 50 of his men. As a final act of heroism, Colonel Crittenden refused to kneel with his back to the firing squad, saying that he knelt only to God. Shot while proudly facing his execu-

---

Horses were plentiful in Cuba and the revolutionaries proved to be good riders, enabling them to field effective cavalry troops. They did not, however, carry traditional cavalry swords in battle. Instead, they were armed with machetes, the broad flat-blade cutting instruments many had known from boyhood as they cut sugar cane during the annual harvest. In two views of cavalry charges during the Three Years' War, with their carbines slung across their backs or in saddle holsters, Cuban cavalrymen charge out of the rain forest that provided them with excellent concealment, enabling them to repeatedly surprise their foes.

Opposite, T. de Thulstrup

Center for Cuban Studies

tioners, Crittenden's body and those of his men were then subjected to "all manner of indignity" according to an eyewitness account. Even greater indignity over the incident arose throughout the United States, but the growing disintegration of the Union focused the attention of Americans closer to home, giving Spain a few years' reprieve, time that she foolishly squandered by increasing rather than alleviating her harsh and bloody rule of Cuba.

Despite the seriously deteriorating sectionalism problem in the United States, earnest efforts continued on behalf of Cuban independence. In 1853, another famous Mexican War veteran, Major General John A. Quitman, then governor of Mississippi, sponsored an expedition to aid the Cuban patriots. Again enforcing the neutrality laws, the Federal government launched a suit against Quitman for complicity in the Lopez invasion, thereby aborting the new attempt. The hopeful Cubans who awaited the arrival of the Americans were rounded up by the Spaniards and shot, making Washington an unwitting accomplice in the Cuban terrorism. The 1861-1865 Civil War period curtailed virtually all American concern with Cuba, but no sooner had the rebellion ended when the United States again regained its indignant interest.

The most serious incident involving Americans occurred in 1873 and nearly precipitated a war between the United States and Spain. A small wooden side-wheeler flying the American flag, the *Virginius* may well have been on a filibustering mission to Cuba when she was seized in international waters by a Spanish cruiser and taken to Santiago, where Captain Joseph Fry, his crew and the passengers were condemned as pirates. On November 7, 1873, Fry, 36 of his crew and 16 of the passengers were executed by firing squad. The remaining 112 were literally spared at the last moment when Sir Lampton Lorraine, of the British ship *Niobe,* took it upon himself not only to represent his Queen, but the United States as well. Landing unannounced in Santiago, he threatened to bombard the city if the massacre of Americans was not immediately halted. His audacious courage saved the survivors and earned the gratitude of the American government.

After the *conquistadores* had massacred the native population of Cuba within a few decades after its discovery by Columbus, a new breed of "natives" — descendants of the earliest Spanish settlers, Creoles and Negroes (some of the latter free, but most still slaves) — became the resident citizenry. As the centuries passed and more generations separated the populace from their ancestral settlers, Spain found that "ever faithful" Cuba had become riddled with the spirit of rebellion — much as England had discovered in its North American colonies in the 1770s. Finally, in 1868, a major uprising, which lasted a decade and became known as the Ten Years' War, erupted, and to the chagrin of the mother country, it was led by some of the most prominent and wealthiest business and plantation owners. Sugar cane was rapidly becoming the world export crop of Cuba and the millionaire *azúcar* dons were not only patriotic Cubans who loathed the Spaniards for granting them absolutely no say in the affairs of their own country, but were being crushed by the ever-increasing tax burden imposed by Madrid. Again, in the manner of the *Norteamericanos* a century earlier, the grievous policy of "taxation without representation" acted like a bellows to the embers of revolt among the business community. The colonial authorities had hoped that the black slaves would rebel against their masters, but many of the planters, including the leader of the uprising, Carlos Manuel Céspedes, one of the richest Cubans, freed their slaves, and the newly freed men, patriots in their own right, often enlisted in the rebel cause and fought with distinction.

Business owners in Havana and other metropolitan centers, however, were more likely to be among the 200,000 resident Spaniards who were intensely dutiful to the Madrid government and who were to become, through the volunteer military units they formed, the most vicious and atrocious of Spain's loyalist forces. At the outbreak of the Ten Years' War, there were but 10,000 Spanish regulars, scattered in small garrisons throughout the island, incapable of defending the government prior to the arrival of tens of thousands more from Spain. The volunteer Spaniards on Cuba, having much to lose if the rebellion succeeded, were hastily organized into battalions. Well trained, armed with the finest new weapons and perhaps as motivated as the Cuban patriots, they soon went on a bloody rampage against the non-Spanish populace. In their actions and demeanor, the spirit of the *conquistadores* Cortez and Pizarro of more than 300 years previously, lived on.

In such fights for freedom, women often become directly involved in the conflict and Cuba saw its share of distaff bravery under fire. After witnessing the firepower of the Volunteers, many women sought refuge — then vengeance — against the perpetrators, especially after the Villanueva Theatre incident in Havana. It was early in the Ten Years' War, on January 22, 1869, that a company of Volunteers, apparently drunk, with their officers unable or unwilling to control them, and armed with new rifles obtained from a Spanish arsenal, opened fire on an unarmed theatre audience, composed mainly of middle- and upper-class Cuban families. After mowing down scores of men, women and children with repeated volleys, the Spaniards made an encore performance a few weeks later, at the nearby Louvre coffee house, then began a reign of terror, shooting indiscriminately into buildings in the Cuban neighborhoods. Women were repeatedly molested by the Volunteers, so many joined their husbands, fathers, brothers and fiancées in the forests and mountains, some as cooks, nurses and armorers in the camps. Many took up arms against their enemies. According to a contemporary account in *L'isle de*

Cuba, by Hippólyte Pirón, written during the Ten Years' War: "These implacable tyrants have inspired even the women of Cuba with the same lively hatred, as is manifest in all of their actions. These women . . . have been transformed into heroines by an overmastering love for their outraged country. Fighting . . . they display the most veritable valor, and give up their lives with the sublimest courage."

Pirón continued: "One day a dozen women, roaming through a forest, met, most unexpectedly, a column of the Volunteers. The lieutenant in command asked these ladies if they knew of any encampment in the vicinity and upon responding in the negative, they were bound two by two and carried off prisoners . . ." Later, a firefight with insurgents ensued and the Volunteers won the skirmish. The female captives were looking at the bodies ". . . and one, quickly recognizing her husband among the dead, betrayed her womanly weakness . . . casting herself upon the lifeless body . . . and covers it with her kisses and her tears. What does our lieutenant do? He orders his men to shoot these twelve women down upon the spot, and the barbarians execute the order instantly."

The bloody Ten Years' War dragged on inconclusively, leaving hundreds of thousands of casualties and hundreds of millions of dollars in war costs and destroyed property. Considering their difficulty in getting supplies and holding permanent garrisons, the *insurrectos* performed very well using classic guerilla tactics, severely

When the Spaniards wished to conserve gunpowder and sword blades or to impress the local populace with a ceremony of execution, they utilized a brusque and crude device of their own invention: the garrote. The condemned man was seated with his back against a vertical plank upon which was mounted a vice-like collar, with a screw mechanism protruding out the back. Since Spanish colonial authorities were rarely concerned with painless treatment of prisoners, a tightening of the screw resulted in the strangulation of the victim; by the 19th century it had been somewhat modified so that one quick turn would shatter the spinal column at the base of the brain, resulting in a quicker death. Garroting of prominent prisoners was usually done before a large public audience as a warning to rebel sympathizers, as in the case of the execution of Cuban patriot General Goicouria, shown in a contemporary engraving of the event at Havana, on May 7, 1870, during the Ten Years' War.

crippling the Spanish forces. By 1876, it was reported in Spain's national parliament, the Cortes, that 145,000 soldiers had been sent to Cuba from Spain and that not enough of the original troops remained to man a single regiment! The Cuban patriots had acquitted themselves well and had received important assistance from Americans and other sympathetic foreigners, but they too, were exhausted — and ready to accept a final act of treachery from the mother country. Even though Spain had carried out a "no prisoners" policy and had executed more than 40,000 political and military captives, while in most instances the Cubans disarmed their prisoners, then turned them loose, the rebels went into a negotiated settlement, the Treaty of El Zanjón, signed in February 1878. Subsequent reports claim that Spain never abided by the vaguely worded terms of the treaty, that she continued her brutal policies and that even first-generation children in Cuba, born of immigrants from Spain, considered themselves *insulares* (islanders) rather than *peninsulares* (from the Spanish peninsula) and grew up hating the mother country and her representatives.

With the Cuban *insurgentes* largely disarmed (although thousands of firearms and much ammunition had been secreted for future use) a demoralized populace of Cuba entered the 1880s still very much under the capricious and vindictive rule of the *peninsulares*. Sporadic incidents and sabotage were the norm, the former often dismissed as "insignificant Negro riots" by the authorities, and in 1888 another uprising failed due to a delay in the arrival of a filibuster expedition. Then, on February 24, 1895, the Cubans began their final bid for freedom, known as the Three Years' War, which was to be superseded by the American invasion in 1898.

The Cuban patriot, José Martí, led the 1890s insurrection in its early months, but was killed in an ambush. Throughout the first year, Spain brought in thousands of reinforcements as Cuban veterans of the Ten Years' War returned to join the ever growing guerrilla forces in the field. As in the earlier conflict, the rebels obtained most of their weapons, ammunition and supplies by attacking Spanish supply trains and convoys. Yellow fever proved once again to be their ally, afflicting mostly the Spaniards which had just arrived from home and were not acclimated to the tropical weather and diseases. By January 1896, much of the 800 mile-long island was securely under the control of the Cubans; most of the formidable Spanish units were holed up in the fortified cities, many isolated and impossible to resupply. Strong rebel units were attacking towns so close to Havana that the loyalists in the capital began to panic at the sight of distant smoke columns and the sound of both Cuban and Spanish artillery.

The Spaniard who ruled Cuba in the early 1890s was Captain General Arsenio Martínez Campos, a moderate by colonial standards, who became increasingly despised by the Volunteers and other military factions for his sometimes humane policies towards the *insulares* and the rebel soldiers. Demanding leadership who would reinstate the give-no-mercy policies of the recent past, Madrid responded by sending Captain General Valeriano

---

There were numerous skirmishes, hit-and-run guerilla raids and major battles involving cavalry and artillery units on both sides during the on and off 30 years' struggle for independence in Cuba. When a large detachment of marines from the Spanish gunboats *Alcedo* and *Vigia* went ashore near the mouth of the San Juan River, they were promptly ambushed by a strong force of Cubans concealed in the tall grass and trees on a hill overlooking the beach. It was to be the constant intense attacks by the *insurrectos* — operating in rough terrain that they knew so well and choosing times and places to their advantage — that inflicted heavy casualties on Spanish units, frustrating their commanders and demoralizing the soldiers.

Artwork by T. de Thulstrup

Weyler y Nicolau, Marquis of Tenerife, who became governor of Cuba on February 10, 1896. The *Westminster Review* reported that "Campos, having failed to satisfy the bloodthirsty cravings of his countrymen, was recalled, and returned to Spain to face unpopularity and the general abuse which was heaped upon him. His successor, General Weyler, interpreted far better the popular longing for an energetic policy — which meant nothing less than a savage scouring of a people who had dared to raise their voices against the violence of masters inherently sanguinary." When the United States Senate Committee on Foreign Relations called the author of a popular book, *The Real Condition of Cuba To-day* to testify, he was asked: "What justification do they (Spaniards) give for shooting women and children?" He answered: "The women might breed and the children may grow up." He added that the colonial authorities actually spoke in such terms.

"Weyler the Butcher" soon became very popular among the *peninsulares*, who believed that "with him in command, this policy of extermination will be carried out to its logical conclusion." "General Weyler . . . is our man," said a Spanish businessman in Santa Clara, "he is bloodthirsty and he is the man we want." Prime Minister Canovas del Castillo emphasized that "the government of His Majesty approves every act of General Weyler's policy in Cuba and accepts the fullest responsibility for him and his acts." Weyler's first proclamation concerned the *reconcentrado* policy of establishing concentration camps into which the local populace would be herded within the provinces under siege. The citizenry was given eight days to obey: "Any individual found outside the lines in the country at the expiration of this period shall be considered a rebel and shall be dealt with as such" — meaning that they will be shot. Weyler lived up to his reputation as his troops descended on villages, indiscriminately gunning down *pacíficos* — peaceful civilians — among them foreign nationals, including Americans. In the concentration camps food was scarce, medical care nonexistent and disease rampant; most of the weakened internees starved to death under the indifferent watch of Spanish guards. As Weyler led his army in the field in 1896 and 1897, thousands of noncombatants were shot on sight or consigned to the slower death of the camps. This, according to Weyler, was "the due process of military law."

During Weyler's reign of terror, as more than 400,000 Cuban civilian noncombatants were confined to the "starvation stations," the American people were contributing money and survival necessities to send to Cuba to alleviate the suffering. Lieutenant General Máximo Gómez, the aged commander of the Cuban Army, expressed his appreciation in a letter to President McKinley: "However true and minute may be the reports that you have heard, never will you be able to form a just conception of the bloodshed, the misery, the ruin, and the sorrow caused to afflicted

Cuba to obtain her independence, and how the despotic power of Spain, irritated to the last degree before the most just of all rebellions, has revelled in the most implacable destruction of everything, lives, and property. The nation which at one time accepted the Inquisition and invented its tortures lastly conceived the concentration scheme, the most horrible of all means, first to martyrize and then to annihilate an entire people; and if it has stopped in the path of destruction, it is due in great measure to the cry of indignation which the knowledge of such horrors unanimously has drawn from the States over which you govern."

Repeatedly defeated, the popularity of Weyler rapidly waned, and on October 31, 1897, his successor, Ramón Blanco, recently governor of the Philippines, arrived in Havana as the replacement governor and captain general of Cuba. "My policy will never include concentration," Blanco stated. "I fight the enemy, not women and children. I shall immediately extend the zones of cultivation and allow the *reconcentrados* to go out of the towns and till the soil."

Among the considerable number of Spanish soldiers who had deserted to the rebel side was Captain Don José Palacio, who, after fighting bravely, was captured with 15 of his men and, after handing over his sword, awaited a bullet to his head. To his amazement, Cuban General Antonio Maceo made a speech to his command, praising the defeated captain's bravery and returned his sword. Captain Palacio's reaction was to shout "*¡Viva Cuba Libre!*"; his men resounded the chorus and immediately joined the insurgents. As the fateful year of 1898 approached, the Cuban situation had become the primary concern of the U.S. President William McKinley, in his annual message at the end of 1897, informed the nation that intervention on humanitarian grounds had received his "most anxious and earnest consideration."

On January 24, 1898, the second-class American battleship the *USS Maine*, a staunch, fast vessel, frequently described as "the pride of the Navy of the United States," steamed out of Key West, Florida, with orders to Captain Charles D. Sigsbee to sail into Havana Harbor on "a visit of courtesy." While preparing for war, the U.S. government was still trying to maintain peace with Spain. And the last thing that the Spanish government wanted was a conflict with the regional coastal power so close to its rebellious colony. The Americans officially stated that the purpose of the visit was "simply the resumption of friendly naval relations with Spain" and the Spaniards were quite enthusiastically in favor of this gesture. Of course, the presence of the impressive warship also would send a message of naval power not to be ignored. Welcomed by multi-gun salutes from the forts and every Spanish war vessel, the *Maine* arrived triumphant in the harbor of the Cuban capital the next morning, but a violent destiny that was to lay the foundation of international politics and warfare throughout the following century awaited the peaceful visitor.

The side-wheel steamer *Virginius* (above) was run down on the high seas off Cuba in 1873 by the Spanish Navy, and the 165 officers, crew, and passengers on board were taken to Santiago de Cuba, where they were sentenced to death as filibusterers. Fifty-three were actually executed by firing squad (below) on November 7, including Captain Joseph Fry (left), before a Royal Navy captain intervened to save the rest. It was along the Alamenda Wall (opposite top), pock marked by thousands of bullets over many years, that the Spaniards executed prisoners, including the Americans from the *Virginius*, at Santiago. The detail (opposite, center) of the sign on the wall reads: *You who pass here learn that this land is sacred ground. For over 30 years blessed it has been by the blood of patriots burned by tyranny.* It was erected when Cuba was liberated in 1898. The 30 years' reference dates to the start of the Ten Years' War in 1868. A drawing by a crewman of the small steamer *Perrit*, shows her unloading weapons, supplies, and men (opposite, bottom) on a moonlit night in the Bay of Nipe. Filibustering missions to Cuba, like gun running through several centuries up to the present time, was a dangerous enterprise; international law recognizes the rights of the occupying authorities to execute foreigners who engage in smuggling contraband to rebels.

1868   1898

Tú, que pasas, descúbrete este lugar es tierra
consagrada. Durante treinta años bendecida
ha sido con ... sangre de Patriotas inmolados por la libertad

One of the last great cavalry charges took place near Puerto Principe, Cuba, on October 8, 1896, when General Máximo Gómez with about 600 mounted cavalrymen and 300 infantry, caught up with a force of 2,500 Spaniards led by General Castellano. As the ten yards visibility fog lifted, the two forces were just 400 yards apart, the Spaniards well covered, but Gómez ordered his cavalry to attack. According to American Lieutenant Colonel Frederick Funston (who, just three years later, was a U.S. Army general during the Philippine Insurrection), the Chief of Artillery of the Cuban Army of Liberation and commander of American filibusterers, the bloody fight that day was a "Cuban Balaklava." He was referring to the infamous charge of the light brigade, for the Cuban scenario in the battle, in which he was to

participate, was nearly identical, with hundreds of cavalrymen galloping across a wide-open field into a well-manned and heavily-armed superior (by a margin of almost three-to-one) stronghold. The Cubans rode right up to the Spanish front line, firing their Remington carbines and revolvers, staying back just far enough not to use their swords and machetes. Soon they overwhelmed the position and the Spaniards quickly retreated, but the patriot casualties were tragically high, with barely a hundred men still sitting in their saddles, the rest all killed, wounded, or their horses shot. A final comparison with Balaklava: the light brigade suffered a staggering 37 percent casualties, while Gómez' cavalry had to sacrifice 52 percent of its men (more than 300) to win the day.

Artwork by W.A. Rogers

During the height of the Ten Year's War, in August 1873, Máximo Gómez was promoted to General-in-Chief commanding the Cuban insurgents. Addressing his troops, he cautioned: "Do not risk your life unnecessarily. You have only one, and you can best serve your country by saving it. Dead men do not fire guns. Keep your head cool; keep your machete warm; and we will yet free Cuba." Although past the age of 70, Gómez took command of the Cuban patriot army during the Three Years' War, leading his forces in grueling campaigns through rough countryside, inflicting serious losses on the Spaniards.

While the American population had long been outraged by the Spanish administration in Cuba, some took great risks to assist the patriots, mostly by filibustering forays. Others went ashore and fought for the rebel cause, exploits which could stand them before firing squads if they were captured. When Spanish General Suárez Inclan attacked an insurgent camp, his troops were mowed down by Gatling guns manned by Americans, who may have even worn Cuban uniforms.

Like Gómez, Antonio Maceo was a lieutenant-general in the Cuban Army during the insurrection just prior to the Spanish-American War. Both men returned to Cuba from exile shortly after the fighting began in February 1895 and both proved to be brilliant field commanders, whether conducting joint operations or campaigning individually. A synopsis of Maceo's fervent opposition to Spanish rule, as related by *Harper's:* "After the Ten Years' War, Antonio Maceo, refusing to acknowledge the Treaty of El Zanjón, kept up the ferment of rebellion for two more years, and then retired to the continent to plot further revolt. At the outbreak of the Three Years' War he was living in Costa Rica, whence he was in uninterrupted communication with Marti and other Cuban leaders. On the 31st of March, with his brother José and 22 other revolutionists, he effected a landing in Baracoa ... In the first brush with Maceo, the Spaniards were repulsed with a loss of ten killed and nine wounded ... with only two or three of his original companions, he fell in with a band of patriots and was received with wild enthusiasm." The Cuban insurgentes, less than two months after the fighting began in 1895, had the commanders which would bleed their oppressors until the arrival of their liberators from the U.S.

T. de Thulstrup

Artwork by T. de Thulstrup

After a battle, the wounded were cared for as best as was possible under the primitive hot and humid circumstances. A Cuban infantry company is shown marching from the field with wounded comrades being carried by litter-bearers and on horseback, while the *soldado* in the foreground brings in their rifles. On the horse, the wounded man sits in the saddle holding the reins, while the man behind him keeps him erect. José Martí (right) as he looked in 1892, three years before he returned to Cuba to lead the 1895 rebellion. He was living in the United States, as were 40,000 other Cuban expatriates in the early 1890's, raising sympathy and money for the cause of *Cuba Libre.* He developed his war plan by December, 1894 and the uprising was scheduled for February 24, 1895, but the trio of filibustering ships were intercepted by the U.S. Navy, delaying the arrival of Martí, other leaders and equipment until after the revolt began. A month after the Three Years' War commenced, Martí was back in Cuba and along with commanding general Máximo Gómez, issued a manifesto calling for fair treatment of all residents — especially Spaniards, but left no doubt that "Steel will answer to steel; friendship will answer to friendship." They added that "Cowardice, with its pretext of prudence, may seek to hide behind its pretended fear of the negro race — a senseless fear never justified in Cuba. The menace of a race war, with which our Spanish beneficiaries have long sought to inspire . . . is indignantly denied by the martyrs . . . of our revolutionary past." On May 19, 1895, less than two months after the fighting began, Martí, escorted by 50 cavalrymen, was on his way to the coast, to leave for the United States to gain more support, when he was ambushed by 800 Spanish troops and, leading a charge to escape, was killed. José Martí is still a national hero in Cuba, with Havana's International airport, among other places, named in his honor.

While Cuban *insurrectos* during the wars for independence held some towns for long periods, they were more likely forced by circumstances to operate out of crude forest camps, with even thatched huts being a luxury. During the Three Years' War, officers planned their next attack (above) in their makeshift headquarters. Using their rifles not only to kill Spanish soldiers, but local game as well, Cuban soldiers (below) cooked the meat on a rough rack of tree branches.

Lieutenant-General Calixto García, commander of one of the Cuban armies, assumed a more prominent role in the command structure after General Maceo, "the most daring warrior of the Cuban conflict," was killed in action on December 7, 1896. With Captain-General Valeriano Weyler enforcing his *Reconcentrado* orders in the field by gunning down hapless *pacíficos* between pitched battles with Cuban forces that he usually lost, Gómez, García, and Maceo kept up a relentless pressure. García, shown in a mountain camp with his staff officers and in a more formal portrait, went on to command the troops which fought alongside the American expeditionary force that finally liberated Cuba 18 months later.

Below, National Archives

29

In the vast areas of countryside held by Cuban rebel authorities, they levied taxes on the Spanish *grandees* and wealthy Cubans who owned businesses, mills, and farms. Any who balked at paying soon found their holdings attacked and destroyed by insurgent forces. Often Spanish soldiers would wreak similar destruction to deny the patriots sources of supply and income, the whole process resulting in economic chaos on both sides. Cuban cavalry and sympathizing workers (above) wielding torches set fire to a sugar mill near Trinidad.

The Cuban *insurrectos*, like many revolutionaries who lived off the land and depended on sympathetic civilians and attacks on the enemy supply lines for support, were often a scraggly rag-tag lot, with courage and motivation the only assets in boundless amounts. Shown are two Cuban rebels of the 1890s, posing during the Three Years' War. Impressed with the valor of the Cubans and appalled by the lack of military bearing and equipment, Theodore Roosevelt wrote that they were "armed with every kind of rifle in all states of dilapidation." The fact that Cuban and Spanish soldiers wore similar white uniforms exacerbated the confusion of the battle for both sides.

Typical of Spanish Army units fighting the Cuban *insurgentes* was the 3rd Company, 1st Battalion of Navarra's Regiment (above), whose area of operations was Mantanzas. The most notorious of the oppressors in Cuba were the Spanish Volunteers, composed of resident Spaniards who stood to lose their homes, possessions, and their livelihoods if the Cubans won independence, unlike the regular soldiers who would just sail back to Spain after a few years' duty in the Caribbean. Motivated by a much greater personal stake in the suppression of the Cuban patriots, the Volunteers fought hard and committed the worst atrocities, including the enthusiastic enforcement of Captain General Weyler's *Reconcentrado* internment of the provincial rural population. Two of the ranking officers of the Havana Urban Volunteer Battalion during the Three Years' War were Lieutenant Colonel D.N. Díaz (lower left) and Major Celestino Blanch (lower right), posing in their field uniforms.

Three photos, Biblioteca Nacional, Madrid

The only place in the Cuban capital where *campesinos* driven out of the farming villages of Havana province were interned was the disease-ridden, overcrowded district of warehouses with barred windows derisively named "The Ditches" by the inmates. The Spaniards allowed photographer Harold Martin to take pictures of their ghetto of human misery, and one of the foremost American illustrators, W. A. Rogers, painstakingly studied his prints to create this moving portrait of the *Reconcentrados* sentenced to a slow death in The Ditches.

T. de Thulstrup

Many Spanish soldiers recognized the immorality and futility of their government's colonial rule in Cuba and fought lackadaisically against the patriots. Others became so guilt-ridden and disgusted that they switched allegiance, and some actively joined the rebel cause. Among the most renowned was Captain Don José Palacio who, having fought bravely, was overwhelmed; he and 15 of his men were captured by General Maceo's soldiers. When Maceo returned Palacio's sword (above), the Spanish officer shouted for Cuban liberation and along with his men, joined the cause of freedom.

The picture below shows two of the rifles most commonly used in the Three Years' War, both from the collection of Richard G. Hendrikson. The .30-calibre Remington rolling block rifle (above) was an 1870s American arm, many of which were acquired by the Cubans. This one is fitted with a bayonet. The 8 mm German Mauser (below) was widely used throughout the world at the turn of the 20th century; it was the standard rifle of the Spanish Army. At first, Spain purchased Mausers from Germany; later they manufactured them in their own arsenals.

Ron Ziel

Biblioteca Nacional, Madrid

Newspapers in Spain sent reporters to cover the Three Years' War. Five of them, at least one of whom carried a revolver, posed for an informal picture. Each was employed by a major metropolitan Spanish newspaper. With telegraph cables already in service across the Atlantic by the 1890s, the dispatches sent by these correspondents reached their employers and other continental periodicals quickly, providing timely reportage of the progress of the war.

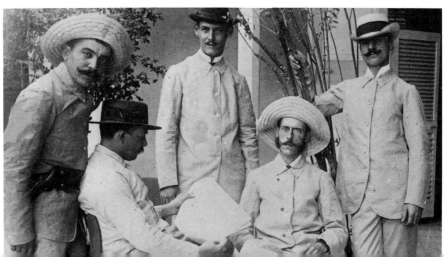

Entitled "Los Heroes de 'Sao del Indio y la Pimienta,'" this picture of the officers of a Spanish battalion which suffered heavy losses in a furious engagement with Cuban rebels was taken moments after they returned to their secure camp. Described as "the remains of the Spanish forces that survived the very heroic combat," they are (left to right): Lieutenant Colonel Segura, Captain E.M. Irles, Colonel Canella, Military Doctor Valderranca, Captain Miranda and Major Garrido. The doctor has just finished treating and bandaging the wound that Canella received in his left foot. The scene dates from 1895, at the beginning of the final Cuban uprising. "Butcher" Weyler was relieved of his command and replaced by Captain General Ramón Blanco late in 1897. Blanco, shown wearing the sash and medals of his distinguished career, was a definite human rights improvement over his predecessor, and he immediately promised to release the concentration camp prisoners and return them to their abandoned burned-out villages to resume farming. His reforms were slow to be implemented, however, especially by the disappointed Weyler supporters who had no desire to have the peons back in the countryside, giving aid, food, and new recruits to the insurgent army. Blanco's more benign administration of Cuba, including limited autonomy, proved to be too little and too late, especially when the autonomy policy included attempts at bribing the rebels to desert. Blanco was to be the last Spanish Governor General of the rebellious island; less than a year after superseding Weyler, he presided over the surrender to the American liberators.

Some of the fine artwork to come out of the Spanish-American War era was sketched by artists at the scene. A few works were based on photographs and much of the finished art depicting events in Cuba in this volume came from highly accurate sketches done by artistic participants and witnesses, then sent to the U.S. for a final rendering by the best illustrators. Often, the on-the-scene drawings were accompanied by elaborate descriptive notes, making the final work a definitive record of places and events. Spanish war criminals, including Weyler, seemed totally unaware of the uncivilized and abhorrent realities of their acts. They made hardly any effort to conceal them, even allowing high-ranking American government officials, correspondents, and artists to visit the concentration camps. The resulting scenes, such as this showing Spanish cavalrymen forcing a family into a camp while half-starved inmates scrutinize the new arrivals, were published in the U.S. and Europe, bringing a hail of invective and indignation toward Spain, but the Spaniards, so immersed in their colonial problems and apparently convinced that the righteousness of their cause justified any means to achieve victory, could not comprehend the foreign exasperation. So appalled was renowned American artist Frederic Remington at what he saw and sketched that he terminated his contract with William Randolph Hearst and came back to New York in 1897, vowing to return to Cuba only if he went with the U.S. Army. The following year, employed by one of Hearst's competitors, he did just that!

W. A. Rogers

The first-class battleship *USS Massachusetts* was a fine example of the immense progress which had been made in warship design in just 25 years. Even in 1870, wooden ships with muzzle-loading cannon, powered by sail and steam, were still to be found active in the fleets of leading naval powers. Vessels weighing under 1000 tons, struggling to attain speeds of six knots, with guns that fired iron balls at ranges measured in terms of a few hundred feet, had been superseded by armor-plated behemoths weighing 11,000 tons, mounting 13-inch guns weighing 67 tons each that could fire high-explosive shells weighing up to 500 pounds and capable of penetrating 30 inches of iron, with ranges up to 11 miles, at speeds approaching 20 knots! That one generation had seen the greatest period of naval architectural development the world has ever known, and the *Massachusetts* and her sisters built in the mid-1890s

would soon be challenged by more advanced ships already under construction. Her armament consisted of four 13-inch guns (two each, in turrets fore and aft), eight 8-inch guns (two each, in four side turrets), plus numerous smaller calibre rapid-fire guns. She played a vital role in the blockade of Cuba and was the flagship of the fleet which invaded Puerto Rico. The original 1898 caption describes well the lower photograph: "INTERIOR OF TURRET — These are 13-inch guns in a turret of the first-class battleship *Massachusetts*. The neatness and cleanliness that are cumpulsory aboard a battleship are in no part of the vessel better exemplified than in the turrets where the monster instruments of destruction are situated. Not only does the machinery work with clock-like accuracy, but it is kept as clean as a watch."

Rising and Falling Empires

When the *USS Maine* sailed into Havana Harbor, the Spanish Empire was in decline, with only a small portion of its overseas possessions still under its control. Spain was able to field well-armed infantry and artillery units, equipped with Mauser rifles and Krupp guns, and its fleet of warships was considered superior to those of America. The training, experience, expertise and motivation of American soldiers and sailors were held in low regard by virtually all of the military and naval circles of Europe except Great Britain; the fact that the United States had just realized its Manifest Destiny by defeating the Plains Indians who, although brave and cunning as individual fighters, were lacking in command structure, strategy and mobility and were totally bereft of an industrial base, mass transportation or economic resources, only reinforced the miscalculations of the continental powers. Unfortunately for the Spaniards, they were among the "true believers" of the erroneous underestimation of the Americans, genuinely convinced that if hostilities should commence, they would win a speedy victory. It was to be the Spanish as fighting forces on land and sea, who would prove to be lacking in combat. The fact that the large Spanish Army could not keep Cuba under control for almost a half-century was apparently written off by Madrid as more the result of guerrilla tactics and fanatical motivation on the part of the Cubans, than being attributable to ineptitude of the officer corps of Spain or the poor training and low quality of many of her soldiers and sailors, who were often backwards draftees with little education or fighting spirit.

Conversely, Americans tended to be more adventurous, creative and self-reliant, and being the products of a democratic society, even the lowest-ranking soldiers might question orders and think for themselves. While Spanish military personnel were assigned to maintain a hated exploitative regime against the wishes of its people, U.S. forces believed themselves to be the liberators of the sorely oppressed. Even as the Spanish Empire was declining over the past century, the United States, since the 1790s, was in rapid — indeed, phenomenal — ascendancy. America was on a swift forward momentum, buoyed by self-confidence and well aware of its accomplishments in war and peace, and in science, industry and economics. Having secured its continental expansion after nearly three centuries of westward movement, it seemed only logical that sheer momentum could carry the American flag into the Caribbean Sea and across the Pacific Ocean. While liberation of the oppressed was the high calling, the wholesale imperialism of the European powers was also an inducement to the Americans; if the Europeans were establishing colonies all over the world, perhaps the United States could have a few as well — and they would be administered much more benignly, a claim that the American Indians so recently herded into reservations in poverty might question!

The "Gay Nineties" in America was a time of great expansion and invention: 5,000 miles of new railroad routes were being opened each year, the northern tier of states, from the Dakotas to Washington, plus Utah, had just entered the Union, and new inventions — from the X-ray and motion pictures to the automobile and electric appliances — were being patented. The restlessness of the American people was played upon by the "yellow journalists," especially Joseph Pulitzer and William Randolph Hearst, whose horror stories of Spanish excesses, especially in Cuba, were to become the foundation of media influence of government policy and public opinion, so well established in the United States a century later. Indeed, when President William McKinley expressed his concern over the sensationalism of Hearst's newspapers and the effect on the American people, the publisher repled: "Mr. President, you supply the Army and Navy, I will supply the war!"

All was not going smoothly in the United States however, for a raucous national debate was raging over whether the country should become involved in overseas problems. While Spanish oppression was deeply offensive, many Americans honestly maintained that it was not their business to intervene. President McKinley was reluctant to involve the country in tropical quagmires and he was continually prodded by the warhawks in the press, Congress and his own administration — including his Assistant Secretary of the Navy, Theodore Roosevelt. The assistant secretary, ever astute and forward-looking, firmly believed that war with Spain was inevitable, but his efforts to whip the Navy into a high state of readiness were frequently slowed by his boss, Secretary of the Navy John D. Long. Often, Roosevelt would wait until Long left his office, then he would order coal, provisions and powder to keep the ships well supplied; he also exerted considerable influence in the appointment of senior officers who were, like himself, aggressive and competent. Largely because of the at times virtually insubordinate actions of the assistant secretary, the Navy was far better prepared for conflict when it finally came, than was the Army. His final act in the Navy Department was to resign his position, stating that when war comes, he wanted to be in the thick of the fighting, but that "I would be totally useless on a ship." He then petitioned President McKinley to raise a volunteer cavalry regiment with himself as lieutenant colonel and his good friend, army surgeon and frontier Indian-fighter, Colonel Leonard Wood, as commander. By these two actions Roosevelt showed that while he was self-confident —

perhaps even egotistical — he also was aware of his limitations, hallmarks of a truly great leader. His honesty was also respected, when surprised high-ranking government officials commented that he was rising fast in the capital and why give it all up to be executive officer of a regiment? His somber reply was that he could not, in good conscience, sit out the war safely behind a desk, while his countrymen went off to die, partly because of his encouragement, and that he too would be at the front, in action.

A comparison of the armed forces of Spain and the United States during the winter of 1898, just before the commencement of hostilities, illustrated both the similarities and the differences between the two combatants. In the category of warships, both navies were almost equal in number but they differed greatly in their missions and fitness for combat. Spain had one first-class battleship, the 9,900 tons *Pelayo*, six first-class armored cruisers of about 7,000 tons displacement each, 28 torpedo boats and torpedo boat destroyers, and about 100 smaller torpedo craft and gunboats, mainly for harbor defense. Against approximately 135 craft of Spain, the U.S. fleet also exceeded 100 vessels, designed more for coastal defense than for projecting seapower over oceanic expanses to defend distant colonial islands. The four first-class American battleships, *Indiana, Iowa, Massachusetts* and *Oregon*, as well as the second-class battleships *Maine* and *Texas*, were larger partly because of their home-defense mission, and, more importantly, mounted heavier, longer-range guns. They also presented a lower silhouette, offering less exposure to the enemy. The *New York* and *Brooklyn* were the only American armored cruisers and their armor plate was lighter than the Spanish cruisers. The U.S. Navy had 14 protected cruisers, four double-turret monitors and 12 torpedo boats. The dynamite cruiser *Vesuvius*, armed with three huge pneumatic guns which propelled 500-pound charges of nitroglycerin, and the ram *Katahdin*, designed to sink enemy ships by ramming below the waterline although in fleet service, were still experimental and unproven, as well as surrounded by as much controversy as they were surrounded by water. The remainder of the American fleet consisted of small gunboats and long-obsolete (some dating back to the Civil War era) harbor-defense craft.

In the category of ground forces lay the biggest paradox: while existing Spanish military personnel at the outbreak of hostilities was far larger in number, it was the American side that had the potential to train and equip vastly greater legions of fighting men. At the beginning of 1898, regular army troops that Spain had on active duty numbered approximately 250,000, of which 150,000 were in Cuba, with 60,000 garrisoned in the home country, the remaining 40,000 in the Philippines, Puerto Rico and the rest of the colonies. The Spanish government could also rapidly call up the 160,000-man active reserve units and if required,

there were approximately 1,000,000 additional inactive reservists, bringing the total to over 1,400,000 men that Spain could field within a 90-day period. But the financial resources of the government were disastrously low, and the citizens, both in the home country and the colonies, were already under an intolerable tax burden. These fiscal factors were due mainly to the almost constant warfare in Cuba.

Conversely, under the McKinley administration, the U.S. economy was booming, the vast majority of Americans paid no taxes (the first income tax, which only affected a small amount of the earnings of the wealthiest Americans, was still 15 years into the future) and enjoyed a much higher standard of living. The strength of the U.S. Army on the eve of the war was a mere 18,000 men — below the already anemic strength of 25,000 authorized by law — less than one thirteenth the number of Spain's regular forces. While Spanish troops had gained much combat experience in the colonies, it had been 33 years since Americans had last fought in major battles at the close of the Civil War. However, most officers and senior noncommissioned officers had fought in the campaigns against the Indians, which ended just seven years earlier. Their experience was comparable to that gained by the Spaniards fighting in Cuba against paramilitary guerrilla units. The State Militias (National Guard) totalled perhaps 200,000, but the completely new concept of an American president activating them to fight overseas posed serious legal questions. There was solid precedent in nationalizing the militias for duty within the United States (the Civil War, Indian fighting, railroad strikes and other labor unrest), but not for foreign expeditions, prompting the powerful peace factions to bring up the issue. Of course, the majority of the individual officers and men in the militia units were as anxious as the regulars to disembark from U.S. shores to fight anywhere that Spanish forces were entrenched, and most were annoyed at the isolationist obstacles to their doing so. McKinley then instituted a procedure by which entire militia units resigned and immediately volunteered for the regular Army.

The longer-range advantage of the Untied States was its pool of qualified men of fighting age: at least 10,000,000, or seven times the number that Spain could raise. Most of the Spanish men would serve reluctantly, disinterested in dying to defend distant colonies administered by corruption and brute force, while the morale of the Americans was high and they felt a genuine calling and sense of mission — a most crucial contrast that was to be a major element in the outcome of the war. These factors, while favoring the United States, by no means ensured its victory. While the *esprit* and the motivation, as well as training and tactics of the Spaniards, were questionable, their sense of duty, despite some glaring exceptions, was often high and they were courageous; the American admirals and generals regarded them as dangerous and very formidable opponents.

In addition to raising a huge army quickly, the U.S. government was deeply concerned about defending the coast line of the eastern United States and the Gulf of Mexico and, to a lesser extent, the west coast. Political and military leaders feared that Spanish squadrons, crossing the Atlantic undetected and just a night's sail from Cuba to Key West, or little over two days to New Orleans, could suddenly begin bombarding American cities, ports, naval bases and bridges. Congress passed a large appropriation to quickly reinforce coastal defenses with long-range guns and patrol craft. Although the fears proved groundless, due to the Spaniards wisely not wishing to risk their ships before engaging the American fleet, as well as concentrating their ships to defend Cuba and the Philippines, in early 1898 the threat seemed very real and was taken seriously by Washington.

A debate continued across the Atlantic Ocean concerning how the American Army, comprised of few professionals and mostly of state militias and volunteers, would perform against the large standing army of Spain. Spanish military intelligence had published a report, *Poder Militar y Naval de los Estados Unidos*, which expressed accurate insight into the problems faced by the United States in a conflict over Cuba: "The State Militia, although their instruction has been recently improved, owing to assembling where they have had brigade exercises, could not without difficulty answer the demands upon them if suddenly called into service. The complex duties which in that event they would at once have to perform, such as preparing subsistence, mounts and transportation, mustering in quite large masses for the execution of military operations to which they are unaccustomed — fulfilling, in a word, all the duties of a soldier, without taking into account all his necessary education — are circumstances of abrupt change to which such troops, in view of their civic-military organization, could not readily adapt themselves. Moreover, such troops have no transportation service, sanitary corps, or even a staff by means of which the forces of various states might be able to cooperate with the regular army or mingle harmoniously with each other in order to be able to mobilize and concentrate as part of an army of operation." The Spanish report continued: "There exists in the (American) Republic no uniformity in armament, for while the standing army uses the Krag-Jorgensen rifle, the various state militia organizations have rifles of different models and calibers, and generally greatly inferior to the regulation arm of the standing army." It was acknowledged, however, that if war came, such problems would be quickly rectified.

The Spaniards were perhaps the first foreign power to appreciate the great American industrial capacity; the failure to do likewise would prove to be disastrous to the Germans and the Japanese in the major 20th century wars: "The industries of the country, on the other hand, can produce arms in

Small, swift and maneuverable, torpedo boats had the perilous mission of speeding towards enemy ships and launching torpedos at a close enough range so that the target would not have time to avoid being hit. The wood-hull *Stiletto* was a little vessel — the most diminutive of all American torpedo craft — displacing just 31 tons, 88 feet in length, armed with six small-calibre rapid-fire guns and a crew of only one officer and five men. She is seen launching a torpedo from her single bow tube.

great quantities in a short space of time. According to statistics set forth by our military attaché, the North American government could at once arm about 100,000 men, the government works could construct 1000 rifles and 1,000,000 cartridges daily, and private manufacturers could turn out 3000 rifles and as many revolvers with 2,000,000 cartridges in the same time. In this way something like 20,000 men could be armed, and with two months of preparation one might easily arm 280,000 by utilizing the material on hand in stock and manufacturing it in the said time, without counting on what the army and the militia already have." That high degree of industrial capacity was already on line in America at the end of the 19th century!

Understandably, even the English underestimated American power, know-how and resolve, as the commander-in-chief of the British army, Lord Wolseley, was to observe just days before the war started: "The United States would make a mistake in attempting to invade Cuba with volunteers who are not fully drilled and disciplined. If that was done, the United States might expect heavy reverses when those troops encountered the trained Spanish troops on land. It would be a grave error to underestimate the strength of the adversaries of the American troops. I would regret to see the Americans even temporarily beaten, as all my sympathies are with them. It is fortunate for the

United States that this war is not with a first-class power, for it is evident that in such an encounter they would be badly beaten at the beginning, though I believe that *the Americans are able to defeat any nation in the long run*" (emphasis added).

Coincidentally, although the acquisition of the Hawaiian Islands by the United States occurred at the same time as the war with Spain, the two events were unrelated, except that they dove tailed perfectly ensuring that the foundations of America's sudden rise to world power status would be permanent and strategically secure. But initially, when the U.S. government realized that a defeat of Spain would mean American occupation of the Philippines — 7,500 miles from California — Hawaii loomed as a vital naval base and coaling station. Still, Manila was 5,500 miles beyond the planned base at Pearl Harbor, Hawaii, so as early as May, 1898, astute American naval strategic planners were briefing Congress on the absolute necessity of not only annexing Hawaii, but additional Spanish possessions westward, to form a line of naval stations to support what they correctly envisioned as a large future Pacific fleet. Intrigue and debate concerning American annexation of the Hawaiian archipelago had been going on for years and the Navy had already attempted to build a base on Midway Island, 1,200 miles to the northwest. In the fast unfolding events of the spring of 1898, two forces were driving the United States to immediate annexation: the national security necessity of naval facilities and the growing realization that if the Americans did not seize Hawaii quickly, the government of Japan would.

It had been less than a half century since American Admiral Matthew Perry had opened the way for Japan to become an important player on the world power stage and, while growth and expansion in the United States had been unprecedented, that of Japan was proportionately even greater! The Japanese were expanding their power and influence in all directions and an interesting and prophetic concern of the anti-imperialists in Washington, D.C. in 1898 was that if the United States was to annex Hawaii and hold on to the Philippines, it would undoubtedly cause a major conflict with Japan a few decades into the 20th century. While the small native population of Hawaii was being overtaken by thousands of American immigrants in the early 1890s, the Japanese were also arriving in increasing numbers. The revolution which overthrew the weak native government declared the archipelago an independent republic, with President Sanford P. Dole as head of state. Shortly before leaving office in 1893, American President Benjamin Harrison sent a treaty of annexation of Hawaii to the Senate; it was promptly withdrawn by his successor, Grover Cleveland and resubmitted by President McKinley in 1897. While debate in the capital raged over the role of the U.S. government in clandestinely having supported the overthrow of the natives and demands even were made that the Americans

should not only reestablish the ousted regime, but should pay reparations as well (strongly supported by Cleveland), the agenda of the Japanese was becoming increasingly evident. By 1898, the 109,000 population of Hawaii was nearly one-fourth Japanese and growing at a rate of almost 75 percent annually, while natives numbered a little over 30,000. The rest were from various other Pacific and European nations, plus a large American presence.

On May 18, 1898, Rep. Newlands of Nevada — a far western state where concern for Pacific affairs was high — introduced a joint resolution in the House of Representatives which clarified the issue as a direct challenge to American interests: "The native Hawaiian race cannot in any contingency control the islands. (They) must fall to some foreign people . . . The Japanese (on Hawaii) are intensely Japanese, retaining their allegiance to their empire . . . The Japanese government demanded of the Hawaiian government . . . that the Japanese in the Hawaiian Islands should have equal privilege. (to) include voting and holding office. This claim was made when a flood of Japanese subjects, under the supervision of the government of that country, of from 1,000 to 2,000 per month, were being poured into the Hawaiian Islands, threatening a speedy change of the government into Japanese hands, and ultimately to a Japanese possession. The demand was resisted by the little republic, and a treaty of annexation with the United States arrived at for a time.

"With the Japanese element in the ascendant and the government under Japanese control, the treaty would be promptly terminated . . . the first step taken . . . toward the complete incorporation of the islands into the Japanese Empire and their possession as a strategic point in the northern Pacific, from which her strong and increasing fleet would operate. Annexation, and that alone, will securely maintain American control in Hawaii . . . Annexation imposes responsibility, but will give full power of ownership and control."

The day before — on May 17 — the Hawaiian government had decided to unconditionally assist the United States in the war with Spain, including the use of all facilities and harbors, thereby repudiating any neutrality policies which, Honolulu claimed, did not apply in this case, and in a reply to a strenuous protest from the Spanish consul, answered: ". . . owing to the intimate relations now existing between this country and the United States, this country has not contemplated a proclamation of neutrality . . . your protest can derive no further consideration than to acknowledge its receipt." The joint resolution overwhelmingly passed in the House and after weeks of Senate debate, was adopted by a 42—21 vote — precisely the two-thirds required for a treaty — on July 6. Ceremonies commemorating the raising of the American flag over Hawaii took place on August 12; firmly establishing the main base of U.S. power in the Pacific through the upcoming century and beyond.

Good photographs of Spanish warships of the 1890s are virtually impossible to find, so pictures such as these, taken from contemporary publications, must suffice. The small, light cruiser *Nueva España* (above) displaced just 630 tons (about the same weight as the biggest land-bound American railroad steam locomotives of the 1940s), was 190 feet long and produced 2,600 horsepower. Her batteries consisted of two 4.7-inch Hontoria guns; four 2.2-inch rapid-fires; one additional rifled gun, and a pair of torpedo tubes. Her speed was 18 knots and she was manned by a crew of 91. The famed *Vizcaya* (below), of 7,000 tons displacement, 340 feet in length, and 13,000 horsepower, was more heavily armored than most American men-of-war and had two turrets, each mounting a single 11-inch gun, plus ten 5.5-inch rapid-fire, two 2.7-inch, eight 2.2-inch, four 1.4-inch, and two muzzle-loading rifled cannons. With six torpedo-tubes and a speed of 20 knots, she was a formidable adversary, but her 500-man crew was not as well-trained as the American sailors she was to fight in Cuban waters. The high expense of modern American weaponry was an issue a century ago, just as it is at the turn of the 21st century. Just as criticism for spending over a $1,000,000 for a single tank was muted after their spectacular success in the 1991 Gulf War, so it must be noted that the *Vizcaya* was built and outfitted 100 years earlier for just $600,000, while comparable U.S. Navy vessels such as the flagship of Commodore Schley's flying squadron, *USS Brooklyn*, cost exactly five times that amount. But after the two ships faced off at Santiago Bay in 1898, there could be no doubting the wisdom of the Americans in spending the extra money to make their ships technological and engineering marvels!

U.S. Naval Historical Center

Suffolk County Historical Society

Smaller, with lighter armament than the battleships, cruisers were quite formidable, capable of lobbing eight-and ten-inch shells several miles and carrying large batteries of rapid-fire guns. A port stern view of *USS Wilmington* (upper left) shows her at anchor with two of her boats being rowed back from shore. A sister, *USS Helena* (lower left) as she looked in 1896, also possessed a tall, slender funnel and an identical mast which mounted a circular gun platform, large searchlight, and a crane boom. Ships of this type were often named after American cities (*Olympia, New York* (the city, not the state), and *Brooklyn* were flagships); many cruisers and smaller warships were to be named for cities in the U.S. The names *Helena* and *Olympia* are of interest, since both were insignificant little towns in the mid-1890s – the former recently a frontier settlement in Montana Territory, the latter in Washington Territory. When both were admitted to the Union in 1889, the two towns became the capitals of the new states, so the big, powerful warships named for them were sure to instill deep pride in the citizenry of those states. It was a fine act of welcoming them into the Union! The *USS Aileen* (above) was a trim and speedy little craft, typical of the former yachts acquired by the Navy for Spanish-American War service. She is towing a tiny steam launch in Peconic Bay, which separates the twin forks of eastern Long Island. On that station, she may have been assigned to defend the approaches to New York Harbor. The *USS Newark* (right) was receiving coal from a barge tied alongside as she was conducting operations during the war.

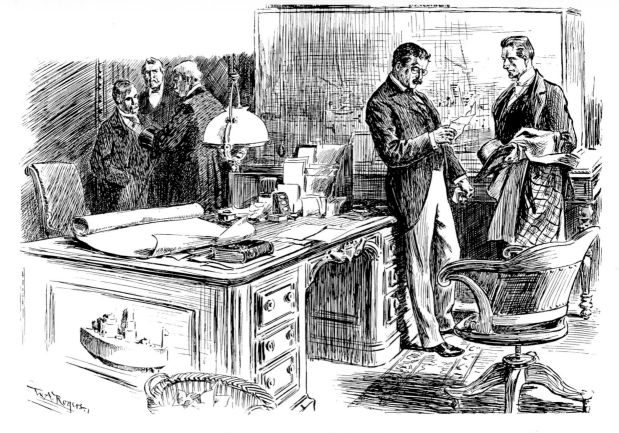

Largely due to the frenetic activity of Assistant Secretary Theodore Roosevelt, the Navy Department was always busy and a primary source of juicy news copy during the year ending in April 1898, when he left to become executive officer of the Rough Riders regiment. The assistant secretary is shown at work in his office (above), with a large drawing of *USS Olympia* hanging on the wall. The older, more sedate Secretary of the Navy, John D. Long (center) was unusually complacent in tolerating the whirlwind

of commotion and opposing ideas that his assistant brought to the office. The correspondents' corner in the Navy complex (below) was well lit by electric lamps by 1897, providing adequate working space for the reporters assigned to writing about the rapidly unfolding preparations for the war that most believed was inevitable. A pair of bored telegraph messenger boys waited to run the stories to their offices, to be sent to the newspapers' headquarters.

Photo, Library of Congress   Artwork by W. A. Rogers

THE CORRESPONDENTS' CORNER, NAVY DEPARTMENT.—Drawn by W. A. Rogers

The view of the U.S. Navy first-class protected cruiser *Brooklyn* in drydock accents the bulbous hull that was so typical of 1890s warships. The large twin screws drove her at speeds of 22 knots and the ample rudder made her highly maneuverable. The cramped environment of her fire room several decks down illustrates the horrendous conditions under which the stokers and engineers labored when called upon to produce the prodigious amounts of steam required to get maximum performance, as during the battle of Santiago Bay when she was Commodore Schley's flagship. Stripped to the waist, with inadequate ventilation, the men toiled in temperatures up to 160° Fahrenheit! The statistics of the *Brooklyn* were impressive and confirm her role in running down and destroying several of Spain's best cruisers: 9,153 tons displacement; length, 400 feet, 6 inches; breadth, 64 feet; mean draft, 24 feet; 18,770 horsepower; armor, 3 inches on the sides, 5.5 inches on the turrets and 4-8 inches on the barbettes; main battery, eight 8-inch guns and twelve 5-inch rapid-fire guns; secondary battery, twelve 6 pounder and 4 one-pounder rapid-fires and four Gatlings; and crew, 46 officers and 515 men. She cost almost $3,000,000 (about $50,000,000 in 1997 dollars).

Several classes of smaller American warships in 1898 carried a terrific wallop, mounting large-calibre guns on relatively short, shallow-draft hulls. Among these were the fast and low monitors, some having one and the larger examples carrying two heavy two-gun turrets, plus smaller rapid-firing batteries. The double-turret monitor *USS Miantonomoh,* is shown under full steam, forging through rough seas while on patrol.

New naval recruits (above) during their apprenticeship duty on board *USS Atlanta*, a period which will ascertain their aptitudes and fitness for seafaring. In the realm of racial integration, the Navy had, at the turn of the 20th century, black sailors in many job categories on warships, including the four snappy-looking ones in this picture, but regressed in 1921, when it issued a policy restricting new colored recruits to the Stewards Branch (black sailors who held other rates continued in their duties). According to E.C. Finney, Jr., of the Naval Historical Center: "Then in World War II the restriction to the Stewards Branch was dropped, but segregation still continued. When President Truman told the armed forces to integrate, the Navy said 'aye, aye, sir' and did it. It may not have been a cheery 'aye, aye,' but the USN does not disregard presidential orders." In the

Army it was quite different with colonels and generals who were racist, sometimes blatantly disregarding the order. Unlike in the period between the World Wars, in 1898 black sailors were not confined to scrubbing kettles! Twenty-two colored sailors perished along with the battleship *Maine*—nearly ten percent of the fatalities in that incident. Building and maintaining the late 19th century ironclads was heavy work, as the task of installing a 10-inch gun (below) in the turret of a monitor illustrates. The breech-loading rifled cannon, weighing more than 30 tons, was lowered with the barrel carefully eased through the firing port of the turret, then the breech end was placed on the mountings, and according to the 1898 caption: "In a very short time the cumbersome weapon is working with oily smoothness."

There could be little doubt as to the extent of the role of the U.S. Government in the overthrow of the native regime of Queen Liliuokalani of Hawaii in 1893. Supporting the faction of American businessmen who had precipitated the revolt, the U.S. Ambassador John L. Stevens "arranged" to have marines from the *USS Boston* landed in Honolulu to protect Americans and their property, despite the fact that there was absolutely no

evidence of danger to either. Their armed presence intimidated the natives and rallied the elements that had overthrown the government. President Sanford B. Dole, in long beard and white suit, third from left (above) reviewed a parade in Honolulu in 1893, with Captain Wiltse of the *Boston* standing at potbellied attention next to him and U.S. Marines with the Stars and Stripes just a few feet away. Pearl Harbor (left) was a bucolic and peaceful estuary in the 1890s; it had already been leased to the U.S. by the king of Hawaii in 1887, but had the Japanese seized the archipelago, that treaty would have been rendered meaningless, leaving the new owners' imperial navy to develop a huge base. The American flag-raising ceremony in front of Iolani Palace (opposite, above) took place on August 12, 1898, with sailors from the *USS Philadelphia* and a large white dog forming the honor guard and artillery pieces in the foreground ready to fire a salute. That night, the palace was illuminated by hundreds of electric lights (opposite, bottom) for the annexation ball. At the ceremony, President Dole (opposite, center), in no small part due to his leading the quest for annexation and siding with America in the war with Spain, was appointed to continue as head of state and was made territorial governor by President McKinley in 1900. He was a native Hawaiian, born in Honolulu to an American missionary couple in 1844, and except for his postgraduate education in Massachusetts, he spent his life on the islands. As the 1898 war progressed at lightning speed in favor of the United States, Great Britain accelerated her program to develop a transatlantic alliance with the U.S., and the U.S. was quick to reciprocate with displays of the Stars and Stripes and the Union Jack in the most prominent locations at official functions. The Hawaii ceremony on August 12 – coincidentally the same day that the armistice which ended hostilities was signed – was typical, with the British and American flags centered on the podium in front of Sanford Dole. Had the 1996 national election in the U.S. been won by the Republican candidate Bob Dole, there would have been a second President Dole in American history!

Five photos, Hawaii State Archives

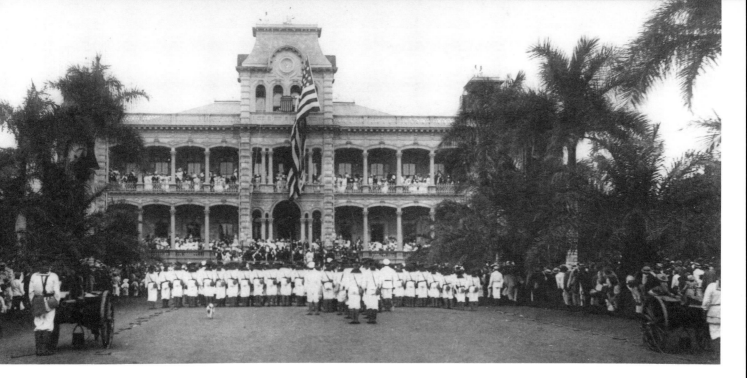

"Remember the Maine"

On the evening of February 15, 1898 at 8 p.m., various officers in charge of security of the boilers, coal bunkers, magazines and the watch on the decks of the U.S. battleship *Maine*, which had been anchored in Havana Harbor the past 21 days, reported to Captain Charles D. Sigsbee that all was in proper order for the night. Thus informed, as was the standard procedure each day at that time, the captain knew that all directives and arrangements required by naval regulations and his own orders had been complied with, including visual inspection and, most importantly, temperature checks of each powder magazine and coal bunker. All was normal and peaceful on board and surrounding the *USS Maine*, as she performed her uneventful mission as a visitor of good will during the tense period of deteriorating relations between the governments of Spain and the United States.

One and a half hours later the skipper was in his cabin, writing personal letters in the pale yellowish glow of electric lights, the power generated by two of the six boilers maintained at 80 pounds pressure, one-third less than the 120 pounds when the ship was under way. Most of the other officers were relaxing in their cabins or socializing in the ward room, their quarters being on the upper decks. The sailors and marines, all off-duty except the few on watch or firing the boilers, were on the lower decks; many had already retired for the night. The duty officer that evening, Lieutenant Blandin, related his experience at the time of the 9:40 p.m. explosion: "I was on the watch and when the men had been piped below I looked down the main hatches and over the side of the ship. Everything was absolutely normal. I walked aft to the quarter deck behind the rear turret, as is allowed after 8:00 in the evening, and sat down on the port side, where I remained for a few minutes. Then for some reason I cannot explain to myself, I moved to the starboard side and sat down there. I was feeling a bit glum, and, in fact, was so quiet that Lieutenant Hood came up and asked laughingly if I was asleep. I said: 'No, I am on watch'. Scarcely had I spoken when there came a dull, sullen roar. Then succeeded a sharp explosion, some say numerous explosions. I remember only one. It seemed to me that the sound issued from the port side forward. Then followed a perfect rain of missiles of all kinds, from huge pieces of cement to blocks of wood, steel railings, fragments of gratings and all the debris that would be detachable in an explosion ... I was struck on the head by a piece of ce-

ment and knocked down, but not hurt, and got to my feet in a moment. Lieutenant Hood had run to the poop (deck) and I supposed, as I followed, he was dazed by the shock and about to jump overboard. I hailed him and he answered that he had run to help lower the boats. When I got there, though scarce a minute had elapsed, I had to wade in water to my knees, and almost instantly the quarter deck was awash. On the poop I found Captain Sigsbee, as cool as if at a ball, and soon all the officers except Jenkins and Merritt joined us. The poop was above water and the *Maine* settled to the bottom..."

Captain Sigsbee's account was similar: "I find it impossible to describe the sound or shock, but the impression remains of something awe-inspiring, terrifying, of noise-rending, vibrating, all-pervading. There is nothing in the former experience of anyone on board to measure the explosion by ... After the first great shock — I cannot recall how many sharper detonations I heard, not more than two or three — I knew my ship was gone. In a structure like the *Maine*, the effects of such an explosion are not for a moment in doubt ... I made my way through the long passage in the dark, groping from side to side, to the hatchway and thence to the poop, being among the earliest to reach that spot. As soon as I recognized the officers, I ordered the high explosives to be flooded, and then directed that the boats available be lowered to the rescue of the wounded or drowning ... Discipline in a perfect measure prevailed. I cannot form any idea of the time, but it seemed five minutes from the moment I reached the poop until I left, the last man it was possible to reach having been saved. It must have been three-quarters of an hour or more, however ..." After giving the order "abandon ship," Captain Sigsbee was the last man to leave the already totally destroyed hulk.

The explosion set the entire Cuban capital city into shock and panic. The bright flash in the night, followed instantly by the noise and shock wave, brought thousands of residents of Havana streaming out of houses, restaurants and theatres. The initial reaction was that the rebels must have blown up part of the fortifications and were advancing into the city, or that Morro Castle, overlooking the harbor, had been targeted. As soon as the flames were seen emanating from the *Maine*, a vast multitude rushed to the waterfront, to gaze in disbelief and helplessness at the tragedy which had claimed the lives of 266 American sailors — just two of whom were officers. One eyewitness reported: "I strolled down to the riverfront for a breath of fresh air. I was about two or three hundred yards from the *Maine*. The first intimation I had of an explosion was a crunching sound. Then there came a terrible roar, and immense pieces of debris flew skyward from the *Maine*. Some of them must have been thrown at least three hundred feet. It looked as though the whole inside of the ship

The *USS Maine* and the *USS Texas* were the two U.S. Navy second-class battleships. The *Maine* was commissioned in 1895 and assigned to the North Atlantic Squadron. She was a fast, modern, efficient vessel, considered to be one of the best of her class in the world. In the waters of her namesake state shortly after she entered service, she is seen in a stern view (opposite) at Bar Harbor, Maine.   U.S. Naval Historical Center

53

A starboard angle of the *Maine* in 1895, at the beginning of her brief career of less than three years.   U.S. Naval Historical Center

had been blown out. Many persons on the pier were nearly thrown from their feet by the force of the explosion. The air became stifling with smoke."

The Ward Line steamship *City of Washington* had been moored close by the *Maine* and many of her passengers witnessed the disaster, leaving vivid impressions, such as this: "Suddenly we were startled by a loud report. As by a single impulse our little group rushed to the portholes and saw an immense flash shoot up in the air with a horrible grinding, hissing noise that might have been an earthquake or a cyclone. Debris of all kinds and a large number of bodies were thrown upward. It was first believed that the *Maine* was being fired upon, but afterward as the *City of Washington* was struck by what turned out to be falling debris and she careened, it was thought she was being fired upon. A second explosion took place, and following it we heard groans and cries of 'Help, Help us'. The boats of the *City of Washington* and those of the Spanish cruiser *Alfonso XII* were hurriedly launched and went to the rescue. I went into one of the boats of the *City of Washington*, and the scenes I witnessed were heartrending beyond description ... Two of the small boats on board the *City of Washington* were stove in by the debris from the *Maine*. The battleship sank even with the water in abut thirty minutes after the explosion ... Many of the rescued men were brought on board almost nude and the passengers gave them clothing."

The immediate reaction to the destruction of the American battleship from the Spaniards was of shock and sympathy. Some of the survivors were rescued quickly by boats from the warship *Alfonso XII* and brought to hospitals in Havana; within a half hour, both the civil governor of Havana and Captain General Blanco's chief of staff were on board the *City of Washington*, conferring with the American officers and offering aid and condolences. However, it was noted immediately that while the Cubans were genuinely bereaved by the American loss, most of the *peninsulares* were not. The expressions of the Spanish authorities were regarded as diplomatic niceties, while many ordinary Spaniards seemed indifferent and not a few even quite satisfied with the fate of the *Maine*. Virtually all of the Cuban women dressed in black mourning clothes the next day, "while the Spanish women wore colors," according to one American who had been "received politely" aboard the Spanish cruiser. Two days later, "while driving to the cemetery (where the 266 victims were interred) with two American friends, I was assailed with jeers and someone threw a large stone at our carriage. In fact, one or two children yelled after us that they had blown up the '*Americano*' and that they were glad of it. I did not hear one expression of regret for the terrible loss of life from any Spaniard during the time that I was in Havana."

Captain Sigsbee apparently realized that the reaction at home might well force irresistible pressure on the McKinley administration and Congress to declare war, since who but the treacherous Spaniards could have perpetrated such a vile deed? His first message to Secretary of the Navy Long was indeed restrained: "*Maine* blown up in Havana Harbor at 9:40 and destroyed. Many wounded and doubtless more killed and drowned. Wounded and others on board Spanish man-of-war and Ward Line steamer. Send lighthouse tenders from Key West for crew and few pieces of equipment still above water. No one had other clothes than those upon him ... Public opinion should be suspended till further report ... Many Spanish officers, including representatives of General Blanco, are now with me and express sympathy."

The shock and outrage felt throughout the United States the next day was indeed tempered by Captain Sigsbee's message and the attitude of the administration that, until a thorough investigation was made, no conclusions should be drawn regarding culpability. The gnawing question on everyone's mind: was it an internal explosion, possibly caused by spontaneous combustion of the highly volatile gases in a coal bunker or carelessness in monitoring a powder magazine, or had there been a deliberate act of sabotage by exploding a subsurface mine or torpedo beneath the ship? Both the U.S. Navy and the Spanish navy immediately formed investigative boards of officers to try to resolve the issue. Their findings, upon which might hang the issue of war between the two powers, arrived at totally differing conclusions.

The officers of the American Naval Court of Inquiry were led by Captain William Thomas Sampson, who would distinguish himself in the Battle of Santiago Bay the following July. The American government, emphatically rejecting Spain's suggestion that a joint investigation be conducted, carried on an exhaustive inquiry, bringing in divers, lighters and a large salvage team to recover all that could be brought up in the shallow six fathoms in which the ship had sunk. The Spanish navy carried on its own study; both reports being completed six weeks after the event, with President McKinley transmitting the American findings, along with his own message to Congress a week later, on March 29, 1898.

Excerpts from the findings of the Spanish Court of Inquiry:

"First. That on the night of February 15th last an explosion of the first order, in the forward magazine of the American ironclad *Maine*, caused the destruction of that part of the ship and its total submersion in the same place in this bay at which it was anchored.

"Second. That it is learned, from the diagrams of the vessel that there were no other substances or articles in that magazine, the only one which exploded, than powder and shells of various calibres.

"Third. That the same diagrams prove that said magazine was surrounded on the port side, the starboard side, and partly aft by coal bunkers containing bituminous coal, and which were in compartments adjoining the said magazine, and apparently separated from it only by metal bulkheads.

"Fourth. That the important facts connected with the explosion, in its external appearances, at every moment of its duration, having been described by witnesses, and the absence of all the circumstances which necessarily accompany the explosion of a torpedo, having been proved by these witnesses and experts, it can only be honestly asserted that the catastrophe was due to internal causes."

Captain Don Pedro Del Peral y Caballero, the investigating officer, made several additional points, including the assertions that he was unable to determine the exact "internal origin of the disaster," and "the impossibility of establishing the necessary communication, either with the crew of the wrecked vessel or with the officials of their Government . . ." implying official American lack of cooperation.

Excerpts from the findings of the American Court of Inquiry:

After describing in detail such factors as excellent discipline on board the *Maine*, security of the magazines, proper stowage of the other combustibles and the good condition of the coal supply, and the fire alarm system, the report continued: "There were two explosions of a distinctly different character, with a very short but distinct interval between them, and the forward part of the ship was lifted to a marked degree at the time of the first explosion. The first explosion was more in the nature of a report like that of a gun, while the second explosion was more open, prolonged and of greater volume. This second explosion was, in the opinion of the court, caused by the partial explosion of two or more of the forward magazines of the *Maine*.

"The evidence bearing upon this, being principally obtained from divers, did not enable the court to form a definite conclusion as to the condition of the wreck, although it was established that the after part of the ship was practically intact, and sank in that condition a very few minutes after the forward part.

"The following facts in regard to the forward part of the ship are, however, established by the testimony: A portion of the port side of the protective deck, which extends from about frame 30 to about frame 41, was blown up, aft, and slightly to starboard, folding the forward part of the middle superstructure over and on top of the after part . . . caused by the partial explosion of two or more of the forward magazines of the *Maine*. At frame 17 the outer shell of the ship, from a point 11½ feet from the middle line of the ship, and six feet above the keel when in its normal position, has been forced up so as to be now about four feet above the surface of the water, therefore about 34 feet above where it would be had the ship sunk uninjured. The outside bottom plating is bent into a reversed V shape ($\wedge$), the after wing of which, about 15 feet broad and 32 feet in length (from frame 17 to frame 25), is doubled back upon itself against the continuation of the same plating extending forward.

"At frame 18 the vertical keel is broken in two, and the flat keel bent into an angle similar to the angle formed by the outside bottom plating. The break is now about six feet below the surface of the water, and about 30 feet above its normal position. In the opinion of the court this effect could have been produced only by the explosion of a mine situated under the bottom of the ship at about frame 18 and somewhat on the port side of the ship. The court finds that the loss of the *Maine* on the occasion named was not in any respect due to fault or negligence on the part of any of the officers or members of the crew of said vessel.

"In the opinion of the court the *Maine* was de-

55

stroyed by the explosion of a submarine mine, which caused the partial explosion of two or more of the forward magazines. The court has been unable to obtain evidence fixing the responsibility for the destruction of the *Maine* upon any person or persons."

The American people had, for the most part, made up their minds the day the news of the tragedy broke: it was indeed an external explosion and the Spaniards, if not directly involved, were at best criminally liable for not having protected their peaceful visitor. The question of whether or not Captain Sigsbee should have posted more guards or had the surrounding water watched more closely was never raised, at least not publicly, but in such a volatile situation as existed in Cuba, with rebellion, corruption, ineptitude and insubordination rampant, it would seem that the *Maine* should, perhaps, have been on a status of higher security and vigilance.

There was little doubt, from the subsurface condition of the hull of the *Maine*, that the initial muffled explosion was caused by a device beneath the exterior of the ship. With the passing of a century and much research, the identity of the culprits is still not certain and barring discovery of previously unknown documents, the riddle will never be resolved. One theory of a small minority of cynical historians suggests that the grisly affair was rigged by the United States as an excuse to go to war with Spain. Certainly President McKinley would never have entertained such a plot; he was fighting against the drift toward conflict and he was well aware that no excuse was needed — the American people were already spoiling for a fight. The powerful capitalists in America who would gain by war profiteering also realized that no provocation was needed and that war was all but inevitable by 1898.

Despite the outcry and the vindictive accusations hurled at Spain, it made no sense to even imagine that Madrid wanted a war with America; her diplomacy, while often clumsy and incompetent, showed a deep desire to avoid an altercation. Certainly the Cubans desperately wanted the United States to become involved, raising the logical question that one of their factions may have been responsible. Such a possibility cannot be ruled out; it seems much more plausible than the dominant belief in the United States at the time that the Spanish government was the culprit.

A bizarre but logical possibility gives credence to both the American and Spanish beliefs: could renegade, insubordinate Spanish officers, disobeying their government's policies, have planted the explosives? When the behavior of the Spanish Volunteers in Cuba at the time is studied, including their loathing of even their governor generals, it is not difficult to believe that a clique of them, driven by a fanatical loyalty to the home country and an obsessive hatred of the United States, may well have engineered the destruction of the *Maine*. Below the waterline, 1890s warships were quite vulnerable — and the location of the high-explosives magazines was no secret. A relatively small charge, perhaps carried by as few as two or three strong swimmers, could have been placed against the hull. A huge hole in the mud under the ship may have been caused by a larger charge assembled on the harbor floor, just a few feet beneath the keel of the *Maine*. If, in fact, renegade Spaniards were responsible, the American populace was correct: the Spaniards did it and the vociferous disclaimers of the Spanish authorities in Madrid and Havana were also true: the government of the Queen Regent knew nothing of the affair and honestly condemned those responsible, if it was an external explosion.

On January 25, 1898, the *Maine* entered Havana Harbor, steamed past the famed Morro Castle at the entrance and went to her violent destiny, which occurred three weeks later. Although Captain Sigsbee was in no way blamed for the explosions which destroyed the warship on February 15, there were suppressed reports that his ship was not always maintained in the finest Navy traditions of spotlessness and strict observance of security regulations concerning close scrutiny of the coal bunkers and the powder magazines. Still, his subordinates were well-trained, experienced officers and seamen who, like all Navy men, were extremely duty-conscious. Whether heightened vigilance on the deck-watch could have prevented external sabotage (if, as most experts believe, it was a beneath-the-hull explosion), will, of course, never be known.

U.S. Naval Historical Center

Rather opulent for a man-of-war, rare interior photographs of the ill-fated vessel show that not all of the large expenses that made American warships superior to their Spanish opponents were lavished on their combat capabilities. Even the rooms where the torpedo-firing tubes (or guns) were mounted (above), were paneled in fine wood over the steel plating. Such superfluous wood, while handsome, hardly was an asset in case of fire! Like most battleships of the nations of the world at the time, the *Maine* was armed with torpedoes; she carried four tubes. Just a few years later, it was realized that huge battleships with their long-range guns, were hardly going to be within visual range, much less in torpedo range so those weapons were most appropriately consigned to the newest ocean weapons system, the submarine. Morale has always been important to counter the boredom and crowding onboard ship during long cruises, but it was conspicuously ignored until the late 19th century, when admirals finally began to realize that contented sailors performed better than intimidated ones. Entertainment became an important factor, and the Bachelor's Glee Club on the *Maine* (below) never failed to delight the officers and the men with their cheerful, salty singing. Some — perhaps most — of these happy young salts perished in the violent explosion the night of February 15, 1898.

Lieutenant-Commander Adolph Marix is shown at work in his tight yet ample stateroom on the *Maine* prior to his transfer from the ship in 1897. Virtually all of the senior officers' cabins were identical in size and wooden Victorian furnishings, except the one occupied by the captain, which was considerably larger. While heavy riveted steel plates formed the ceiling, the deck and walls were less intimidating. Marix was to partake in writing the final chapter in the tragic story of the *Maine* when he was appointed Judge Advocate of the five-officer board of inquiry, headed by Captain William T. Sampson, which investigated the disaster on orders from President McKinley.

The contemporary caption of this photograph is an apt description: "Master at Arms mess aboard the *Maine*. A generous diet is never begrudged American seamen by the citizens of the country, and the exposure and training undergone by naval men justify good living, which tells in time of war when muscle, nerve, and sinew are called into action, and victories that set the world awondering are recorded against the expenses of keeping a powerful Navy. There are no dinner tables on land or sea to equal a sailor's mess for good humor and good appetites — the prelude to deeds of daring."

A view of the quarterdeck of
USS Maine, exhibited the spit
and polish of a well-main-
ained U.S. Navy battleship.
The gleaming wood plank-
ing of the deck, the fresh
paint on the masts and the
superstructure, the tightly-
stretched canvas canopy, and
the neat rigging all presented
an impression of readiness
and competence. The vertical triple-expansion engines,
shown before being installed
in the ship, were of the latest
design and highest capacity
available in 1895.

In a painting by American illustrator H. Reuterdahl, the *USS Maine* is shown firing a salute to the Spanish flagship *Alfonso XII*, just after she anchored in Havana Harbor. The *Alfonso XII* is in the right background, while the German school ship *Charlotte* is moored astern. Captain Charles D. Sigsbee is shown (opposite, top) while writing an entry in his log book in his wood-paneled cabin. The last known photograph of the ship was taken with a cheap little Kodak camera at four o'clock in the afternoon of February 15. Riding peacefully at her mooring to buoy No. 4 in the harbor at Havana (opposite, bottom), the proud American warship was destroyed by massive explosions less than six hours later.

Opposite, bottom, U.S. Naval Historical Center

Yellow journalism in the U.S. reached a summit with the reporting of the destruction of the *USS Maine* over the following days and weeks. On the morning of February 17, 1898, William Randolph Hearst, on the front page of his *New York Journal* milked the story for all he could, blending fact, fancy, fabrication, and financial flimflam to boost the sales of his newspaper. His $50,000 reward for the apprehension of those responsible, would be worth almost $1,000,000 in the dollars of 100 years later, but he could be confident that the perpetrators (if indeed there were any) could not be identified. The illustration, showing how the *Maine* could have been destroyed by a mine, was equally fanciful, showing the ship anchored in about 20 fathoms of water; the harbor was just six fathoms at that spot. Of course, in his sensationalism, Hearst writes only of a "Spanish" mine; never mentioning that Cuban *insurgentes* or other factions could have been involved.

$50,000 REWARD.—WHO DESTROYED THE MAINE?—$50,000 REWARD.

EDITION FOR GREATER NEW YORK.

NEW YORK JOURNAL

AND ADVERTISER.

The Journal will give $50,000 for information, furnished to it exclusively, that will convict the person or persons who sank the Maine.

The Journal will give $50,000 for Information, furnished to it exclusively, that will convict the person or persons who sank the Maine.

NO. 5,572.   Copyright, 1898, by W. R. Hearst.—NEW YORK, THURSDAY, FEBRUARY 17, 1898.—16 PAGES.   PRICE ONE CENT In Greater New York, Elsewhere and Jersey City. TWO CENT

DESTRUCTION OF THE WAR SHIP MAINE WAS THE WORK OF AN ENEMY

$50,000!

$50,000 REWARD!

For the Detection of the Perpetrator of the Maine Outrage!

The New York Journal hereby offers a reward of **$50,000 CASH** for information, **FURNISHED TO IT EXCLUSIVELY**, which shall lead to the detection and conviction of the person, persons or government criminally responsible for the explosions which resulted in the destruction, at Havana, of the United States war ship Maine and the loss of 258 lives of American sailors.

The **$50,000 CASH** offered for the above information is on deposit with Wells, Fargo & Co.

No one is barred, be he the humble but misguided seaman eking out a few miserable dollars by acting as a spy, or the attache of a government secret service, plotting, by any devilish means, to revenge fancied insults or cripple menacing countries.

This offer has been cabled to Europe and will be made public in every capital of the Continent and in London this morning.

The Journal believes that any man who can be bought to commit murder can also be bought to betray his comrades. **FOR THE PERPETRATOR OF THIS OUTRAGE HAD ACCOMPLICES.**

W. R. HEARST.

Assistant Secretary Roosevelt Convinced the Explosion of the War Ship Was Not an Accident.

The Journal Offers $50,000 Reward for the Conviction of the Criminals Who Sent 258 American Sailors to Their Death. Naval Officers Unanimous That the Ship Was Destroyed on Purpose.

$50,000!

$50,000 REWARD

For the Detection of the Perpetrator of the Maine Outrage!

The New York Journal hereby offers a reward of **$50,000 CASH** for information, **FURNISHED TO IT EXCLUSIVELY**, which shall lead to the detection and conviction of the person, persons or government criminally responsible for the explosion which resulted in the destruction, at Havana, of the United States war ship Maine and the loss of 258 lives of American sailors.

The **$50,000 CASH** offered for the above information is on deposit with Wells, Fargo & Co.

No one is barred, be he the humble, but misguided, seaman eking out a few miserable dollars by acting as a spy, or the attache of a government secret service, plotting, by any devilish means, to revenge fancied insults or cripple menacing countries.

This offer has been cabled to Europe and will be made public in every capital of the Continent and in London this morning.

The Journal believes that any man who can be bought to commit murder can also be bought to betray his comrades. **FOR THE PERPETRATOR OF THIS OUTRAGE HAD ACCOMPLICES.**

W. R. HEARST.

POWDER MAGAZINE

MINE

WIRE

NAVAL OFFICERS THINK THE MAINE WAS DESTROYED BY A SPANISH MINE.

George Eugene Bryson, the Journal's special correspondent at Havana, cables that it is the secret opinion of many Spaniards in the Cuban capital that the Maine was destroyed and 258 of her men killed by means of a submarine mine, or fixed torpedo. This is the opinion of several American naval authorities. The Spaniards, it is believed, arranged to have the Maine anchored over one of the harbor mines. Wires connected the mine with a powder magazine, and it is thought the explosion was caused by sending an electric current through the wire. If this can be proven, the brutal nature of the Spaniards will be shown by the fact that they waited to spring the mine until after all the men had retired for the night. The Maltese cross in the picture shows where the mine may have been fired.

Hidden Mine or a Sunken Torpedo Believed to Have Been the Weapon Used Against the American Man-of-War---Officers and Men Tell Thrilling Stories of Being Blown Into the Air Amid a Mass of Shattered Steel and Exploding Shells---Survivors Brought to Key West Scout the Idea of Accident---Spanish Officials Protest Too Much---Our Cabinet Orders a Searching Inquiry---Journal Sends Divers to Havana to Report Upon the Condition of the Wreck.

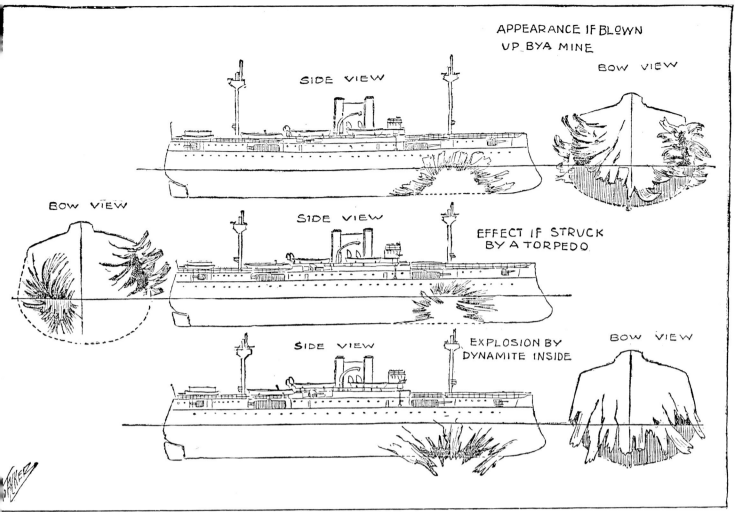

THE ENEMY'S BLOW OR ACCIDENT? HOW THE DISCOVERY MAY BE MADE.

The Government can without doubt learn whether the loss of the Maine was due to the treachery of the Spaniards or accident. An inspection of the sunken vessel will be made by divers. A blow delivered from the outside would bend the plates inward and if the explosion occurred in the powder magazine the plates will show it. The upper picture shows the Maine as she appears if a mine was exploded under her. If a torpedo, secretly launched by Spaniards, struck the big war ship the second picture shows the condition she is in. An explosion inside the vessel would tear a big hole in her bottom, bending the plates outward, as shown in the third picture.

The *New York Journal* ran a series of drawings showing the possible effects of explosions of three most likely causes of the destruction of the *Maine:* a mine, a torpedo, or an internal explosion. Under the banner headline "NOTED NAVAL AUTHORITIES DECLARE IT WAS NOT AN ACCIDENT," the subheadlines at left show how pure speculation was given unquestioned credence, weakly supported by terms such as "Experts think," "People convinced," and "Some say." The accompanying articles reveal much prejudice: "The (American) government is holding its breath. There is an outward calm which marks a Northern race. Paris would be filled with a mad mob, Rome would howl, Madrid would riot with savage fierceness." Also gross errors: "...the explosion was too far forward for ...coal bunkers or magazines..."; actually the massive secondary explosion was the main magazine — adjacent to a coal bunker — where the reaction was either initiated or was set off by an external hit on the hull encasing it. Under the headline "LONG AND ROOSEVELT AT LOGGERHEADS. THE SECRETARY MAINTAINS THAT THE DISASTER WAS AN ACCIDENT, BUT HIS ASSISTANT DOESN'T THINK SO," the *Journal* reported "Secretary Long and Assistant Secretary Roosevelt are at total variance over the calamity, and both of these officials have chafed at their departmental moorings all day in consequence of the opposite directions from which they view the cause of the Havana horror.

"Whether the disagreement between them will go beyond a mere conflict of opinion will be determined in the future, but at the present time the relations between the Secretary of the Navy and his valuable and aggressive Assistant Secretary are strained, to say the least.

"Secretary Long has followed the lead of the President and publicly insisted that the explosion aboard the *Maine* was an accident. Privately he has said that he feared it was not.

"Secretary Roosevelt, backed by the ablest and most experienced officers of the Navy, has taken the opposite view of the situation, and with his characteristic vigor has contended that the circumstances as reported in the official and unofficial returns from Havana show that it was an act of treachery.

"Thus the two ranking officials of the Navy Department have virtually been breaking lances with each other throughout the day, and the result has been more or less confusion among the subordinates."

The two hands show just two small areas used for torpedo warheads. Totally ignored are two 6-inch shell magazines, two 10-inch round magazines, a 6-pounder and small arms magazines; the four large-caliber storage areas much more lethal than torpedo heads! The most dangerous location on the ship was the powder magazine, situated between the forward 6-inch and the 6-pounder magazines, virtually the center of the explosion. Had a knowledgeable group of saboteurs planned to hit the hull beneath the surface of the water, as is generally believed, this is the exact location they would have chosen to inflict the most damage. Also, this sectional drawing shows just one small coal bunker, directly ahead of the forward boiler room; the ship required much larger coal storage areas, so the accuracy of the illustration is in doubt. The berth deck, where virtually all of the enlisted men had retired for the night, was directly above the magazines which blew up, accounting for the tremendous loss of life. The illustration by renowned political cartoonist Homer Davenport (opposite) showing bereaved Uncle Sam, reverently standing alongside a coffin draped with 45-star American flags, accurately expressed the somber mood of a nation in mourning.

The victims of the *Maine* catastrophe whose bodies were immediately recovered were interred in a section of a Havana cemetery; their funeral procession (above) required the use of virtually every hearse for miles around. Contemporary accounts noted that the *Insulares* were genuinely grieving over the American loss of life, while most of the *Peninsulares* either seemed indifferent or even haughtily satisfied concerning the results of the disaster, the latter well aware that war was probably inevitable. A cutaway diagram of the ill-fated warship (below), also published in the *New York Journal,* was a further exercise in media ignorance, referring to "The hands point-(ing) to the compartments where explosives were stored."

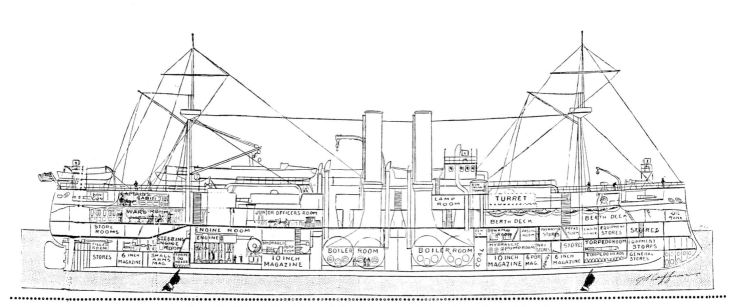

A SECTIONAL VIEW OF THE MAINE.

The battle ship was 324 feet 4 inches over all.   The scale in this sketch is 20 feet to the inch.   The hands point to the compartments where explosives were stored.   It was near the forward compartment of the vessel that the explosion occurred.   The berth decks above the compartment were occupied by the sleeping sailors, and no second glance is necessary to tell what awful havoc would be wrought among the sleeping tars by an explosion in it.

Top, National Archives   Bottom, Collection of Richard B. Wettereau

U. S. Navy divers and salvage men went immediately to work to ascertain the cause of the *Maine* disaster, supplying much of the information on which Captain Sampson's Court of Inquiry based its final report. With the mast still upright, the crow's nest was draped in black mourning bunting (top) with a flag flying at half-staff above it, as salvage boats worked alongside. Salvagers were at work (above) on the midship section. Oddly enough, it would not be until 1911 — 13 years after the *Maine* blew up — that she was finally raised, towed out to sea, and sunk. On March 17 of that year, her remains (bottom) were being readied for her final, melancholy journey.

Monuments and memorials commemorating the sinking of the *USS Maine* sprang up in abundance. Some, such as the elaborate floral display which featured the ship and two field artillery pieces (Naval guns would have been more appropriate) with the slogan of the Spanish-American War "Remember the Maine" (above), were high points of Victorian-era sentimentality. On the waterfront in Havana, a masonry monument which cradled two guns entwined with anchor chains from the ship (below) still reminds natives and visitors to Cuba of the tragedy. An American eagle once was perched atop the columns, but Fidel Castro supposedly ordered it removed. As far as he was concerned, the 266 American sailors did die for *Cuba Libre*, but they also perished for *Imperialismo Yanqui!*

The equestrian arts reached their zenith in the cavalry units of the regular armies of the world and the Americans, being among the frontier nations so dependent on horse transport, excelled in fine horsemanship. Elite military establishments have always prided themselves in precision drill, be it by individual soldiers or entire units, and the cavalrymen were especially adept at impressive maneuvers. Three troopers, each standing on the backs of a pair of horses (above), competed in a Roman Race in the Riding Hall at Fort Myer, Virginia. In an incredible display of precise timing, superb horsemanship, and well-trained mounts, a cavalryman straddled three horses (below) as they jumped over hurdles, also at Fort Myer, in 1898. The renowned artist Frederic Remington created both of these wash drawings.

United States Declares War

At the time that the *USS Maine* steamed into Havana Harbor, Spain's ambassador to Washington, D.C., Señor Dupuy de Lome, expressing the approval of his government and acknowledging that a Spanish vessel would soon reciprocate, made a comment that could have been prophetic: "the only remote contingency which might lead to unpleasant consequences would be some overt act on the part of insurgent sympathizers with the hope of embroiling Spain and the United States." After the *Maine* went down, de Lome's thoughts could be interpreted according to the convictions of the listener: the anti-imperialists could reason that the Spanish diplomat had warned that there was at least a possibility of sabotage beyond the control of his government, implying that the Americans should be on guard. Those who favored war conversely could cite the warning as proof that not only was treachery planned by Madrid, but a disclaimer had been already issued, weeks before the event! When the Spanish armored cruiser *Vizcaya* sailed into New York Harbor two days after the destruction of the *Maine*, she attracted much attention; not necessarily hostile, but more as an opportunity to compare her to the American warships that she might soon engage at sea. A week later she departed for Havana and naval authorities from several major powers seemed to agree that while the vessels of both nations were comparable, Americans were superior in gunnery. These factors, according to the experts, made both fleets equal; but U.S. naval officers knew better, as Admiral George Dewey was later to say regarding his victory at Manila Bay: "...the first lesson of the battle teaches the importance of American gunnery and good guns... combats are decided more by skill in gunnery and the quality of the guns than all else."

As the Spaniards prepared for war, the European onlookers who had recently believed that they would quickly overcome the Americans in battle began to reconsider, as evidenced by dispatches from correspondent Wolf of the Berlin *Tageblatt*, of the preparations at Cadiz, during the *Maine* crisis: "Gun practice here is a lost art. 'The captain general does not think much of it' said a black-eyed señora to me; 'it is so hard on one's nerves, and such a waste of powder.' The soldiers lounge about and the officers gamble and flirt. (The captain general's) intimations of war secrets was a bluff; there are no secret preparations." Commenting on Spain's sole first-line battleship, the *Pelayo*, Wolf wrote: "The *Pelayo* is a fine ironclad. It makes a good impression. There are four big guns on deck and a good many smaller ones at the sides. But I have been talking with people who know the *Pelayo* well, and I gather from their intimation and hints that she is one of those belles who are beautiful only when in repose. She only shows off in the safety of harbors, and then is much admired. Only once did she venture out to sea, I am

told, and the experiment was disastrous... A naval officer told me Cadiz had fifteen or sixteen new Krupp guns. Whether there is any ammunition for these guns I could not learn. The Cadiz people doubt it. I have not heard a shot fired during the week I am here." The German reporter concluded: "I am almost ashamed of this letter. I was sent to report a war, or at least war preparations; and though I searched high and low, I cannot discover any..."

Only the British had appreciated the skills, motivation and determination of the Americans from the start, as Henry Norman, the respected English correspondent, wrote in the *Chronicle* of London, as he covered Washington at the beginning of the war: "After admitting every reasonable criticism, (the U. S. Army) is a triumph of organization. I doubt if so much, from so little, has ever been accomplished so expeditiously and so uneventfully before. And look at the display of American patriotism. When the volunteers were summoned by the President they walked on the scene as if they had been waiting in the wings... As I was standing on the steps of the Arlington Hotel, a tall, thin man, carrying a large suitcase, walked out and got on the streetcar for the railway station, on his way to Tampa (the embarkation port for the Cuban invasion). It was John Jacob Astor, the possessor of a hundred millions of dollars. Theodore Roosevelt's Rough Riders contain a number of the smartest young men in New York society. A Harvard classmate of mine, a rising young lawyer, is working like a laborer at the Brooklyn Navy Yard... He is a naval reserve man and sent in his application for any post 'from the stokehole upward'. The same is true of women. When I called to say goodbye to Mrs. John Addison Porter, the wife of the Secretary to the President, whose charming hospitality I had enjoyed, she had gone to Tampa to ship as a nurse on the Red Cross steamer for the coast of Cuba." Norman then commented on American courage and bravado, and in an interesting observation, he inadvertently mused on the future alliance of Great Britain and the United States: "...this is the old daring of our common race. If the old lion and the young lion would ever go hunting side by side." It was the Spanish-American War that would make Norman's fanciful introspection come to fruition.

Although these two correspondents' writings may seem slanted against Spain, it must be remembered that they were neutral, indeed the Germans had leaned more towards the Spaniards. In the final analysis, while Spain had some fine commanders and experienced soldiers and sailors, the long colonial struggles and the failings of their domestic society left them unprepared for a fierce conflict with such a vigorous and aroused people as were the Americans. As Congress debated the issue of war and appropriated $50,000,000 for immediate defense requirements, especially coastal fortifications, the entire country prepared for the inevitable conflict. It was also noted that the average young American male was somewhat of a machinist and a mechanic and most were trained as marksmen with the rifle from boyhood, traits that were indispensable in a late-19th century combat situation — and in the conflicts of the 20th century as well.

Meanwhile, with the report of the Naval Commission concerning the sinking of the *Maine*, Congress moved closer to war. When Senator Redfield Proctor of Vermont returned from a fact-finding trip to Cuba, he delivered a revealing speech relating his observations of the intolerable affairs on the island. On March 16 he spoke in the Senate to his enraptured colleagues and the press. Proctor's oratory was calm and unemotional, purposefully avoiding sensationalism or incitement. He reported what he saw of the devastated countryside, the untended fields and the starving *reconcentrados*, many of whom had not been returned to their homes and farms as Captain-General Blanco had promised. He spoke of the *trochas* — the armed entrenchments surrounding the towns where the local citizenry were interned — as well as the other violations of human dignity and civilized behavior. Senator Thurston of Nebraska had also just returned from Cuba and addressed the Senate in a more emotional speech on March 24. As was written at the time, in the *History of the Spanish-American War*, by Henry Watterson, these and other senatorial speeches "... awakened the conscience of the nation and formulated in the popular mind a declaration of war."

Two weeks elapsed between the sending of the *Maine* report to Congress by President McKinley and his "war message" of April 12, when he released to the nation's deliberative body its constitutional prerogative to declare war. Even at that late date, the President avoided belligerence and did not ask for war, contrary to the clamoring demands of a majority of the citizenry, as well as Congress. With straightforward clarity, McKinley, while not outrightly requesting a war declaration, issued four propositions which left little maneuvering room to avoid the now imminent conflict:

First — In the cause of humanity and to put an end to the barbarities, bloodshed, starvation, and horrible miseries now existing there, and which the parties to the conflict are either unable or unwilling to stop or mitigate. It is no answer to say this is all in another country, belonging to another nation, and is therefore none of our business. It is especially our duty — for it is right at our door.

Second — We owe it to our citizens in Cuba to afford them that protection — and indefinitely — for life and property which no government there can or will afford, and to that end to terminate the conditions that deprive them of legal protection.

Third — The right to intervene may be justified by the very serious injury to the commerce, trade, and business of our people, and by the wanton destruction of property and devastation of the island.

Fourth — And which is of the utmost importance, the present condition of affairs in Cuba is a constant menace to our peace, and entails upon the government enormous expense. With such a conflict waged for years in an island so near us and with which our people have such trade and business relations — when the lives and liberty of our citizens are in constant danger and their property destroyed and themselves ruined — when our trading vessels are liable to seizure and are seized at our very door by warships of a foreign nation, the expeditions of filibustering that we are powerless to repress altogether and the irritating questions and entanglements thus arising — all these and others that I need not mention, with the resulting strained relations, are a constant menace to our peace and compel us to keep on a semi-war footing with a nation with which we are at peace.

After several days of reports from the committees on foreign relations of both houses of congress, intense debate and voting, the final declaration of war emerged from Congress as a joint resolution:

"WHEREAS, the abhorrent conditions which have existed for more than three years in the island of Cuba, so near our own borders, have shocked the moral sense of the people of the United States, have been a disgrace to Christian civilization, culminating as they have, in the destruction of a United States battleship, with two hundred and sixty-six of its officers and crew, while on a friendly visit in the harbor of Havana, and cannot longer be endured, as has been set forth by the President of the United States, in his message to Congress on April 11, 1898, upon which the action of Congress was invited; therefore,

"RESOLVED, By the Senate and the House of Representatives of the United States of America in Congress assembled,

1. That the people of the island of Cuba are, and of a right ought to be, free and independent.

2. That it is the duty of the United States to demand, and the Government of the United States does hereby demand, that the Government of Spain at once relinquish its authority and government in the island of Cuba and withdraw its land and naval forces from Cuba and Cuban waters.

3. That the President of the United States be, and he hereby is, directed and empowered to use the entire land and naval forces of the United States, and to call into the actual service of the United States the militia of the several States to such an extent as may be necessary to carry these resolutions into effect.

4. That the United States hereby disclaims any disposition or intention to exercise sovereignty, jurisdiction or control over said island, except for the pacification thereof, and asserts its determination, when that is accomplished, to leave the government and control of the island to its people."

The strenuous efforts of McKinley to maintain peace had ended — not because of any failure of his efforts, but due largely to the refusal of

Spain to alleviate its repressive rule and the excuse afforded by the *Maine* incident. The President quickly signed the joint resolution into law; the United States was now at war with Spain, fulfilling the demands of a majority of its citizens. What began as a modest effort to liberate Cuba quickly grew into a much greater endeavor even as Commodore Dewey was readying his well-provisioned Asiatic Squadron of the U.S. Navy at Hong Kong, to sail to the Philippines, where a powerful enemy fleet lay waiting in Manila Bay. On the home front, the response was immediate and overwhelming: when the President issued a call for 125,000 volunteers, more than three-quarters of a million responded within ten days! Training camps were established in every state and territory, and America's robust manufacturing, shipping and railroad industries swung into action to produce the armaments and supplies and to move them to the embarkation ports.

With but 10 percent of the American population composed of black or "colored" citizens, fully one-third of the regular army at the start of 1898 was filled by Negro units, commanded by white officers. Many had been the legendary "Buffalo Soldiers" of the frontier Indian engagements, and they were to add to their accomplishments in the battles just ahead. Colonel Leonard Wood headed for San Antonio, Texas, to establish the training camp for his 1st Volunteer Cavalry Regiment and to begin accepting the cowboys, U.S. marshals, mine foremen and Indians whom he knew were

Typical of American industrial might of the 1890s – both military and civilian – was the Watervliet Arsenal in New York State. Here, large-calibre naval guns (above) were mass-produced either for use on battleships or for coastal defense.

already well experienced for the task ahead. Meanwhile, his Lieutenant Colonel, Theodore Roosevelt, remained in Washington awhile longer, locating the best in weaponry and equipment that he could requisition and bringing some of the brightest and most athletic graduates of Yale, Harvard and other fine universities into the regiment, which was immediately nicknamed the "Rough Riders" by the admiring press.

While blacks and Indians served with distinction in combat roles during the Spanish-American War and women fought just as heroically in their tasks as nurses under appalling circumstances, the distinguished service rendered by a rapidly-growing minority in the 1890s — the country's Jewish citizens — deserves respectful acknowledgment. Perhaps the best-known Jew in the service at the time was Lieutenant Commander Adolph Marix, who had been the first executive officer of the *USS Maine,* but was reassigned in early 1897 when he left the doomed ship to be replaced by Richard Wainwright. After the Battle of Manzanillo, for which he was promoted and cited for eminent and conspicuous conduct, Marix's Navy career advanced and he was a vice admiral at the time of his death. Approximately

5,000 Jews served in the war, with only 100 reported in the Navy — a figure which seems unreliably low, considering that 15 the *Maine* fatalities were Jewish. It seems unlikely that 15 percent of all Jews in the Navy served on one ship — maybe more if any Jews survived — those sailors being of a far greater number than the total Navy casualties due to enemy action!

Roughly two percent of Army and Navy personnel were wounded or killed by enemy action and disease during the conflict; the casualties among Jewish soldiers and sailors — 29 killed in action, 47 wounded, and 28 deaths from disease, was also about two percent. In the officer corps, there were 30 Jews in the Army and 20 in the Navy (another suspiciously low number, a mere one percent of Jewish personnel). Like Marix, Lieutenant Joseph Straus eventually attained the rank of admiral, as did Lieutenant Edward D. Taussig, who not only occupied Wake Island, but later was assigned to administer Guam, as it was transformed from a desolate Spanish possession into a large strategic American naval base.

The elite Rough Riders included Jewish troopers, such as Jacob Wilbusky, just 16 years old, who was one of the earliest to be killed at Las Guasimas. Colonel Roosevelt later spoke publicly of his experience with Jewish soldiers: "One of the best colonels among the regular regiments who fought beside me was a Jew. One of the commanders of the ships which blockaded the coast so well (Taussig, ed.) was a Jew. In my own regiment, I promoted five men from the ranks for valor and good conduct in battle. It happened by pure accident (for I knew nothing of the faith of any of them) and these included two Protestants, two Catholics and one Jew." Of course, so diverse a regiment as the Rough Riders would concoct picturesque nicknames for its members, among them a Jewish trooper fondly known as "Porkchop" and the gentile with the foulest mouth who was dubbed "Prayerful James!" The most appropriate moniker of all came from a Sioux Indian trooper who, when he first saw Roosevelt's famed toothy grin, named him "Laughing Horse."

The American diplomats in Madrid, Havana and other Spanish possessions were "handed their passports" — the diplomatic language of the era — as were the Spanish embassy personnel in Washington, who returned to their home countries. All of the great powers were observing with deep interest, for they were well aware that the outcome of the conflict would have a salient impact on the world order, even if most Americans had not yet come to the same realization. All that the United States seemed concerned with was to evict the Spaniards from Cuba; the rest would manifest itself in the weeks ahead, to the bemusement and surprise of a people somewhat naive in the realm of world geopolitics that they were thrusting upon themselves.

The reaction to the declaration of war by the ruling classes in Spain was one of defiance and ve-

hemence, of contempt for the "Yankee pigs" who had dared to challenge the millennia-old country whose pioneering efforts and vision had brought the nations of the western hemisphere — including the upstart United States — into being. Queen Christina and her son, the adolescent King Alfonso XIII, appeared before the Cortes in Madrid, where the Queen Regent read her speech from the throne with her young son standing next to her. The Queen of Spain was regal and noble and the gathered dignitaries cheered most exuberantly as she prepared to address them. Those who were more reflective and familiar with the depth of the tragedy they were embarking upon felt the more sobering emotion of sadness as Her Most Catholic Majesty spoke in an elegant yet somber tone of the insults and intolerable provocations from the United States which compelled her government to sever relations. She requested that the "supreme decision of parliament" support her in defending the rights and the honor of Spain. The highlight of her courageous speech brought forth the patriotism and heartfelt loyalty of all Spaniards: "I have summoned the Cortes to defend our rights, whatever sacrifice they may entail. Thus identifying myself with the nation, I not only fulfill the oath I swore in accepting the regency, but I follow the dictates of a mother's heart, trusting to the Spanish people to gather behind my son's throne, and to defend it until he is old enough to defend it himself, as well as trusting to the Spanish people to defend the honor and the territory of the nation."

On April 25, 1898, the American Congress passed the bill which formally declared war, dating it from April 21. Already the U.S. Navy had blockaded the north coast of Cuba and was sending vessels to patrol around the southern shores. Several Spanish ships had been immediately captured and brought to Key West as war prizes. Throughout the island of Cuba, the *insulares* rejoiced and renewed their revolutionary efforts, while the *peninsulares*, more than ever before, felt besieged from all sides. In the Philippine Islands, all was quiet; the proverbial calm before a rapidly approaching storm.

The monitor *Monterey* in action
during the Spanish-American War.

Within three weeks after President McKinley issued a call for 100,000 volunteers, more than 750,000 responded, crowding into recruiting stations all over the country. A potential volunteer seriously studied a recruiting poster (above) in New York City, while two soldiers and several civilians looked on. Once inside, the new enlistees began their processing by noncommissioned officers (below) within the same branch post office in lower Manhattan.

President William McKinley (opposite top) possessed a great aversion towards the demands swelling up in government offices and among the American citizenry that the U.S. go to war with Spain if that country continued to refuse to relinquish sovereignty over Cuba. In not-so-private conversation, his Assistant Secretary of the Navy Theodore Roosevelt had referred to him as a "white-faced cur" and reportedly had described him with a backbone "as soft as an eclair" for not rushing into conflict with Spain. Totally understanding and devoid of vindictiveness, McKinley had once observed that he substantially agreed with the bellowing of Roosevelt then solemnly intoned that "mine is the greater responsibility." When army surgeon Colonel Leonard Wood was the President's personal physician, McKinley jokingly inquired: "Have you and Theodore declared war yet?" Wood's answer was forthright: "No, Mr. President, but we think you should." After traveling every road seeking a peaceful outcome and finding nothing but washouts, McKinley's resolve immediately focused on prosecuting the war to a quick and overwhelming conclusion. During the conflict he posed with his war cabinet (right) consisting of (left to right): himself; Lyman T. Gage, Secretary of the Treasury; John W. Griggs, Attorney General; John D. Long, Secretary of the Navy; James Wilson, Secretary of Agriculture; William R. Day, Secretary of State; Russell A. Alger, Secretary of War; Cornelius N. Bliss, Secretary of the Interior; and Charles Emery Smith, Postmaster General. Navy Secretary Long had become accustomed to the vigorous insubordination of his assistant, Theodore Roosevelt; now it would be the task of War Secretary Alger to cope with the same situation, as the newly-commissioned lieutenant colonel embarked on a three-and-a-half-months' military career which was to have a greater impact than many which lasted for three-and-a-half decades! Despite the unpreparedness and the blunders associated with the prosecution of the Spanish-American War, it was these high U.S. government officials who would lead the United States out of the 19th century as the emerging great power of the 20th century.

Among the most stalwart and powerful of the jingoes in the U.S. Senate were Republican Senators Redfield Proctor of Vermont (opposite, left) and Henry Cabot Lodge of Massachusetts (near left), both of whom exerted great influence on the administration. Proctor delivered a moving speech in the Senate, calmly describing in detail, the abominable human rights violations in Cuba, from whence he had just returned. Consulting closely with Assistant Naval Secretary Roosevelt, he also successfully lobbied McKinley to appoint his friend and fellow Granite State native, Commodore George Dewey, to command the Asiatic Squadron. Lodge, one of the most puissant men in the Senate, strongly backed the war buildup and was a close confidant of Roosevelt during his rapid rise to the presidency and his seven-and-a-half year administration. Lodge served 31 years in the senate, ending with his death in 1924. His son of the same name was ambassador to the United Nations in the Eisenhower Administration and vice presidential candidate in the Nixon Campaign in 1960. The fact that one of just four American first-class battleships during the war with Spain was named *USS Massachusetts* may well have been due to the influence of the senator.

In the early spring of 1898 with the final report of Captain (soon to be promoted to Rear Admiral) Sampson's court of inquiry having concluded that the battleship *Maine* had indeed been a victim of unknown enemy agents, the American people interpreted those findings to be an indictment of the Spanish government, a conclusion based on ignorant emotions since it was inconceivable that Spain, in a dire predicament economically and morally, would provoke a conflict with the prosperous and powerful U.S. The manhood of America — all social classes, races and ethnic groups — were ready to respond to the call to arms whenever it would be sounded. At the National Rifle Range at Creedmoor, Long Island, which became a political segment of New York City that very year, officers watched (above) as cavalry troops practiced their marksmanship. Proudly posing in his new uniform and armed with a sabre and revolver, young Lieutenant Godfrey A. S. Weiners (left), a resident of College Point, was newly commissioned in the 17th New York National Guard Regiment headquartered in Flushing, in the county of Queens which became a borough of the vastly enlarged city of New York in 1898. One of the few photographs taken at Camp Wood, outside of San Antonio, Texas where the 1st Volunteer Cavalry Regiment was organized and trained, shows a group of officers (upper right) at lunch on homemade benches. At the head of the table sits the commander of the Rough Riders, Colonel Leonard Wood and his executive officer, Lieutenant-Colonel Theodore Roosevelt, in May 1898. Roosevelt wanted to lead a regiment that was not only militarily elite, but that would be a cross-section of the U.S. population. While many of his troopers were frontiersmen, cowboys, tough mine foremen, and Indians, others were eastern aristocrats whom many observers believed would not mix well and could wind up fighting more among themselves than against the Spaniards. One of the most famous and prominent was the commander of Troop K, Captain Woodbury Kane (lower right), a socially notable cousin of John Jacob Astor. A classmate of Roosevelt at Harvard, Kane was an accomplished athlete and internationally-renowned yachtsman. His superb horsemanship was a great asset for a cavalry officer, and although a dandy of the "Fifth Avenue Boys" faction of the regiment, he "fought with the same natural ease as he dressed," according to Roosevelt. The lieutenant colonel had picked his men well, for the eastern society dudes soon proved to be as hardy and aggressive as the western roughnecks, and they quickly bonded in mutual respect.

The greatest and the least of Spanish warships are shown in these two illustrations. The mighty cruiser *Vizcaya* (above) as she steamed into New York Harbor just two days after the American battleship *USS Maine* exploded and sank in Havana, on February 15, 1898. One of her aft guns is firing a salute, as tugboats and other harbor craft steam around her in a combination of halfhearted welcome and curiosity about what many Americans were already considering to be an enemy ship. She remained less than a week, then sailed off to join Admiral Cervera's squadron, and less than five months later, went down fighting before the heavy guns of the U.S. Navy. The diminutive little gunboat *Guantanamo* (below), is shown as she rode at anchor in the harbor of Cádiz on October 28, 1895, just after she was built. Coastal vessels such as *Guantanamo* and other boats of her class — *Almendares, Baracoa, Cauto, Mayarit* and *Vumuri* — were intended mainly for harbor defense, both in Spain and in the colonies.

Art work by H. Reuterdahl   U.S. Naval Historical Center

Queen Christina (above, left) was the mother of Don Alfonso XIII (above, right), the young King of Spain. Since Alfonso was barely into his teen years, his mother was the real power behind the throne. The Queen-Regent appeared regal and deeply concerned for her country and her subjects, yet her government officially stood firm in support of Weyler and his concentration camps as well as the other criminal policies pursued by Spanish colonial rule. It is probable that she and her son were never told the truth concerning the genocidal treatment of the *pacíficos* in Cuba. Praxedes Mateo Sagasta (below) was the prime minister of the Spanish government during the war with the U.S., having succeeded Canovas del Castillo.

COMMODORE
GEORGE DEWEY U.S.N.

Battle of Manila Bay

George Washington Dewey was born December 26, 1837, in the Green Mountain city of Montpelier, Vermont, at an altitude and distance from the sea hardly conducive to the breeding of a naval warrior. The house of his birth stood across the street from the state capitol building and his constant view of the impressive structure which symbolized democratic government, citizenship and stability during his formative years, influenced his development into a patriotic, dutiful and courageous public servant. Appointed to the U.S. Naval Academy in 1854, largely through the influence of his father, Dr. Julius Yemans Dewey, one of the most prominent Vermonters, the young naval cadet, returning home, noticed that a statue of the Revolutionary War hero, Ethan Allen, had been erected on the portico of the capitol building. Admiring the statue, he wondered if ever such a monument would be made of him. A century after his great triumph, visitors in the rotunda of the building are confronted by a painting of Dewey and his officers on the bridge of his flagship, *USS Olympia,* during the Battle of Manila Bay, but a few yards from the statue which had prompted his youthful musings.

After graduation as a midshipman in 1858, Dewey immediately went to sea, serving on the *USS Wabash* in the Mediterranean, where he first saw Spain, but the thoughts of naval conflicts were back home and, shortly after his return, the Civil War began. As a lieutenant on the *USS Mississippi* of Admiral Farragut's West Gulf Squadron, he distinguished himself early when, as he was the last to leave his burning ship, he saved a drowning sailor as he was swimming away; an act of bravery and coolness, according to his commanding officer, Captain Smith. By the end of the war between the states, Dewey had attained the rank of lieutenant commander, a singular achievement for an officer still in his mid-twenties. During the following 30 years, Dewey was to hold a great variety of commands and assignments, gaining the valuable experience for the supreme test of his remarkable career. When Spain and the United States went to war, Commodore George Dewey was 60 years old and in his 40th year of active duty.

Fortunately, fate, with severe prodding from Senator Proctor and Assistant Naval Secretary Roosevelt, had indeed placed the right man in the right position, as told by one of Dewey's confidants, diplomat and war correspondent John Barrett, in his unabashedly hero-worshipping book, *Admiral George Dewey,* published in 1899: "Dewey had never had a high command on the Asiatic Station, and did not feel familiar with that part of the world; but he was deeply interested in its progress and development. There was considerable competition for the Asiatic Station. Secretary Long was not in favor of sending Dewey there. He was not opposed to Dewey personally, and he had no lack of confidence in his naval ability, but he had made up his mind that, as far as his influence could go, it should be given to another officer. At this juncture Senator Redfield Proctor (a fellow Vermonter)...a trusted friend of (Dewey) went to the President and urged that Dewey should be given command ... The President agreed . . . and before Secretary Long made his nomination, he found that the President had promised the place. It could not be said that the President overruled Long, but he made the independent choice of Dewey on the strong recommendation of Senator Proctor, supported by Assistant Secretary Roosevelt, who was strongly in favor of Dewey's appointment from the first consideration of names. Remembering the foresight with which Dewey, as chief of bureau, had prepared for possible war with Chile and the opinions of his ability expressed by naval men, Roosevelt earnestly favored his appointment to the Asiatic Station, where the Assistant Secretary then foresaw, with characteristic acumen, a probable scene in any war with Spain."

Unlike Cuba so close to home, Americans had scant knowledge of the Philippines and conditions there, also under Spanish colonial rule for nearly 400 years. Dissimilar to the island of Cuba (with a mere handful of close by smaller islets), the Philippine archipelago consisted of more than 1,200 separate islands, many uninhabited and some populated by the most savage and cannibalistic people on earth. Many were pirates, attacking coastal shipping and communities, sometimes within 30 miles of Manila Bay. The Spaniards wisely never tried to subdue and occupy vast portions of their far-flung colony. Those areas that were held by the Spaniards, especially the largest islands of Luzon, Mindanao, Panay, Mindoro and others, experienced the usual autocratic Spanish rule, with natives allowed no decision-making powers in their own affairs, sparking numerous bloody insurrectionist movements, but on a smaller scale than in Cuba. The government of the Philippine colony was a *junta* composed of a governor-general sent from Madrid and his most powerful cabinet member, the Roman Catholic Archbishop of Manila, as well as the admiral of the Pacific naval forces and the captain general of the army. The actual political and legal powers were held by the governor-general, the archbishop and the religious orders of the Church, which were the governing bureaucracy — the archetypical example of church-state rule and oppression. Without exception, all of the priests and civil servants who had any role in administrating the colony were native-born Spaniards, whose sole allegiance and responsibility were to the crown and the Church. The Philippines became the place for Spaniards favored by the Madrid establishment to spend a few years in service to the government and to return home with considerable personal fortunes — at the expense of heavily taxed natives and foreign nationals. In the same manner, the religious orders had acquired enormous wealth.

In addition to explaining the heterogeneous population of the Philippines, composed of several distinct racial groups, often at war with one another, as well as the Spaniards and able to wage effective guerilla warfare in the jungles, mountains and narrow waterways, Henry Watterson wrote: "All civil servants and priests . . . sent to take their instructions from those already adept in oppression, and ambitious to surpass their predecessors in the fortunes to be accumulated for the home churches or by the court favorites who returned to Spain to dazzle the supporters of the crown with the glories of a short term abroad in the service of their country. The trying climate of the Philippines, which is tropical, subjected to violent monsoons, seasons of drenching rains, and an almost intolerable heat lasting from March to July, has made it necessary to change continually the Spanish administrators. From the governor general down to the private soldier, five years was the average length of service possible, so that the native population, estimated at from 8,000,000 to 15,000,000 in numbers, was always under the rule of transient strangers, having no continuing interest in their welfare. There have been, of course, individual instances of honorable and just governors. Among these . . . was General Blanco, who was afterwards selected to establish the weak experiment of autonomistic government in Cuba. It was, however, the rule, under the very nature of the colonial system, that temptation to oppress, rob, and enslave the natives was held out to every administration in succession, and such temptations are not long resisted by those appointed over uncivilized and ignorant people."

That was the formidable and perilous — and mysterious — situation into which the Asiatic Squadron of the U.S. Navy was preparing to sail and fight, as it lay at anchor in the friendly harbor of Hong Kong, which had been for 150 years ceded to British rule in 1847, to be returned to China in 1997. Having been well provisioned with coal and supplies, its magazines full, crews well trained and of high morale and under the able command of Commodore George Dewey, Assistant Secretary of the Navy Theodore Roosevelt had paid particular attention to this strategic squadron and more than any other official, he deserved credit for its high state of readiness. But the light flotilla, consisting of six warships and but three auxiliary vessels, was exposed to severe threats, other than the Spanish men-of-war and the fortress guns of Manila Bay, once war was declared. The problem confronting American authorities was well anticipated when, on April 25, President McKinley chose the riskier, but far more courageous and geopolitically daring missions for the Asiatic Squadron. Assuming that Spanish Admiral Montejo would sail his force out of Manila Bay to attack American targets on the west coast, many U.S. officials favored Dewey's squadron rushing 7,500 miles eastward to augment the small complement of just the battleship *Oregon*, one gunboat and two monitors — only four vessels — guarding the whole Pacific shore.

The alternative, cabled to Dewey on that day that Congress declared war, came right from the President: "Seek the Spanish fleet and capture or destroy it." If enemy ships could be engaged in or near Philippine waters, there would be no need to race them across the Pacific and no danger to U.S. territory. The great additional risk in that course of action was brought into sharp focus that same fateful day, when the British authorities at Hong Kong, under the international laws of neutrality, gave Dewey 24 hours to sail his squadron out of the harbor. The American ships were 7,000 miles from the closest U.S. bases and coaling stations. Possibly, they could have reached home directly on coal in their full bunkers, but once they sailed south to the Philippines and went through the high fuel consumption of a major battle, the only recourse would be to capture Spanish supplies at Manila Bay, or to wait — perhaps for a month — for colliers to reach them. Undaunted and anxious to — in Dewey's words — "find the Spaniard and smash him," he immediately left the British protectorate, never taking advantage of the additional hours available to him. Fortunately, one of the auxiliary ships was a British collier which had been hastily purchased, loaded with coal, in Hong Kong, with its English captain still on the bridge. According to Barrett: "Both of them (British skippers of the pair of purchased supply vessels) told me that while they fully realized the great risk they were running, and the certainty of being put to death if captured, they left their first conference with (Dewey) supremely impressed with the idea that such a man knew what he was about and could not be beaten. Therefore they would be safe in continuing as captains of their steamers. They were paid double what they received in times of peace, but even that inducement would not have sufficed if they had not been moved by reliance on the Admiral's judgement and courage."

Although the British, up to that point, had been the sole foreign element with any faith in American men and arms, they believed that Dewey had a chance, they felt that the odds were greatly against his command, given the quality of the Spanish ships, the fortresses defending Manila and the unfamiliarity of the Americans with the area of operations, while to their enemies, it was virtually home waters. At least one Royal Navy officer remarked that the Yanks had been fine chaps during their stay at Hong Kong and it was sad that the British would never see them again! The Commodore and his men entertained no such thoughts as they steamed across the South China Sea, the sailors and their commandant amply charged with complete faith in their ability, patriotism, their ships and guns and the righteousness of their cause. In Manila, Admiral Montejo was more concerned with plans to bombard San Francisco once he had destroyed Dewey's fleet, than he actually was preparing to engage the Asiatic Squadron!

The warships under Dewey's command consisted of his flagship, the protected cruiser *Olympia*, displacing 5,900 tons, with heavy long-range guns, capable of high speed and considered among the world's best; the smaller protected cruisers, *Baltimore*, at 4,400 tons; *Raleigh*, 3,200 tons; and the 3,000-ton *Boston*. There were a pair of gunboats: *Concord*, at 1,700 tons and the 890-ton *Petrel*. Awaiting them in the wide bay at Manila were 14 ships, mostly small gunboats, but the Spaniards' largest vessels also were comprised of four protected cruisers, albeit smaller with lighter, shorter-range guns. Montejo's flagship was the 3,500-ton *Reina Cristina*, and the others were *Castilla, Don Juan de Austria,* and *Velasco*, all of lesser armament. Although the Spanish fleet more than doubled the Americans' in number, its combined size and total of guns did not match that of America. Countering the superiority of the American ships and guns were the heavy artillery mounts on Corregidor Island, guarding the entrance to Manila Bay, as well as the batteries at Manila and at Cavite, south of the city. It was beneath the protecting crossfire of the modern, heavy guns at the latter two fortresses that the Spanish ships waited.

The Spaniards first sighted the incoming American flotilla off Cape Bolonao on the west coast of central Luzon, steaming south, on the morning of April 30, still 12 hours' sailing time from the entrance of Manila Bay. All men aboard the ships were manning their battle stations, ready for action. On board the despatch boat *McCulloch*, Emilio Aguinaldo, the Filipino insurgent leader, and his aides were also on their way to Manila. Although Dewey had not requested that Aguinaldo accompany him, nor had he invited the rebel chieftain, he recognized the value of putting him ashore to organize resistance to Spain and to lay siege to Manila from the land while the U.S. ships controlled the bay. Sailing parallel to the Bataan peninsula, Dewey ordered the two gunboats to reconnoiter Subic Bay, where it was believed the Spanish squadron might be waiting. Having seen no sign of the enemy and with all lights extinguished, the Americans rounded Luzon Point in darkness; directly ahead lay the searchlights and the heavy guns of Corregidor.

Although it seemed incredible to the Americans that the Spaniards apparently were not preparing a welcome of fire and steel for them, Dewey made the decision to sail through the Boca Grande, the southern — and larger — of the passages around Corregidor. The island and its batteries were quiet, the searchlights turned off, instead of anxiously sweeping the channels into Manila Bay. By 11:00 p.m., with Dewey on the bridge of the *Olympia* in the lead, his squadron was in range of the enemy batteries. Corregidor remained dark and silent as the American flotilla was passing unnoticed! Noiselessly, at steady speed, with all officers and gunners on the decks on high alert for mines and torpedoes as well as action at the batteries, the cruisers and gunboats proceeded. In the boiler rooms, the temperature was as high as 160 degrees, but the stokers seemed undeterred, not a man flinching, except for an engineer on the *McCulloch*, who died of a heat-induced heart attack.

After half of the ships were past Corregidor, a few sparks erupted from a funnel of one of them, giving away their positions. The fortress guns began firing immediately, bringing a brief reply from the *Boston* and the *McCulloch;* then the Spanish batteries again fell silent, to the relief and bewilderment of the Americans. Once in the bay, the squadron slowed to a virtual halt and the sailors rested at their stations, awaiting the first light of dawn to close with Montejo's vessels. Virtually unchallenged, the American Navy had sailed past Bataan and Corregidor, places that would become so sadly known to the triumphant sailors and the next two generations of their countrymen 44 years later, as the settings for the worst defeat the United States was ever to suffer, under the invading Japanese.

In the early dawn of May 1, 1898, less than a week since the declaration of war, it was 5:00 a.m. when the American fleet, now steaming five miles from the Manila waterfront, and the Spanish defenders first recognized one another. Soon, the brightening light revealed the line of Spanish ships positioned beneath the heavy guns of Cavite. At 5:15 a.m., opening salvos roared from two batteries at that fortress and three at Manila, as the long-range guns of the ships also commenced firing at the advancing American squadron. To concentrate on the Spanish men-of-war, Dewey ordered that the guns at Manila be ignored; he also did not

A three-man gun crew is shown firing a 6-pounder rifle onboard a Spanish warship. The gunner is bending forward to aim the weapon, while the man to his left holds the next round and spent shell casings litter the deck.

want to subject the densely populated city of friendly natives to a deadly bombardment, even though those guns laid down a heavy barrage — to no effect — for two hours. Heading into the potentially murderous crossfire, the flagship *Olympia* was followed in line by the *Baltimore*, the *Raleigh*, the *Petrel*, and the *Concord*, with the *Boston* bringing up the rear. For the next 26 minutes, the Americans refused to reply to the intense fire being hurled at them, as they headed straight for Cavite and Montejo's ships, his flag vessel already in their sights.

Then Dewey gave his famous order to *Olympia*'s captain: "You may fire when ready, Gridley!" When the eight-inch guns of the forward turret let loose right at the *Reina Cristina*, at 5:41 a.m., a loud cheer and resounding shouts of "Remember the *Maine!*" arose from all six American vessels, their guns coming to bear as each ship came into range. Beginning at a distance of 5,500 yards, the U.S. Navy ships took up a circular formation which came nearer their quarry with every movement, pouring in intensive broadsides from all their guns. Lieutenant L. J. Stickney described the initial engagement as he stood on the bridge as an aide to the commodore: "The Spaniards seemed encouraged to fire faster, knowing exactly our distance, while we had to guess theirs. Their ships and shore guns were making things hot for us. The piercing scream of shot was varied often by the bursting of time fuze shells, fragments of which would lash the water like shrapnel or cut our hull and rigging. One large shell that was coming straight at the *Olympia*'s forward bridge fortunately fell within less than one hundred feet. One fragment cut the rigging; another struck the bridge gratings in line with it; a third passed under Commodore Dewey and lodged in the deck. Incidents like these were plentiful.

"Owing to our deep draught, Commodore Dewey felt constrained to change course at a distance of 4,000 yards and run parallel to the Spanish column. 'Open with all guns,' he ordered, and the ship brought her port broadside bearing. The roar of all the flagship's five-inch rapid-fires was followed by the deep diapason of her turret eight-inchers. Soon our other vessels were equally hard at work, and we could see that our shells were making Cavite harbor hotter for the Spaniards than they had made the approach for us. Protected by their shore batteries and made safe from close attack by shallow water, the Spaniards were in a strong position. They put up a gallant fight.

"One shot struck the *Baltimore* and passed clean through her, fortunately hitting no one. Another ripped the upper main deck, disabled a six-inch gun and exploded a box of three-pounder ammunition, wounding eight men. The *Olympia* was struck abreast the gun in the wardroom by a shell which burst outside, doing little damage. The signal halyards were cut from the officer's hand on the after bridge. A sailor climbed up in the rain of shot and mended the line. A shell entered the *Boston*'s port quarter and burst in Ensign Dodridge's

stateroom, starting a hot fire, and fire was also caused by a shell which burst in the port hammock netting. Both these fires were quickly put out. Another shell passed through the *Boston*'s foremast just in front of Captain Wildes, on the Bridge."

On the fifth pass at the enemy, Dewey's navigator had allowed the flagship to advance within just 2,000 yards, making even the small six-pounder guns effective. On this pass, ". . . the storm of shot and shell launched against the Spaniard was destructive beyond description," according to Stickney. When the *Reina Cristina* sailed out to directly challenge the *Olympia*, she was confronted with fire so intense and accurate that she turned to scurry back to the relative safety of the Cavite breakwater and was struck in the stern by an eight-inch shell which exploded in her engine room, setting her ablaze and drifting. Montejo abandoned her and transferred to the gunboat *Isla de Cuba*, while Captain Cadarso, *Reina Cristina*'s skipper, mortally wounded, refused to leave and courageously went down with his ship, perishing with many of his men. The American flagship had defeated the Spanish flagship head on, making Dewey's victory over Montejo a very personal encounter!

The *Castilla*, long obsolete and never set loose during the entire battle, which had served as a floating stationary fortress — and a fine target — was on fire, when a shell hit the magazine of the *Don Juan de Austria*, blowing her up. In a frenzy of largely inaccurate fire, the remaining Spanish ships and the shore batteries could not deter the Americans, much less stop them. Dewey finally had enough of the Manila batteries and sent a message to Governor-General Augusti, informing him that if the firing at his ships was not immediately halted, he would bombard the city; the guns at once fell silent. At 7:35 a.m., Dewey disengaged and steamed out of range of the Spanish guns, prompting a legend in the press back home that he had withdrawn for breakfast; the story stuck, but was not true, as the Commodore's own report clarifies: ". . . it having been erroneously reported to me that only 15 rounds of ammunition per gun remained for the five-inch rapid-fire battery, I ceased firing and withdrew the squadron for consultation and a redistribution of ammunition, if necessary." It was the ammunition assessment and the need to review the condition of each ship, casualties and other factors that had prompted the withdrawal. Since the crews had been on high alert and in action under severe stress for almost 30 hours, the commandant took advantage of the respite to have his men fed a very bountiful breakfast and to enjoy a much deserved rest.

With all of the American captains conferring on board the *Olympia*, they made the startling and elating discovery that not a single one of their men had been killed and just a few slightly wounded and each ship was still completely fit for battle, despite the ferocity of the fight and the severe damage inflicted upon the enemy. The Spaniards, meanwhile, misconstrued the temporary withdrawal to be a retreat and they began celebrating, as a cable was sent to Madrid where riotous exultation took hold. Just three and a half hours after breaking off the engagement, the Americans, well fed, rested, flushed with victory and anxious to administer the *coup de grâce*, returned. With less need for caution, Dewey ordered "close action" as his squadron poured barrage after devastating barrage into the wounded ships of Spain, whose replying fire was fading fast. The guns of Cavite had become the only threat, as they laid down a continuous fire, so the *Baltimore* broke from the formation, headed straight for the fort and cut loose with all of her firepower. Almost immediately, she scored a direct hit on the magazine, destroying the entire complex, enabling the *Boston*, the *Concord* and the *Petrel* to round the point and take on the gunboats. The Spaniards made no attempt to fight; they scuttled their vessels and set them afire. At 12:40 p.m., the Battle of Manila Bay was done, with white flags of surrender flying over the Spanish positions.

With *Olympia* heading for Manila, the crews of the other U.S. Navy ships began going ashore with the ships' surgeons, to assist the many wounded Spanish sailors and fortress gunners. Every one of Spain's warships had been destroyed, with a few launches and tugboats captured. Approximately 1,000 Spanish officers and men were dead and 600 wounded; the unusual tally of almost two-thirds of the casualties being fatal emphasized the sheer intensity and violence of the engagement. With 14 ships lost, as well as vast quantities of large guns, small arms, munitions, coal, provisions and all manner of equipment, the American victory was so complete that it totally finished Spain's four centuries' role as a major Pacific Ocean power. It became immediately apparent that the United States would soon be sovereign over the Philippines. Even as American surgeons and sailors were caring for the vanquished wounded, the Archbishop of Manila published a pastoral decree which called upon all Christians in the colony to "defend the faith against the Protestant American heretics who intended to enslave the people and outlaw the sacraments." He warned that altars would be desecrated and "churches turned into Protestant chapels." When news of the true outcome of the most one-sided naval battle in history reached Spain, rioting erupted in Madrid, the populace demanding explanations of the deceptions and duplicity.

The superiority of American gunners and their weapons as the decisive factor in his unprecedented defeat, the courageous but inept Admiral Montejo acknowledged in his official report: "The Americans fired most rapidly. There came upon us numberless projectiles, as the three cruisers at the head of the line devoted themselves almost entirely to fight the *Cristina*, my flagship. A short time after the action commenced, one shell exploded in the forecastle and put out of action all those who served the four rapid-fire cannon . . . The enemy shortened the distance between us and, rectifying his aim, covered us with a rain of rapid-fire projectiles. At 7:30, one shell destroyed completely the steering gear . . . another shell exploded on the poop . . . Another destroyed the mizzen-mast head . . . A fresh shell exploded in the officers' cabin, covering the hospital with blood and destroying the wounded who were being treated there. Another exploded in the ammunition room astern, filling the quarters with smoke . . . As it was impossible to control the fire, I had to flood the magazine when the shells were beginning to explode."

On board *Olympia* after the battle, Barrett enquired of a senior gunner from the eight-inch cannon of the forward turret: "Where did you think you were going, and what did you expect to do when you left Mirs Bay (Hong Kong)?"

"'Go and do?' he replied 'Damn little did I or anyone else on this ship care as long as the old man was ordering it. We knew we were going to a hot place, and meant to make it hotter still for the Spaniards; but, man, we would have sailed straight into hell after him.'"

Commodore Dewey, immediately promoted to rear admiral, stressed the first lesson of the battle: "The Spaniards, with their combined fleet and forts, were equal to us in gun-power. But they were unable to harm us because of bad gunnery. Constant practice made our gunnery destructive and won the victory.

"The second lesson of this battle is the complete demonstration of the value of high-grade men. We should have none but the very best men behind the guns. It will not do to have able officers and poor men. We must have the best men filling all the posts on ship-board . . . we must have, as we have in this fleet, trained sailors to carry out commands.

"The third lesson . . . is the necessity for inspection. Everything to be used in a battle should have been thoroughly inspected . . .

"Look at the difference between our ships and the Spanish ships . . . Their shells, their powder, all their materials were practically worthless, while ours were perfect."

Unloading the first American horses from the little steamer used by Commodore Dewey to cut international telegraph cables in Manila Bay.

Few photographs survive of the Spanish colonial period in the possessions liberated during the Spanish-American War and most of those are of poor quality, having been recopied several times, losing focus, contrast, and detail. One of the few pictures of a Spanish firing squad in action shows two Filipinos, their wrists manacled and backs turned to their executioners, about to be shot.

National Archives

The rules governing insurgent strategy in guerrilla warfare are adaptability and improvisation. The *insurrectos* who fought their Spanish rulers in Cuba and the Philippines became adept at living off the land and making do with little resources. Among the cannons which Spanish forces captured from Filipino rebels were several homemade pieces in the foreground, made out of sections of water pipe, sheathed with wood held securely by iron straps, mounted on cart wheels and axles.

National Archives

Whether in the countryside or in heavily-populated towns and cities, the Spanish authorities fought low-intensity skirmishes with Filipino patriots for years before the Americans intervened to eject the colonial regime. Here, Spanish soldiers are firing from sitting positions on the balcony of a barricaded house, using small barrels and stones for cover behind a balustrade.

The flagship of the Spanish fleet in the Philippines was the *Reina Maria Cristina* (above), one of the fastest, most modern vessels in commission for defense of the colonies. Admiral Patricio Montejo Y Pasaron (center) sat for a portrait by G. W. Peters while he was a prisoner of war in Manila awaiting repatriation to Spain, on September 24, 1898. One of the few photographs taken onboard a Spanish man-of-war to survive shows the formality of a Sunday church service (below) on the canvas-canopied deck of Montejo's flagship.

Three paintings were an important record of the Battle of Manila Bay which captured the feelings of action and historical moment for future generations, before the advent of color photography. Dr. Alfonso Saenz, the Spanish naval surgeon, created the work (right) showing *USS Olympia* leading the Asiatic Squadron as it delivers a broadside barrage against Montejo's fleet. The famous painting "Dewey at Manila" (below) hangs in the Vermont State Capitol in tribute to one of that state's most prominent sons. The American flagship (lower right) is shown in her peacetime paint scheme of white and beige. So forgotten and ignored a century later, references to the war with Spain are often incredulous, such as the plaque accompanying the Saenz painting, which hangs in the prestigious Army-Navy Club, just a few blocks from the White House in Washington, D.C. It refers to Commodore *Thomas* Dewey! That a military historian of so prominent a facility could confuse the naval hero of 1898 with the 1940s governor of New York and Republican presidential candidate, is indeed astonishing.

Right, Ron Ziel photo, courtesy of Army-Navy Club

Below, State of Vermont   Lower right, U.S. Naval Historical Center

Captain Charles V. Gridley was the commanding officer of Commodore Dewey's flagship, *USS Olympia*, and in the tragic last month of his naval career and his life, he was to set a fine example of devotion to duty. Even before the squadron steamed out of Hong Kong, he became gravely ill, and when Dewey wanted to replace him, Gridley insisted that he was fully capable of retaining command. Impressed with his earnestness and aware of the disappointment if Gridley would have been left behind, he agreed to the captain's wishes. Within hours after the great victory in Manila Bay, Gridley's condition was rapidly deteriorating, so he was placed on the next ship heading back to the U.S. Just over three weeks after the greatest day of his service, he died while the ship carrying him was making a stopover at Kobe, Japan, on May 25, 1898. Still painted in the peacetime colors of while hull and beige superstructure, the *USS Olympia*, moored atHong Kong, fired a salute (below) in honor of President George Washington's birthday on February 22, 1898. By April, with war either imminent or already declared, she had been repainted dull battleship gray prior to sailing for Manila. *Olympia* displaced 5,870 tons; length, 340 feet; breadth, 53 feet; 17,313 horsepower; main battery, four 8-inch and ten 5-inch rapid-fire guns; and secondary battery, fourteen 6-pounder and six 1-pounder rapid-fires, four Gatlings and six torpedo tubes. She had a speed of over 21 knots and a crew of 34 officers and 416 men.

Below, U.S. Naval Historical Center

The twin-screw steel protected cruiser *USS Baltimore* (above) was second only to the flagship *Olympia* in size and firepower in the U.S. Navy's Asiatic Squadron at Manila Bay. Displacing 4,400 to 4,600 tons (accounts vary), she was 327 feet long, with a beam of 48 feet, and over 10,000 horsepower. Her main battery consisted of four 8-inch and six 6-inch (no turrets); secondary battery: four 6-pounder and two 3-pounder rapid-firing guns, two 1-pounder and four .37 mm Hotchkiss revolving cannons and two Gatlings. Her speed was over 20 knots, and she was staffed with 36 officers and 350 men. One of the heavy 8-inch guns of the *Baltimore* (center) was a modern, powerful breech-loader, still impressive 100 years later. When an enemy shell hit one of the same ship's smaller 6-inchers, wounding eight men, they were the only American casualties during the fierce battle. The 892 ton *Petrel* (below) was an older ship, built during the time when sails were still employed to augment steam power. Her main armament was four 6-inch guns, supplemented with a 1-pounder and a pair of .37 mm Hotchkiss cannons and two Gatling guns. The little gunboat's speed was just 11.7 knots, and she was crewed by ten officers and 122 men. This port stern view shows her with sailors high up on her spars, in Hong Kong on April 15, 1898, just before she got her coat of gray war paint and sailed for the Philippines 12 days later.

Top, bottom, U.S. Naval Historical Center

Center, Library of Congress

A view looking aft from the bow of the *Olympia* (left) shows the forward 8-inch turret and the portside rapid-fire guns unleashed against the Spanish fleet, with Commodore Dewey in the open, exposed reconnaissance tower between the turret and the bridge. This painting by G.W. Peters was made from a description furnished by Dewey. The Americans concentrated first on Montejo's flagship *Reina Cristina*, as is seen (upper left) as Dewey makes one of numerous broadside passes. Left to right, the U.S. ships are the *Boston, Concord, Petrel, Raleigh, Baltimore,* and *Olympia*, with the Spanish passenger steamer *Mindanao* in the distance showing between the two leading American ships. *Reina Cristina* is in the middle right distance receiving at least one hit, while *Castilla* and *Don Antonio de Ulloa* are returning fire, several of their shells falling near Dewey's cruiser. Gunner S.J. Skaw (above) posing with his gun — from which he fired the first American round in the battle of Manila Bay — on the deck of the *Olympia*.

Above, U.S. Naval Historical Center

93

So shallow was Manila Bay where the Spanish ships made their last stand, that their superstructures — even the tops of their hulls — remained above the waterline. Photographed shortly after the battle, *Isla de Cuba* (above) was not severely damaged; she was later refloated and commissioned in the U.S. Navy. Montejo's flagship *Reina Cristina* suffered much worse, intensely aflame as she settled in the shallow water, her superstructure continuing to burn furiously. Little had remained above the waterline (center) except her funnels, bulkheads, and davits. The cruiser *Castilla* (below) was further proof of the deadly effects of American gunnery. Behind her are (left to right) *Olympia, Baltimore,* and *Raleigh.*

Top, center, National Archives Bottom, U.S. Naval Historical Center

In addition to losing her Pacific Fleet in the battle of May 1, 1898, Spain also lost a large number of fortress guns — some modern, but many obsolete muzzle-loaders. The ancient bronze cannon (above) on the ramparts of the Walled City in Manila had long guarded the mouth of the Pasig River. American soldiers, armed with Krag-Jorgensen rifles (center) were watching over the old guns overlooking Luneta. The big, fat cannon on Corregidor (below), which hardly challenged the American squadron as it entered Manila Bay, was ordered disabled by Dewey right after the battle, since he lacked enough Marines to occupy the island fortresses and did not want the guns to fall back under enemy control.

Three photos, National Archives

Life on board U.S. Navy warships a century ago was a combination of comfort and confinement, much as it is today. These photographs, taken on board *USS Olympia* in 1898, offer glimpses of the routine of shipboard duty. Relaxing on deck (opposite, top), a group of sailors are playing with their pet cats, one of them reflecting a shaft of sunlight in front of a tabby. A second cat is snuggled against the man asleep at the right. The birds in the cage at the upper left are probably also pets, not intended as meals for the feline veterans of the Battle of Manila Bay! While pets are forbidden on American warships 100 years later, as late as World War II their presence was at the discretion of each captain. Admiral Dewey's pet dog was often at his side on board the *Olympia*. Navy chow has long been the envy of ground soldiers, and during the Spanish-American War, while the troops subsisted on hardtack and sowbelly, ships' crewmen enjoyed hot meals, including fresh baked bread and cold milk. Suspended from above by ropes, the tables (opposite, bottom) swayed gently as the ship rolled, seldom upsetting the soup bowls. Like the tables, sailors' bedding was also suspended, in the form of hammocks on the berth deck, where off-duty men (below) are seen sleeping, reading and writing letters. It would shock the occupational safety officials of today to see the barefooted sailors of 1898; even when manning their heavy guns in battle, sailors often wore no shoes, as hot shell casings were extracted from the breeches and sharp pieces of shrapnel littered the decks. Officers never went barefoot.

U.S. Naval Historical Center

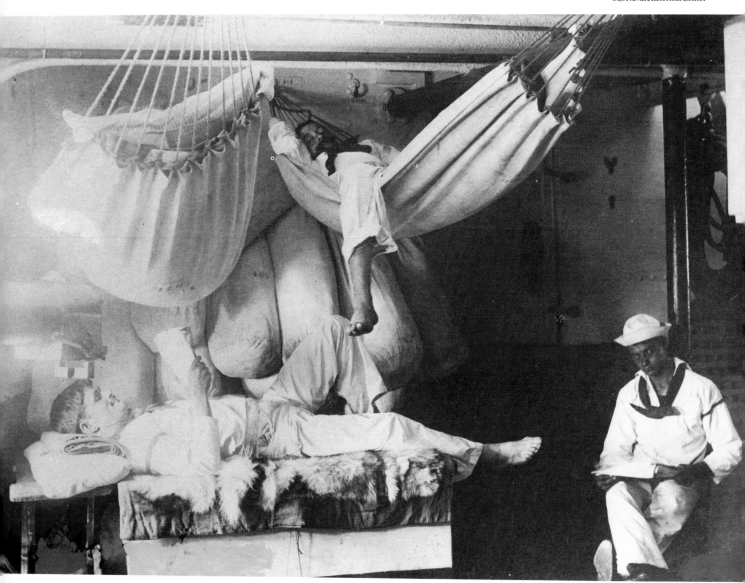

Like Theodore Roosevelt who was a rapidly-rising politician of the Republican Party, William Jennings Bryan was one of the foremost leaders of the Democratic Party and also served as a colonel of volunteers in the Spanish-American War. Bryan had been his party's candidate for President and was defeated by William McKinley in 1896; in their rematch four years later, Roosevelt would be McKinley's vice presidential running mate. Both dynamic politicians had put their public careers aside in 1898 to answer the call to the colors, but it would be Roosevelt who would become a heroic legend in the war, which would soon propel him to the White House. Colonel Bryan reads the latest orders as he sits with the colonel of the New Jersey regiment. While the enlisted men pitched their tents on the ground, officers were supplied with wood platforms for floors.

National Archives

The Shattered World Order

The sheer magnitude of the victory of Commodore Dewey's fleet at Manila Bay startled the American people, evoking a tidal wave of gratitude and patriotism which immediately swept the nation. Its effect on the naval officials and the governments of the great powers of Europe and Japan was absolute shock, followed by admiration and respect, then the sobering realization that, literally overnight, the United States had become a major force in the Pacific, casting all of their intrigues of colonization and establishing spheres of influence into a turmoil of doubt. Now that the Americans could (and obviously would) occupy the Philippines and other Spanish possessions at will, the annexation of Hawaii being a foregone conclusion, how would the proud and arrogant Europeans react to the new interloper which had burst upon the scene in a roaring fusillade of powder and exploding shells? The Germans were the first to probe at the U.S. Navy and to receive an unequivocal reply which combined firm diplomacy with a rough show of Yankee gunnery, courtesy of Vice Admiral George Dewey, victorious warrior turned instant statesman.

The German naval commander in the Pacific was Admiral Otto von Diederichs, who, either acting on his own initiative or on orders from the Kaiser's government, began petty harassment of Dewey's blockading ships in violation of international rules governing such tense situations. While most European powers had sent one or two warships to gain intelligence on what the Americans were up to, there was a squadron of five German vessels weaving about Manila Bay and even taking "noncombatant" Spaniards from Subic to the capital and sending small steam launches to the docks at night. The latter supposedly were carrying officers for a bit of revelry, but were also suspected of smuggling essentials — including small arms and ammunition — to the Spaniards. Diplomatically but firmly, the American admiral sent messages warning von Diederichs to modify his behavior, finally demanding whether the Germans were seeking to fight and, if so, was Berlin aware of it? Whenever Dewey pressed the issue, the Germans would back down, until finally a serious incident occurred. Even the lowest ranking sailor knew that no vessel should ever approach a warship at night without prior announcement and showing lights. Barrett relates how a launch, without running lights, was bearing down on *Olympia*, at a time when German-American relations were most tense: "(The lookout) called out: 'Boat ahoy!' No answer came. He repeated. Again no answer came. This shouting had attracted the attention of the Admiral ... (who) jumped up, ran to the side of the deck, peered out into the darkness, and called to the officer on deck: 'Why don't you fire? It doesn't stop!'"

"There rang out the report of the six-pounder, but the launch kept coming. Then the admiral ordered with an angry tone: 'Fire again, and fire to hit!'

"The searchlight of the *Olympia* was turned full on the bold intruder and displayed a boat flying the German colors. The second shot was well aimed. It struck the water within three feet of the launch and splashed water all over it. It had the necessary effect. The boat stopped. A launch which had been sent out to meet it, then escorted it to the *Olympia*. Up the ladder walked one of von Diederichs's staff officers in full uniform and shaking with excitement or fear. 'Why do you fire upon me? This is a launch from the German Admiral's flagship, flying the German colors, and I am a German officer. Why should you fire? You could see the flag in the light.'

"... the Admiral said: 'Do you appreciate what you have done? Do you know that such a rash act on your part is against all the rules of war and might even have been the cause of serious trouble between your country and mine? Suppose that shot had killed you and sunk your launch, the effect might have been to have brought on misunderstandings and a conflict. It would have been very easy for a Spanish boat meaning us harm to have put up a German flag and sunk the *Olympia* if we did not stop it in time. There is no excuse for such carelessness. You should understand the rules of war in a matter of this kind. Please present my compliments to your Admiral, and ask him to direct his officers to be more careful in the future'."

This incident (which for the Americans was a sobering reminder of the *Maine* affair) and the others were perhaps not all intended to be provocative but, as Dewey asserted, they showed a total ignorance of, or disregard for, the rules of war and blockade observance. When word of the situation in Manila Bay reached Berlin and Washington, D.C., officials helped to smooth it out and the Germans and other Europeans realized that it was best not to aggravate the American Navy!

Above all of Dewey's heavy burdens in May, 1898, loomed the nightmare that a larger fleet could challenge him for control of the Philippines; after all, only his half-dozen ships stood between the imperial ambitions of the great powers and the rich, vast archipelago just wrested from Spanish control. Immediately, Admiral Dewey cabled to his government an urgent request for sea and land reinforcements. President McKinley, instantly grasping the tenuousness of the Admiral's exposed position, ordered that what ships could be spared and a 20,000-man army be dispatched to the Philippines; a priority exceeding all else, including Cuba. U.S. policy and the world order had been completely transposed in just two weeks' time!

On the American home front, the populace, government and industry were immediately caught up in massive mobilization; within a few weeks of Dewey's appeal — before the end of May — the expeditionary force of 4,000 regular soldiers and 16,000 volunteer militia began sailing from San Francisco. Incredibly, this army alone — the first such overseas military venture in American history — was of a strength one-fourth greater than the entire total of all active duty personnel just 90 days earlier! Meanwhile, the regulars and the state militias left behind formed the cadres that began training tens of thousands of volunteers who would soon be sent to fight in Cuba and Puerto Rico and to occupy other Spanish possessions. The American practice of maintaining a small, basic regular army and calling up large numbers of re-servists and volunteer recruits only when abso-lutely required was about to receive its first emer-gency test. Would such hastily raised, trained, equipped and transported forces fight effectively and be able to hold the territory they seized against counterattacks and the vicissitudes of supply lines over thousands of miles? The European powers were watching breathlessly to learn if the Ameri-can system was viable and, if so, how would the les-son affect the Continental military policies of maintaining vast standing armies of often dis-gruntled draftees, costing immense amounts of money which — as in the case of Spain — could drain the national treasury and even spark revolts among a loyal citizenry? In its headlong dash to in-advertently become the great world power of the looming century, the United States was already es-tablishing the philosophy, methodology and mili-tary and naval doctrine that would prove so valu-able in both the attainment and the retainment of that status.

The month of May 1898, was perhaps the most frenetic 31 days in all of American history. Almost 100,000 volunteers reported to half-built training camps, new coast artillery guns were being em-placed to protect port cities, keels were laid for 12,000-ton battleships, all manner of military supplies — from bandages, bugles and bullets to saddles, stoves and ships — were being purchased at home and abroad, and Congress worked late into the spring nights, passing massive appropriations bills, debating Hawaiian annexation and approv-ing resolutions praising and thanking Admiral Dewey and his men. From the start, the Navy had been well trained, equipped and prepared for its dangerous and difficult mission, but the Army, al-though early on showing professionalism and cognizance, began to have serious problems — not through shortcomings of its officers or its own planning, but due to ineptitude on the part of War Department bureaucrats in Washington, D.C. The Cuban expedition was to be especially bungled by desk-bound officials in the capital who had no concept of what was happening in the field; and few having seen military service, were ignorant of the requirements of the generals. All through the process of preparing the Army, sending 25,000 troops, thousands of horses and mules and train-loads of supplies to the embarkation port, landing the forces on hostile soil, then supplying them and even returning them home, the War Department proved unequal to the overbearing task. Field-grade officers were placed in the uncomfortable potential court-martial position of having to resort to insubordination to perform their duties and complete their combat missions.

Singing *The Battle Hymn of the Republic* and shouting "Remember the *Maine;* To Hell with Spain!," thousands of raw recruits were made into trained fighters, with a special emphasis on cav-alry, the coming decline and ultimate demise of that valorous and romantic branch of service al-ready sensed by military strategists who were well aware that the machine gun and motorized trans-port, then in their early development, plus barbed wire, would soon render horse cavalry tactics inef-fective if not suicidal. But, in the last years of the 19th century, master horsemanship could still play a decisive role in combat. Sadly, the ineptitude of the War Department would conspire to rob the proud cavalry of a latter-day rendezvous with glory in the Cuban campaign; even the Rough Rid-ers were to be forced to assault San Juan Hill dis-mounted.

When a people embark on bold new ventures, old problems must first be resolved; in the case of the United States, foremost were the resentments still evident from the Civil War and the period of Reconstruction which followed. President McKin-ley and his War Cabinet were well aware of the bit-ter memories which festered in the land — espe-cially in the states of the Confederacy — so his ad-ministration moved to bandage the rifts. The coming battles paradoxically would help to heal them, as Northerners and Southerners fought side by side, but initially, McKinley instituted a laud-able and controversial policy of appointing vet-eran Confederate officers to high command posi-tions. Although these men had fine records from their service 35 years earlier, most had known no military experience since and had become perhaps too old to endure the rigors of leadership in war-fare in many aspects very different and modern-ized over that which they had known a third-century previously. Still, the appointments of ex-Confederate Generals Fitzhugh Lee and Joseph Wheeler were met with wide approval throughout the nation, as was the commissioning of lower-ranking Confederate veterans. Indeed, it required a new war to finally heal the deep wounds of the old conflict, enabling the American people to ma-ture into eventual world leadership.

The generation of young Americans who re-ported for muster at the training camps for the war with Spain were possessed of the same attitudes, expectations, hopes, and fears as were those in pre-ceding and following times of conflict. Charles Johnson Post, a young artist from New York who, in the 20th century, went on to an illustrious news-paper career, enlisted in 1898 and participated in the fighting in Cuba. His book, *The Little War of*

Crowded with ships and railroad cars, thousands of soldiers were moving
supplies and themselves on to the transports from the cluttered quayage.

Private Post, is one of the best-written accounts of
army life to come out of any war and his artwork
remains a priceless record of unfolding history as
experienced by the enlisted soldiers who were
swept along in a torrent over which they had no
control. A few of Post's observations as he was
training at Camp Black, on the Hempstead Plains
of Long Island, just 20 miles from Manhattan,
which he had known so well, reveal the anecdotes
of resigned and sardonic feelings so familiar to recruits in many wars: "Clearly, nature had designed
me for mere cannon fodder, so I enlisted, taking
the step that qualified me for a drink on the house
almost anywhere between Eighth Street and
Twenty-Third Street, between the Hudson and the
East Rivers.

"I had a uniform — cerulean-blue pants...and
they fitted reasonably well. But my blouse! I had
always thought that a 'blouse' was specifically an
article of feminine apparel, a sort of loose shirt-
waist with a snappy, come-hither effect. But in that
man's army, a blouse was anything worn outside a
shirt and inside an overcoat, and instantly provocative of a sergeant's acute anguish if it wasn't
buttoned. Also, it was supposed to fit . . . The
turned-back sleeves reached my elbows; it folded

around me so that its buttons were at all times under my arms; and it reached down to my knees like
a frock coat.

"The cooking apparatus was what was officially designated as a 'Buzzacot Oven'. This was a
series of huge pots and pans (including a wash
boiler) nesting one within the other, all enfolded
within two sections of an iron grill. The Buzzacot
could cook for a hundred men with ease, and
burned fuel like a blast furnace. In those days,
when war was not waged by machinery...no more
effective cooking device could have been invented.

"It was (company commander) Captain Raf-
ferty who, in broad daylight, broke into a string of
freight cars on the Hempstead siding containing
our regimental food and issue, when army red tape
had got gummed up. He became, in army law, no
better than a common burglar and bandit, a looter
of the sacred supplies and quintuplicate vouchers.

"The plains of Hempstead swarmed with spec-
tators and friends and relatives. And it seemed as if
every friend had brought all the whisky he could
carry. I doubt if there remained a canteenful of
water in the entire regiment. It was dumped for
whisky. Every rolled blanket atop the Merriam

pack (the knapsack of those days) had a quart rolled inside. The blanket was formed into a long roll across the top of the pack and down each side. This blanket could accommodate three bottles, one atop and one each to port and starboard, and the pack straps held it securely so that every bottle was safe and well padded. Beneath the Merriam pack were two more straps. These were for one's rolled overcoat, which could accommodate another bottle or, better yet, a moderate-sized demijohn."

The recoil of the issue .45-calibre round ". . . could, properly directed, knock down two men; the one it hit and the one who fired it.

"The hacks at Hempstead did a roaring business. They pulled up along the siding and trundled the civilian folks off to the Long Island Rail Road station, where the good people embarked for Long Island City to prepare for another reception in the railroad yards for which our troop train was bound."

The experiences of the 1st Volunteer Cavalry Regiment in traveling via seven special trains from their mustering camp near San Antonio, Texas, to the embarkation docks at Port Tampa, Florida, vividly illustrated how the hatreds from the Civil War had subsided; loading them, all of their animals and equipment aboard ship, and sailing for Cuba, became a debacle of condemnation of the War Department. The Rough Riders, a regiment of more than 1,000 cavalrymen, were in a race to reach the Gulf piers, a planned two-days journey through east Texas, Louisiana, Mississippi, and Alabama, then down the west coast of Florida to Port Tampa. In actuality, they spent nearly four days crossing the heart of what little more than a generation before had been the Confederate States of America; the already famous fledgling elite unit leaving its mark as it rolled east and southward. At every station along the route, crowds gathered to see the Rough Riders and to cheer them on their way. Lieutenant Colonel Theodore Roosevelt was particularly impressed with the unexpectedly warm reception and the profusion of American flags waving from the hands of the Confederate veterans. Melons and fruit by the wagon-load awaited the troopers at every stop and beautiful young women brought fresh pies and pails of cold milk. With one of the extra trains pulling out of an engine or crew-change stop, or to water the horses and mules (and many of the men, for the sergeants were obliged to constantly patrol every nearby saloon at each halt), the next would soon follow. As the Rough Riders continued on to Florida, the adoring citizenry at every station would call out the names of the celebrities who had so recently become troopers: William Tiffany, Woodbury Kane, Hamilton Fish — and always a chorus of "Teddy, Teddy," hopeful of getting a glimpse of the famed executive officer.

Port Tampa, Florida, in 1898, was a very modest facility, the docks served by just a single-track rail-road. How the War Department arrived at the decision to dispatch an Army of 25,000 men, thousands of animals and the vast supplies, equipment and arms and ammunition they would consume, from so inadequate a terminal was incomprehensible to every person — military and civilian — who was to witness the debacle. Apparently, the officials ensconced nearly 1,000 miles away in the nation's capital had simply looked at a map and deduced that since Port Tampa was the closest deep-water facility on the Gulf coast to Cuba that could handle large ships and had rail service, it was preferable to Mobile or New Orleans, which would have required a longer sea journey. It seems inconceivable that Secretary of War Russell A. Alger had not been briefed on the limited capacity of Port Tampa, but apparently nobody in his department had thought to investigate! The resulting chaos and demoralization of the soldiers, as well as the dangers to their health and even their lives, threatened the entire mission to liberate Cuba.

The scene that greeted the 1st Volunteer Cavalry on their anxious arrival was one of complete turmoil. Trains sat, caboose to locomotive, in a line miles long. Thousands of soldiers and their equipment were bivouacked for nine miles along the railroad track, having pitched their tents where they left their halted trains. At the docks, regiments were being ordered to board the transports, but they could not find the freight cars loaded with the equipment which had been assigned to them, so their officers committed court-martial offenses by commandeering carloads and even trainloads of stores for their units, even though the cars were clearly assigned to others. They astutely perceived that the war would be short and no commander was going to risk having his unit left behind, waiting for their own supplies to arrive on the pier.

Colonel Wood and Lieutenant Colonel Roosevelt, being audacious senior officers of a crack cavalry regiment, were among the most daring of leaders and they wasted no time getting their unit to the docks and on a ship. Roosevelt noticed a wheezing old switch engine pushing a train of coal cars to the dock. As he later wrote, referring to the cars, "These we seized," enabling the Rough Riders to ride roughly onto the dock. While other colonels were misappropriating boxcars, Wood pulled off the most brazen *coup* of all when he jumped into a steam launch, then ordered its crew to sail out into Tampa Bay, where he virtually shanghaied the transport *Yucatán*, displacing one of the other regiments assigned to it. By the time his second in command arrived with his men in the coal train, Wood had made all of the arrangements to board the steamer.

The most incredible of all blunders — one of the worst in American military history — occurred when the commandant of the Cuba invasion force, Major General William R. Shafter, made the unbelievable discovery that the War Department had not sent him enough transport ships, leaving only the space to carry two-thirds of his army! In the case of cavalry units, that translated into having to leave almost half their men behind and *only senior officers could bring their horses!* The very mission of the cavalry had to be discarded; they would go into battle dismounted, fighting as infantry.

Thus reduced in numbers by one-third and bereft of vital cavalry support, the possibility of total annihilation must have troubled the American generals; if it did, they never showed any concern as they dutifully continued with plans to carry out their orders, as loyal soldiers must do, even under the command of totally inept governmental superiors. Once the 31 transport ships were loaded to the gunwales, dangerously cramped in the tropic heat of June, yet another fiasco was perpetrated by the War Department bureaucracy, one which had the very real potential of annihilating much of the army without an angry shot being fired. The convoy had barely steamed from its moorings when the ships were ordered back to the quayage. Unidentified warships had been reported in the Gulf of Mexico and the Navy was sent out to scrutinize them. For the next six days, the overloaded transports languished at anchor in Tampa bay, the 16,000 troops forced to remain aboard, since orders to sail immediately to Cuba could come at any moment.

Conditions aboard the tightly packed ships quickly deteriorated to an atrocious state of affairs: food spoiled, drinking water turned brackish, and pack mules died of heat prostration. The men, crushingly squeezed on every square foot of deck space, could not shower and the threat of sharks in the bay precluded them from swimming to cool off. While the 1st Volunteer Cavalry had been issued relatively light uniforms, the regular Army troops wore heavy wool attire, prompting Roosevelt to sourly remark that they "were ideally suited for a campaign in Montana this time of the year." By the fifth day, as the ships lay motionless in mid-channel, the men were wallowing in squalid filth, virtually broiling in the stove-like steel hulls. To Army surgeons, such as Colonel Wood, much credit was due; how they were able to prevent outbreaks of epidemics of fatal diseases under such appalling conditions remains a marvelous achievement.

When the officers and men went topside to find relief from the stench of sweating soldiers, mingled with rotting meat, vomit and a myriad of other nauseating odors in the hellish obloquy below decks, they found little respite. The tepid evening air brought some relief, if one refrained from going to the railing to look down into the channel, which had become a veritable open sewer, from the ships having disgorged the effluent of more than 20,000 human beings in so confined an area. Virtually any soldier or ship's crewman who looked over the side could be expected to erupt fresh vomit to the clog of rotting discarded beeves, decaying mule corpses, human excrement and untold other varieties of garbage which was continually eddying about the slime-covered hulls of the ships. Dysentery and typhoid could soon pose a far greater threat than the Spanish Navy, whose unconfirmed presence somewhere over the horizon had kept the Americans bottled up in Tampa Bay for six disgusting and demoralizing days.

Rolls of tent canvas and poles are guarded by a sentry at Camp Black, named in honor of New York Governor Frank S. Black.

The Krag-Jorgensen .30-.40 was to be the last cavalry carbine; it was made the standard arm of the U.S. Army Cavalry for a decade beginning in 1895, to be succeeded by the Springfield 03, at which time it was evident that modern technology would soon render horses in a combat role obsolete. The carbine had a 22-inch barrel, while the infantry rifle version was 30-inch. The Krag was easy to handle, and it was capable of firing 21 aimed shots per minute. This photograph shows a Krag carbine with other Spanish-American War memorabilia: a cavalry saddle, canteen from a New York regiment, cavalry gloves, spurs and campaign hat, and beneath the stock, the famous polka-dot bandanna of the Rough Riders.

Reprinted with permission of the
National Rifle Association of America

Two of the most daring and legendary Confederate cavalry generals of the Civil War returned to active duty in the U.S. Army in 1898. A nephew of the great Confederate commander Robert E. Lee, Fitzhugh Lee (above) turned in stellar performances with the army of Northern Virginia, carrying out daring attacks and being severely wounded. By age 27, he had attained the rank of major general and led the last Southern cavalry charge on April 9, 1865, the day that his uncle surrendered, ending the war. By 1885, he was governor of Virginia and in 1896, President Cleveland appointed him to the most sensitive of diplomatic posts: consul general in Havana, where he remained under the McKinley administration until the declaration of war. Upon his return to the U.S., he was appointed major general of volunteers and commanded the 7th Corps, stationed at Jacksonville, Florida, preparatory to serving in Cuba, a call which never came. In January 1899, when the Spaniards left Cuba, Lee was appointed military governor of Havana and of Pinar del Rio Province – a classic example of the right man for the job! He retired from Army service in 1901 and died at age 69 in 1905. "Fighting Joe" Wheeler (below) lived up to his name during both of his military careers. His life span was the same length as Lee's and occurred just a year later. Early in the Civil War, Wheeler commanded both artillery and infantry units before settling into his renowned role as a cavalry officer. His record in the War of the Rebellion consisted of one spectacular engagement af-

ter another, in which he was wounded three times, had 16 horses shot out from under him, and attained the rank of lieutenant general when just 28 years old. As a congressman from Alabama through the 1880s and '90s, he became chairman of the Ways and Means Committee; that position, adding more honors to his personal popularity and his Civil War record, made him a national symbol of reconciliation between North and South. The whole country then applauded his appointment to command of the cavalry division of the 5th Corps which liberated Cuba. Wheeler — of all the wisdom he bestowed — was to be remembered most fondly by his troopers for an exuberant shout he gave out during the assault on San Juan Hill. In the heat of the attack, as the Spanish forces began to flee their positions, he yelled to a unit comprised mostly of soldiers from northern states: "We've got the Yankees on the run!" He apparently never revealed whether he was joking or if the rallying cry was an unintentional throwback to his earlier command experiences! Quite satisfied with his service in the army of his former enemies, Wheeler remained on active duty after the war with Spain; first commanding the recuperation camp at Montauk, New York, then briefly leading a brigade in the Philippines from August 1899 to January 1900, when he was 63 years old. His illustrious career ended with his death in 1906.

Two photos, National Archives

The tense naval situation between the American and German squadrons in Manila Bay following the destruction of the Spanish fleet sparked world-wide interest, for had Admiral von Diederichs succeeded in outmaneuvering (or in a more serious confrontation – outgunning) Admiral Dewey, Germany, with the connivance of Spain, would have become the dominant power in the South Pacific. With the support of the British, the Americans held firm, retaining control. A witty political cartoon of 1898, captioned with just one word, "JEALOUS!", showed a rejected Germany in the background (below) as Uncle Sam openly flirted with a pretty young native girl labeled "Philippenes" (sic), as U.S. warships were anchored offshore. Already the girl wears a dress woven in the American Stars and Stripes pattern. In a drawing by H. Reuterdahl (above), the German ships are shown in Manila Bay (left to right): von Diederichs's flagship, the 2nd-Class battleship *Kaiser*; 3rd-Class protected cruiser *Gefton*; 2nd-Class battleship *Deutschland*; 2nd-Class protected cruisers *Irene* and *Kaiserin Augusta.* Cutting across the bow of *Irene* is a steam launch carried by the big ships for communication between the vessels; a similar boat approaching *USS Olympia* and ignoring challenges from the American lookout prompted Dewey to open fire.

Jed Clauss collection

JEALOUS!

Long Island, which stretches 115 miles east from New York City, played a prominent role in the Spanish-American War. Camp Black was one of the largest army bases outside the South at the beginning of the war, just a few miles from New York City. Camp Wikoff, at the opposite ends of both the Island and the war, was the recuperation and mustering-out facility for the 5th Corps which had liberated Cuba. There was other defense activity on Long Island and the waters which surround it, since its strategic location dominates the sea lane approaches to New York. In May 1898, just weeks after the onset of hostilities, sailors were hard at work on the bow of an unidentified gunboat (above), one manning a fire hose, while an officer and eight men grappled with an anchor. In the foreground a light rapid-fire gun is mounted next to the anchor chain winch, as the vessel paused in Cold Spring Harbor. The diminutive steam-powered launches were easily carried on board larger vessels and quickly raised and lowered from davits. A launch from the *USS Aileen* towed a lifeboat (below) in Peconic Bay, which separates the twin forks of eastern Long Island. A U.S. Navy Militia landing party stormed ashore and established a small base camp (opposite) in a training maneuver at Centre Island, in the harbor of Oyster Bay, just a mile from Sagamore Hill, the estate of Colonel Theodore Roosevelt.

Four photos, Hal B. Fullerton, Suffolk County Historical Society

One of the largest induction camps in the northern U.S. was Camp Black, hastily established on the Hempstead Plains of Long Island, a short distance from New York City. The 33rd Michigan Regiment (above), after traveling by train from their home state, was marching from the ferry dock at Long Island City to board another train to Camp Black. The rudimentary temporary station (below) was where they reported to drill and continue training until they were ordered out for the disembarkation to their wartime positions. It is here, too, where the civilian friends and families of many soldiers arrived, armed with flasks of whiskey for the boys in blue! All of this fraternizing between military personnel and civilians and the generally festive air surrounding the Spanish-American War, with shipboard naval bands playing the ragtime favorite "There'll Be A Hot Time In The Old Town Tonight!" as they steamed into battle, did much to dull the seriousness of the conflict. While it certainly was an important morale factor at the time, the inconsequential attitude had much to do with the misunderstanding of the great significance of the 1898 war of future generations, which so mistakenly have dismissed it as just a crude grab for power by unsophisticated American imperialist politicians. Studious research alone reveals the global importance of the Spanish-American War's heritage throughout the following century.

Above, Suffolk County Historical Society   Below, collection of Vincent F. Seyfried

With the civilian population of the U.S. overwhelmingly in favor of going to war with Spain, much affection, concern, and admiration was lavishly bestowed upon soldiers and sailors, with citizens of all ages, classes, and genders flocking to the camps to wish their fighting men well. Camp Black, located in such close proximity to New York City, attracted trainloads of well-wishers, including many bicyclists who were able to transport their personal items of mobility in special railroad bicycle-carrying baggage cars. Here, a very businesslike army sentry armed with a rifle and fixed bayonet, challenges two attractive and obviously determined young women cyclists at Camp Black. Both ladies are wearing military-style hats, the one at left with a regimental crest fastened to the front of her headgear. The unit insignia was probably given to her by her beau, whom she has come hopefully to visit, prior to him being sent to Port Tampa to disembark for the liberation of Cuba.

Artwork by T. de Thulstrup

The 3rd U.S. Cavalry Regiment mustered at Camp MacKenzie, Georgia, where two panoramic views (above and below) show a few of the troopers and many of their mounts, tethered in neat, straight lines. Throughout military history, new enlistees into service have had to endure initiations of varying degrees of abuse and humiliation. Sometimes however, it could be fun, as was experienced by the raw recruit (center) being bounced into the air in a blanket toss at the hands of ten comrades. Such high jinks were especially popular among the young sailors and soldiers of the U.S. in 1898, when belief in a just cause and high morale would soon see them virtually dancing off to war. For many, the happy-go-lucky attitudes quickly vanished in the smoke and blood on San Juan Hill.

Above, below, National Archives   Center, University of South Florida

The Plant System steamship and railroad conglomerate may have played a role in the government's inappropriate selection of Port Tampa, Florida as the port of embarkation for the 5th Army Corps. On April 7, with war virtually inevitable, the U.S. government retained the Plant System steamer *Olivette* to shuttle American citizens from Cuba to Port Tampa, and a week later, Consul General Fitzhugh Lee became the last American official to sail from Havana. Then the Plant System supplied one of its speediest 4-4-0 locomotives, a baggage car, a Pullman, and General Superintendent Bradford Dunham's private car to speed Lee to Washington, D.C., averaging a record 54 miles per hour for the 1,274-mile trip, with the train topping 90 mph at times. Dignitaries, military formations and crowds of civilians greeted General Lee's train all along the route, and the journey received national publicity. The Associated Press headline, "Plant System Pleased as Fastest Time is made by General Lee's Special Train to Washington," appeared nationally, and the rousing story stirred patriotism and reassured the American people that the railroads were well prepared to meet the wartime transportation needs. The government then awarded Plant a lucrative contract to transport men and munitions, and promptly designated the company's terminal, Port Tampa, the embarkation port for Cuban operations! Commissioned Major General of Volunteers, General Lee was given command of the 7th Army Corps, headquartered at Camp Cuba Libre, near Jacksonville, Florida. One field expedient utilized by Lee's men was to establish a signal flag platform (above) by stripping the lower limbs off a tall, straight tree. When General Lee (standing above both flags in photo below) reviewed his troops in Jacksonville, the 45-star American flag and the British Union Jack shared the front of the reviewing stand, as the budding alliance burst into bloom. The inscription on the picture, written by a soldier in 1898, read: "You will notice that all through this war that the English and American flags always went together."

Two photos, University of South Florida

As regiments that were to comprise the 5th Army Corps began arriving at Port Tampa from all over the U.S., they were assigned to sprawling bivouac areas while awaiting orders to board their ships. The 69th New York Regiment (above) drilled and tended their equipment as they awaited the call. Each day, cavalry troopers (below), their sabers at right shoulder, exer-

cised their horses and practiced their tactics. An open-air regimental barber shop (upper right) tended the shaving and haircutting needs of the men. With their heads in varying stages of having been scalped by their exuberant barber comrades, men of the 2nd Infantry (lower right) ate dinner in the field.

Three photos, University of South Florida   Lower right, National Archives

One photographer managed to expose good 8-inch x 10-inch glass-plate images of the 2nd New Jersey Volunteers in their camp at Port Tampa. "Tent Streets" (above) were the housing complexes of the Army in the field, with crude amenities of home, such as wooden crates for sitting, washlines stretched between tents, and rifles stacked in the street. A cavalryman, his Krag-Jorgensen carbine and reins ready for action (below), posed in full regalia including sheepskin chaps. Carrying their tin cups and mess kits, baggy-pants soldiers (upper right) lined up for midday chow. Mail call (lower right) is always a highlight in the humdrum, boring camp life of soldiers far from home.

Four photos, National Archives

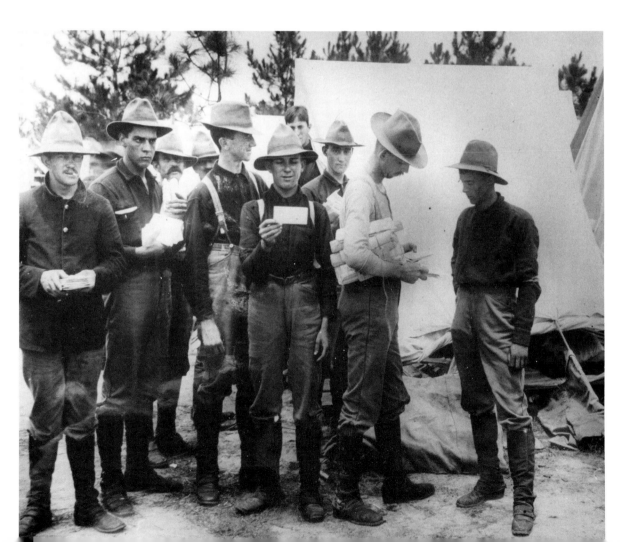

After the battle of San Juan Hill and two days later the great American naval victory at Santiago Bay, the fortunes of both sides deteriorated rapidly on land, but by July 16, the desperate Spaniards were ready to surrender. Shafter's role in allowing Colonel Roosevelt's forceful and insubordinate "Round-Robin" letter to fall into the hands of an Associated Press correspondent was a further example of his courage and his humanity concerning the welfare of the sick and dying men of his command. After the war, General Shafter was sent to command the Department of California and the Columbia, retiring from the regular army in that position a year later. Retaining his volunteer commission until June 1901, he took up ranching near Bakersfield, where he died on November 12, 1906, at the age of 71.

National Archives

William Rufus Shafter had a distinguished combat career during the Civil War, and later, in the frontier campaigns against the last of the hostile Original Americans (or First Americans; the politically correct term of "Native Americans" referring just to the Indians is incorrect and misleading since everyone born in the U.S. is a Native American), rising to the rank of brigadier general in May 1897. A year later, he was appointed Major General of Volunteers and sent to Tampa to build the expeditionary force that would liberate Cuba out of the turmoil and chaos caused by the ineptitude of the War Department. Although a good strategist with a sound battle plan in Cuba, the corpulent Shafter suffered miserably in the heat and humidity of the Cuban summer and was only able to get up to the front lines occasionally and in grave discomfort.

The nickel and the dime novels at the turn of the 20th century thrilled young readers, including teen-age boys and soldiers. *The Starry Flag Weekly* ran a series of "Thrilling Stories of our Victorious Army" (although this issue came out even before the Army had arrived in Cuba, but everyone just *knew* that American boys would rout the enemy at every turn), including this one about "Tampa's Dynamite Fiend."

University of South Florida

The 2nd New Jersey Volunteer Cavalry paraded past the Windsor Hotel in Jacksonville, Florida, prior to being sent to Port Tampa.

As the 25,000-man 5th Army Corps arrived at Port Tampa, chaos and confusion were rampant as the single-track railroad line was clogged with a jam of trains stretching for ten miles, and commanders could not locate the cars with their unit's supplies and equipment. The rough arrival of the Rough Riders on a coal train (above), which had been "seized" by Lieutenant-Colonel Roosevelt, was just one example of many spur-of-the-moment expedients employed by frustrated officers who were desperate to get their men to the transport ships. Hundreds of men at a time were set to work (center) unloading boxcars. The 71st New York Volunteers and at least one Rough Rider, wearing his polka dot bandanna (below), relaxed on the wharf. Another scene shows soldiers carrying crates (opposite, top) from the cars to the ships. Troops with their rifles and field gear (opposite, bottom) double-time up a gangplank and into the hold of a transport.

Below, National Archives   Opposite, bottom, **University of South Florida**

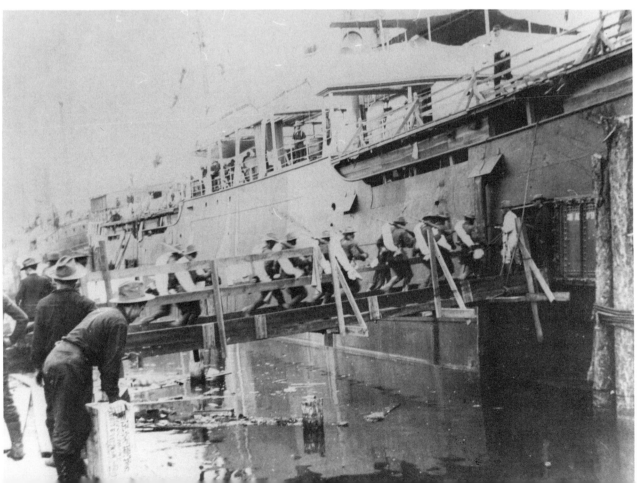

Above, opposite top, University of South Florida

An overall view of the dock (above) shows the loading of the ships at Port Tampa. Henry Plant's famous Port Tampa Inn was built on piles adjacent to the pier and advertised that it was the only hotel in the world where guests could fish right out of their bedroom windows! There can be little doubt that the inn did spectacular business in June 1898. Loaded to the gunwales, a ship (opposite, top) was ready to sail to Cuban waters. Soldiers milled about the deck of the transport *Rio Grande* (opposite, bottom) as they steamed off to their grand historical mission.

Opposite bottom, National Archives

When the keel of the *USS Oregon* was laid in 1891, her proposed size and firepower were impressive indeed, and when called upon to prove her worth, she was to excel in every category. The first big test of the battleship was her dash of 13,000 miles around South America to join Admiral Sampson's fleet in the battle for Cuba. With her outriggers still extended, she is shown in a head-on bow view just before weighing anchor the day she commenced her grand run from San Francisco Bay on March 19, 1898. Her forward 13-inch gun turret and two of her 8-inch turrets just aft and above the big guns show clearly, as does her wide girth of beam and how low her hull rode in the water. Beneath the surface, she was 24 feet of draught. Soon to be nicknamed "McKinley's Bulldog," the vessel boasted a ferocious bite, as Admiral Cervera was later to ruefully acknowledge: Four 13-inch guns, eight 8-inchers and four 6-inch, plus 30 smaller, but no less deadly, rapid-fire guns that virtually cleared the gunners off the decks of the Spanish fleet at Santiago a few months later. Her crew, led by the resolute Captain Charles E. Clark (left), was no less formidable, as they sailed the *Oregon* into battle and naval history in 1898. Her demise was to become a national shame 44 years later, as related elsewhere in this book.

Below, U.S. Naval Historical Center

Sailing off to War

The paralleling campaigns to dislodge the colonial power of Spain from the Caribbean Sea and the Southwestern Pacific Ocean rapidly unfolded in June of 1898. Indeed the first expedition of American Army units, comprised of five companies of the 14th U.S. Infantry, California and Oregon Volunteer Infantry and California Volunteer Artillery, commanded by Brigadier General T. M. Anderson, U.S.V., sailed from San Francisco on May 25, arriving in Manila Bay on June 30. Major General Wesley Merritt had been made commander of the Department of the Pacific on May 16; he arrived in San Francisco two weeks later to command the expeditionary forces so urgently requested by Admiral Dewey. The second expedition embarked on June 15; the third, including General Merritt, on June 27, and four additional convoys left in July. It was an incredible coincidence that the first American occupation troops in the Philippines went ashore at Cavite on July 1, 1898, the same day that their brothers-in-arms won the decisive battle of the war, at San Juan Hill in Cuba, 9,000 miles away!

With no previous experience in seaborne invasions of enemy territory, the United States was busily — and victoriously — embarking on two major assaults simultaneously; in the Philippines the enemy might or might not resist, and in Cuba, they definitely would fight back. It was in the 1520s that the Spaniards — initially under the great Portuguese circumnavigator, Ferdinand Magellan — began their agenda of colonizing *Las Islas Filipinas*, named in honor of Philip, Prince of Asturias, the son of King Charles I. Nearly four centuries thereafter, Spanish rule ended when General Merritt, after occupying the Spanish colony, was appointed military governor of the Philippines by President William McKinley. The Philippine insurgent leader, Emilio Aguinaldo, had fought the Spaniards in "The Insurrection of '96," and while he appreciated the Americans' success in ridding his country of Spanish oppression, he was determined that it should be independent. Aguinaldo and his followers were in no frame of mind to trade bloody Spanish tyranny for American rule, no matter how enlightened or democratic the new foreign masters might prove to be.

Even as the convoys of the American occupation army were enduring the five-weeks trans-Pacific journey, the invasion force that would seize Cuba at last sailed from Tampa Bay, but not before an earlier mini-invasion placed the first U.S. troops on the island and a fierce debate briefly raged within the War Department concerning the desirability of which to liberate first: Cuba or Puerto Rico. The declaration of war had referred only to Cuba, but the earliest fighting was in the Philippines and the commanding general of the U.S. Army, Nelson A. Miles, a gallant and brave Civil War officer who had risen to division commander and later distinguished as an Indian fighter, strongly advocated that Puerto Rico be invaded first, with Cuba to be taken in autumn. Again, lack of experience in long-distance projection of power befuddled the strategic planning of the American government and the Army, since previous conflicts had all been waged on or adjacent to home ground. The most recent combat experience, the closing campaigns of 300 years of fighting against the Indians, offered no lessons in warfare with a European power. The frontier battles were won because, long term, the Indians never stood a chance, no matter how brave or experienced they were. The white man's total superiority in technology and material, his geometrically increasing population which fed westward migration, the railroads and the virtual extermination of the buffalo were the causes of the red man's demise. None of it could be attributed to any advanced strategic doctrine. With the government in Madrid totally inept and Washington, D.C., groping blindly about, it would fall to the generals and admirals and their officers and men to determine the outcome of the unprecedented war in 1898. Fortunately for the United States, this overwhelming burden fell on strong shoulders.

It was incomprehensible to Americans a century later, but in the late 1800s there was often a bitter rivalry between the senior army general and the Secretary of War; never was this more evident than in the relationship between Alger and Miles. When the War Secretary, often displaying incompetence at cabinet meetings, admitted that "the governmental machinery was altogether inadequate to immediately meet the emergency," Miles' pompousness and ego took command and his campaign to get Congress to authorize the rank of lieutenant general went into high gear; he would be the senior officer to be eligible for a third star. Miles further annoyed Alger when, during the last week of May, he proposed the invasion of Puerto Rico, a plan which had merit. With the United States in control of that island, the Navy could easily interdict all the passages to Cuba and prevent the Spaniards from supplying and reinforcing their Cuban garrison, making a later invasion of the larger island less costly. As often happens in crucial war decisions, politics had to be considered as well; for decades, attention had focused only on Cuba and the overriding interest of the press and the public was the liberation of that colony. Strongly espousing his Puerto Rico plans and disagreeing with Alger on Cuban invasion strategy should the original preparations proceed, the two men arrived at an unbridgeable schism when Miles refused to carry out an inspection of the larger training camps. A memo by Alger stated: "Orders not obeyed, General Miles saying he was in the habit of issuing his own orders." On May 31, less than two weeks after McKinley overrode Miles' initial cautious plans when he stated "God willing … we shall end the war before the General would have us begin operations," orders were issued to Major General William R. Shafter, commander of the 5th Army Corps, to embark to the south coast of Cuba.

Even before the 5th Corps invasion force sailed from Tampa Bay, several dangerous and valorous missions were carried out by the U.S. Navy which forever dispelled any remaining doubts in European minds concerning the professionalism and bravery of American sailors and marines. The first was the great race of the battleship *Oregon*, from San Francisco, around South America and up to Key West, in time to play an important role in the Cuban campaign. Once Spain and the United States went to war, the *Oregon* would be needed in the Atlantic, although with just Dewey's Asiatic Squadron in the western Pacific, it was at great risk that the ship was relieved of the duty of guarding the west coast. Still, the decision proved to be sound and in 55 days of actual sailing time, with another 11 days in various ports, coaling and reprovisioning, the 348-foot, 10,288-ton, first-class coastal battleship, manned by 32 officers and 441 men, completed its historic dash, arriving in Florida's Key West waters on May 24. She had come 13,000 miles, with her complicated machinery and skilled crew performing perfectly; not one malfunction or delay for repairs occurred. Upon her arrival, Captain Clark reported that the *Oregon* was ready to sail immediately into action against the enemy. American technology, workmanship, training, and fortitude had proved itself as seldom before or since, and worldwide, naval authorities and the press regarded the feat as an astounding success. Over the next five years, the journey of the *Oregon* was to be cited by high government and defense officials as a stark example of why the United States would have to construct the canal across Central America.

Spanish Admiral Pascual Cervera y Topete had become an elusive sailing ghost around the North Atlantic and the West Indies, as the American Navy sought in vain to pinpoint the location of his flotilla. Finally, he slipped into the harbor at Santiago de Cuba on May 24. Rumors and erroneous sightings had, over the previous weeks, placed Cervera as far north as Labrador, preparing to bombard American east coast cities on his way to Cuba, or hiding in fjords along the southern coast of Argentina, waiting to ambush the *Oregon*. But even as the Spanish government felt relieved that her strongest remaining squadron was "safe" in a harbor which was surrounded by hills and had access by sea only through a narrow entrance framed with steep cliffs, American Commodore Winfield Scott Schley, arriving at the scene with his ships, felt that he had Cervera "bottled up" and trapped. Schley had been at the west end of Cuba to keep Cervera from getting to Havana that way, while Admiral William T. Sampson patrolled the Windward Passage, denying access from the east, as he prepared to escort the planned invasion armada.

The Spanish fleet was far from trapped, however, and serious thought was given to just keeping it in the confines of the harbor until after the invasion and capturing it with land as well as naval forces. Should Cervera decide to sail out under the cover of darkness, he could still give the U.S. Navy a hard fight. To quote Watterson: "… all hope of escape was cut off from Cervera. Still no American ships could venture to enter the harbor, the passage of which was not more than 200 yards in width. The harbor channels were planted with torpedo mines, four land batteries guarded the narrow door, and inside, a battery moored upon an old warship faced the entrance, while Cervera's full squadron lay in wait. For days, the American ships lay off the harbor, like cats before a rat hole, varying the suspense with bombardments of the batteries and with feints intended to draw Cervera out." Admiral Sampson assigned Lieutenant Richmond P. Hobson, an assistant Naval constructor, the task of ascertaining whether it would be possible to scuttle a ship in the narrow mouth of the harbor, thereby assuring that the Spanish fleet could not sail out and releasing the American ships from what had amounted to almost stationary guard duty.

Hobson devised a bold initiative that required but seven men to sail a large transport ship into the gap, turn her sideways to completely block it and sink her — all under the point-blank fire of the overlooking enemy guns. It was to be an heroic mission, for the brave men who were to carry it out were given little chance of getting away with their lives. Sampson agreed to the proposal and, duly impressed with the young officer's thinking and courage, granted his ardent request to be in command of the virtual suicide sortie. His crew was to be composed of one volunteer from each warship in Sampson's squadron, and when the call for men to come forward was made, virtually every sailor enthusiastically responded. The chosen vessel was the *Merrimac*, 330 feet long. In the early hours of June 3, Lieutenant Hobson, his six volunteers, plus an heroic mutineer, a coxswain from Sampson's flagship *New York*, who had been preparing the *Merrimac*, then hid aboard and refused to leave, set out under full steam on the ship, heading for the harbor entrance. The *New York*'s launch followed to rescue the ship scuttlers, if possible.

The fortress gunners did not discover the *Merrimac* until she was nearly to her destination, preparing to lower an anchor that would secure her while the current swung her stern around to block the channel. As time-fuzes were ignited to blow holes in the hull below the waterline, the sea valves were opened and a murderous barrage — both from the fortress batteries and Cervera's warships — raked the doomed vessel, the Spaniards inadvertently assisting in the completion of her mission. The launch which had followed to rescue Hobson and his men, although under heavy fire, searched in vain for the brave men, and it was not until dawn that the quest was abandoned. The following af-

Drawn by Davenport; collection of Jed Clauss

"THE NEXT STRATEGIC MOVE OF THE SPANISH FLEET"

ternoon, a Spanish tug, under a flag of truce, approached the American fleet to report that Hobson and his men had been captured, just two were slightly wounded and they had been received as heroes by Admiral Cervera. When the signal flags on the *New York* relayed the news, loud cheers rolled up above every American ship. During the month of their imprisonment before being released, Cervera ordered that the eight Americans be well treated and shown the respect due such courageous sailors. The *Merrimac*, as it turned out, did not completely block the channel, her hull having filled with water so fast that she had not entirely swung into position before she settled to the bottom. The Spanish officer who brought the news of the survival of Hobson and his crew informed the Americans that by sinking the *Merrimac*, "You have made it more difficult, but we can yet get out." Despite the rapidly developing technology and bloodiness of modern warfare in 1898, both the Spaniards and the Americans could still be chivalrous and even immediately forgiving.

With Cervera safely confined to Santiago Harbor, President McKinley issued the orders for the 5th Corps commanders to proceed with final preparations to invade the south coast of Cuba and capture the city and the Spanish fleet. The warships, now partially freed from their constant watch off Santiago, steamed slowly along the coast in both directions, working in close cooperation with Cuban commanders to select the best landing beach. American ships bombarded several likely sites as feints to confuse the enemy defenders. It was almost two weeks before the arrival of Shafter's expeditionary force that the first American unit — the 1st Marine Volunteer Battalion from New York — landed on the island, established a beachhead and unfurled the Stars and Stripes over Cuban soil. The location chosen was Caimanera, a town about 40 miles east of Santiago at the mouth of Guantánamo Bay, where the sprawling U.S. Navy base would shortly be constructed. The 650 marines were more than a feint; they established a base on June 10 named Camp McCalla in honor of the captain of the gunboat *Marblehead* which was busily laying down protective volleys along the coast. In the late afternoon of June 11, Marines became the first Americans to feel the pain of Spanish Mauser bullets, as 200 enemy soldiers attacked from the dense jungle. The Marines grabbed their Navy Lee rifles and dove into their trenches. About 150 men had been swimming in the surf and at the first shots, they ran up the steep hill, stark naked, retrieved their weapons and wearing just their ammunition belts, leapt into the defensive positions alongside their uniformed comrades. No record survives of the fighting ability of nude marines, but the attack was beaten off, to return that

127

night and tally the first American casualties of the Cuban campaign, with four dead and a number wounded. The majority of this Marine battalion were city boys, who had neither the youthful experience nor the proper training for hit-and-run jungle warfare. Their position had become tenuous and insecure, but the next day, 60 Cuban soldiers emerged from the thick forest to show the once-proud Americans how to take on the enemy in such unfamiliar terrain!

As the American battleships shelled every Spanish fort along the south Cuban coast between Santiago and Guantánamo, the transport ships from Tampa steamed into the waters off Santiago on June 20. The soldiers' morale greatly improved as they saw land and any misgivings about fighting the Spaniards were overcome by their relief at the thought of leaving the miserable quarters on the ships. Some had fared better than others; indeed, although Charles Johnson Post complained of the brackish drinking water, the tepid air below decks and "even the sickly odor of spoiling potatoes (which) lent a sordid accent of drama to adventure," he seemed quite tolerant — even at times enthusiastic — about the time spent on board the transports. In this last war before the advent of submarines and reconnaissance aircraft, the troop ships convoyed at a leisurely pace of under ten knots for almost one week before arriving at the disembarkation points of Daquiri and Siboney, a few miles east of Santiago.

Soon, the inexperience of the Americans in launching massive seaborne assaults became all too clearly evident; it seemed that Nike, the winged goddess of Victory, was intent on favoring their cause despite the lack of preparation and ineptitude of the execution of landing operations. The only way to get the soldiers, burdened as they were with their weapons, ammunition and field gear — almost 40 pounds per man — ashore was to ferry them in the oar-powered lifeboats. Instead of beaching the craft at Daquiri, where the Rough Riders were among the units to come ashore, the boats tossed in the surging waves, discharging the troops onto a dock. That inappropriate procedure resulted in many of the men losing their footing and falling into deep water, and the drowning of two of Roosevelt's troopers. The Lieutenant Colonel of the 1st Volunteer Cavalry was infuriated by his landing experience, losing his self-control and turning crimson when his favorite horse, the ironically named "Rain-In-The-Face" drowned. Because no provision had been made for getting the horses and mules ashore, it was decided to just push them overboard from the transports moored up to a half-mile from the beach, hoping that maybe they could swim through the high breakers. Someone on board the *Yucatán*, out of deference to Roosevelt, made the well-meaning, but disastrous decision to lower Rain-In-The-Face in a cargo sling, rather than just throw her off, like all the other animals. When a large wave came just as the sling reached the water, the horse became entangled and

went under. The final outrage perpetuated on the furious Roosevelt was when the ship sailed off, taking his saddle with it! His other horse, Texas, survived and *New York Journal* reporter, Edward Marshall, who saw his own horse drown, gave his saddle to Roosevelt.

Many of the frightened and confused animals panicked and, being disoriented, swam out to sea. Oarsmen paddled furiously to catch them and point them towards land, but others were lost. When cavalry buglers on shore sounded the calls that the horses knew, most managed to reach safety. In terms of confusion and ineptitude, Daquiri and Siboney proved to be Tampa in reverse. Fortunately for the Americans, the only armed men to meet them were a few scraggly Cuban *insurrectos*. Had a disciplined force of just a few hundred Spaniards been able to avoid the murderous naval barrage and taken up positions just behind the beach, they would have inflicted heavy casualties on the invaders, whose boats were capsizing and being battered against the dock.

The dynamite cruiser *Vesuvius*, the controversial and untried high-explosive launcher, received her baptism of fire (actually, compressed air) during the pre-invasion shelling of the Cuban coast. This ship had three long 15-inch diameter tubes, rigidly mounted at approximately a 30-degree angle, which extended down through three decks and hurled projectiles of up to 1,500 pounds of dynamite with 25 times the explosive power of gunpowder. But the projectile was unstable, and using powder to fire it from the ship could cause it to explode in the barrel, so compressed air was the propellant. The big drawback was that the firing tubes were totally inflexible, having to be rigidly mounted and attached to elaborate air-compressing machinery which virtually filled the hull of the vessel. The only way to sight the guns was by aiming the entire ship, as was later done with fighter aircraft, rendering pinpoint accuracy impossible. When the *Vesuvius* did cut loose, it was with destructive force never before possible, heralding the awesome power which would later be associated with the great World War II battleships.

Just prior to going ashore at Siboney, Private Post witnessed the dynamite cruiser in action: "We could see the *Vesuvius* as she moved in, head-on to the coastline. One might, by watching carefully, see the faint haze at the muzzles of the pipes as she fired and the compressed air was released. Then, after a pause there would come a blast from the jungled hills beyond. It was like a blast from a quarry and a whole section of the hill would be torn off; the dynamite shells were very effective. The whole problem lay in landing on the target — to aim a ship is a problem in itself."

The shortcomings of the compressed-air method of propellant, so obvious to even a young soldier, ensured that the concept would not be used again, especially when, a few years later, methods were devised to fire the most sensitive high-explosives from regular large-calibre guns.

On June 20, even before troops of the 5th Army Corps began going ashore, General Shafter and Admiral Sampson were welcomed by Cuban patriot soldiers on the beach at Aserradero, where they came to plan strategy with Cuban commander General García.   T. de Thulstrup

Mothers, wives, and girlfriends bidding the flower-bedecked soldiers of the California Volunteer Infantry goodbye on the San Francisco wharf as the soldiers prepared to embark for Philippine occupation duty.

Drawing by J. A. Cahill

One of the vessels of the first convoy to leave for the Philippines the last week in May 1898, the *City of Peking*, with hundreds of soldiers waving farewell from the deck, lifeboats, and rigging, slowly pulls away from the San Francisco dock.

As the Spanish-American War progressed with lightning fury on sea and land, U. S. government officials worked long hours trying to coordinate all of the forces, operations, channels of supply, and many other facets to ensure a quick and decisive victory. While there were too many instances of sheer incompetence, much of the problem lay in the great magnitude of a situation which forced a totally inexperienced government to wage two massive military and naval campaigns simultaneously and half a world apart. Secretary of War Russell A. Alger is shown planning strategy with Brigadier General Corbin in the Secretary's Washing- ton office. Alger was an honest and motivated public official who, although overwhelmed by the burdens of his position, freely admitted his shortcomings. His feud with General Miles, the lack of precedent to guide him, and the stunning rapidity of overpowering historical tides which men like Alger had to cope with would have broken men of less fortitude. Despite the scandal and the ineptitude which sullied the prosecution of the war from the start, the final results proved so favorable to the American cause that 100 years later, their grand accomplishments shine as the golden moment in American history!

Assistant Naval Constructor Richmond Pearson Hobson (below) led one of the most daring and courageous missions of the war when he and seven other American sailors ran the collier *USS Merrimac* into the entrance to Santiago Bay, as the fortress guns were firing point-blank at the ship. After opening the sea valves and igniting time fuzes to sink the vessel hoping to block the channel, Hobson and his men were clinging to a life raft as the ship went down. The *Merrimac* (above) as she looked just six weeks earlier, on April 23, as she was being fitted for U.S. Navy service at the Norfolk Naval Yard. Miraculously, all eight men survived. Hobson recalled his capture in *Harper's:* "... we found that one of the pontoons (of the liferaft) was entirely out of the water and the other one was submerged. Had the raft lain flat on the water we could not have got under it, and would have had to climb up on it, to become an excellent target ... we could get under the raft, and, by putting our hands through the crevices between the slats which formed its deck, we could hold our heads out of the water and still be unseen. I swam towards the (Spanish) launch and then she started toward me. I called out in Spanish: 'Is there an officer on board?'" An officer answered in the affirmative, and then I shouted in Spanish again: 'I have seven men to surrender.' I ... was seized and pulled out of the water. As I looked up when they were dragging me into the launch, I saw that it was Admiral Cervera himself who had hold of me. The first words he said to me when he learned who I was were, 'Bienvenido se usted,' which means 'you are welcome.'"

When the 1st Marine Volunteer Battalion from New York came ashore at Caimanera at Guantánamo Bay on June 10, the Cubans at last could believe that their liberation was indeed at hand. As soon as they occupied the crest of the most prominent point, the marines raised the first American flag (above) on Spanish territory. They named their position Camp McCalla in honor of Commander Bowman H. McCalla (center), whose warship *USS Marblehead* was providing the heavy covering fire that kept the enemy at a respectable distance, allowing the marines to land without opposition. A squad of the plucky marines (below) manned a protective skirmish line on the outer perimeter while permanent defensive positions were being dug. These riflemen appear adequately clothed, unlike 150 of their "bunkies" ("buddies" in 1898 military slang) who had to fight off the first Spanish counterattack while wearing not one stitch of clothing. Apparently, the naked marines were actually photographed, for one poor-quality surviving photo shows a group of bare-chested marines in a trench; the pants they are wearing are a rather poor job of retouching, probably required by Victorian-era censorship!

Above and below, U.S. Naval Historical Center

During the first American seaborne invasion of a foreign enemy, U.S. soldiers hit the beach (above) from lifeboats at Siboney, Cuba, on June 25, 1898. Fortunately for the invaders, the incompetent Spanish commanders did not attempt to make a hot reception for them and beat a hasty retreat as the first transports appeared. The power vacuum on the beachhead was quickly filled by eager but ragged Cuban *insurrectos* (below), who warmly greeted their liberators from the north. Two scenes by photographer James Burton show the American troops arriving at Daiquri (opposite), where they crowded the pier, then began their march inland to their first firefight with Spanish forces in the hills in the background.

Above and below, National Archives

The pneumatic-gun vessel *USS Vesuvius* was launched in 1890 and was a radical concept, using compressed air to fire high explosive shells of unprecedented destructive force. She is shown under way on one of her early trial runs (above) in 1891. A view of the forward deck

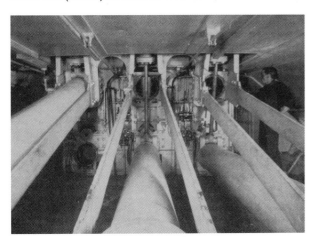

(right) illustrates the stubby muzzles of the fixed barrels and a photo shows the loading room on the lowest deck. Drawings of the ship (below) reveal that she was a slender, fast vessel, with the firing tubes occupying the forward one-third of the hull, the four boilers in the center, and the compressed-air machinery and tanks beneath the firing tubes. The guns were traversed by aiming the ship, and elevation was determined by the strength of the compressed-air charge, rendering accuracy most difficult to achieve. The whole concept was the antithesis of what Admiral George Dewey considered to be the chief reason for the success of U.S. Navy victories in 1898: accurate gunnery. The *Vesuvius* also made history as being, by default, the first modern psychological warfare weapon, when the Spaniards later reported that they had been utterly terrified by it. When any other ship fired its big guns, the roar and, at night, the muzzle flash would give a few seconds' warning. There was absolutely no indication that the compressed-air guns had discharged until a huge explosion tore up the landscape behind Spanish lines!

Photos, diagram, U.S. Naval Historical Center

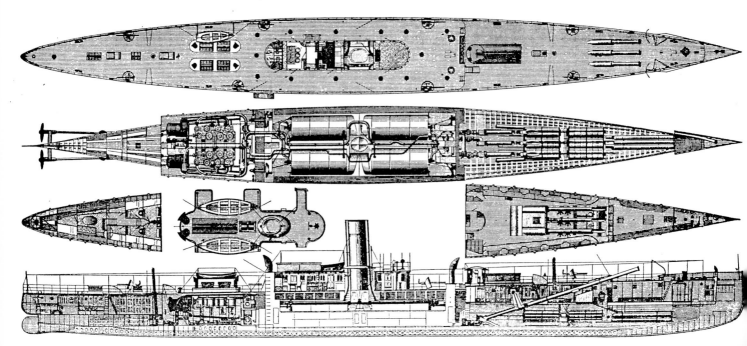

The monitor *USS Monadnock* was escorting one of the convoys to Manila Bay during the Spanish-American War when she was photographed from the *USS Nero* in mid-Pacific. The monitors floated so low in the water that even in just a slightly choppy sea, as in this picture, *Monadnock's* deck was awash, being hardly three feet above the water line. Presenting an extremely low silhouette, making her a very difficult target for enemy gunners, the *Monadnock* almost resembling a surfaced submarine must have been an absolutely frightening ship on which to be during a storm, with waves crashing over her big turret and just her wheelhouse, mast, and funnel above the raging surf. The absolutely watertight construction of the monitors were a credit to their builders. By the beginning of the Philippine Insurrection in early 1899, the *Monadnock* had been transferred to the Asiatic Squadron where she went to work shelling coastal positions on Luzon.

The Cuban Campaign

The Spanish press, censored by the government and not known for the reliability of its reporting as the initial accounts of Dewey's "defeat" showed — produced stories that were among the most farcical of the era, including one about Theodore Roosevelt. Translated excerpts: "The commander-in-chief of the American Army is one Ted Roosevelt, a former New York policeman . . . born near Haarlem, but emigrated to the United States as a youth . . . graduated Harvard Academy, a commercial school . . ." Roosevelt was reported as rampaging all over the U.S. with a ". . . bodyguard of thugs, known appropriately as 'Rough-Rioters!' " The only shred of truth was that he had received his degree from Harvard — the great university, hardly a commercial institution! While the American yellow journalists sensationalized the truth, the Spaniards simply ignored it.

Several of the units that had landed at Daquiri, including the 1st Volunteer Cavalry, immediately had to march for seven grueling miles along a rough coastal trail to Siboney, carrying most of three days' ammunition, equipment and combat rations on their backs, since all of their pack mules had either been left in Tampa, drowned or had been "requisitioned" by the desperate quartermasters of other regiments. Lieutenant Colonel Roosevelt was also on foot, declaring that he would not ride while his men had to march. In Cuba, "Roosevelt's Rough Riders" renamed themselves "Wood's Weary Walkers," and the forced march under the blistering tropical sun proved most exhausting — even for the cowboys, the frontiersmen and the Indians from the southwest who comprised much of the regiment.

General Shafter's plan of battle was to move on the city of Santiago de Cuba, even as the Navy kept Cervera's fleet hemmed in the harbor. Once the city was captured and Spain's warships were destroyed, the Americans would be free to carry on any land and sea operations they wished on Cuba.

Opposite: The Rough Riders firing their Krag-Jorgensen carbines in the initial encounter at Las Guasimas. Captain Allyn K. Capron, still clutching his sword in his right hand, and his left arm entangled in barbed wire, lies mortally wounded in the foreground. Lieutenant Colonel Roosevelt, his sword pointed to his rear, stands behind the nearest troopers. After this battle, Roosevelt had high praise for correspondent Richard Harding Davis who was the first to see the hats of the enemy soldiers and pinpoint them for T. R., enabling the officer to direct the fire of his men. The reporter then grabbed a carbine and, violating the rules governing noncombatants, enthusiastically opened fire. Correspondent Marshall fared worse; he received a paralyzing spinal wound. After Roosevelt's sword became entangled between his legs several times during the battle, he decided that it was an impediment and never wore it in action again.

Artwork by W. A. Rogers

This was sound doctrine, for a direct assault on the capital city, Havana, would have been much more costly in terms of casualties on all sides — especially the civilians, most of whom were allies of the United States — and may have taken too long. Emboldened and supplied by the invading Americans, the Cuban *insurrectos* could begin laying siege to Havana and other strong points and attacking Spanish reinforcements heading for Santiago. Even if the Spaniards did not soon surrender, they were cut off from resupply and would be under murderous harassment from all sides. It would not take long for them to realize the hopelessness of their position. Man-for-man, the ground forces on both sides were well matched and capable of giving a bloody fight. Spanish *soldados* were veterans of warfare in the jungles and sugarcane fields of Cuba and, although oft times poorly officered, they were gallant individual fighters. The smokeless powder of their small-arms ammunition made a well-camouflaged man virtually impossible to pinpoint, while the telltale puffs from the black powder still used by the Americans exposed the location of every U.S. trooper in action. Americans — soldiers as well as seamen — were generally better marksmen, and once an enemy was caught in a rifle sight, his chances were not good. Motivated by a righteous cause and early victories and backed by massive amounts of supplies and a continent-wide war machine just revving up, the *yanquis* felt confident of victory. As for the Cubans, what they lacked in equipment and fortifications they made up for in feelings of having been redeemed and the knowledge that a half-century of horrid persecution and inhuman conflict was about to end in victory.

The first advance inland to do battle with the Spaniards began the day after the amphibious landings when several cavalry units (all dismounted) started off toward the ring of hills which overlooked Santiago de Cuba from the east. First, they had to move through thick tropical rain forest which was virtually a jungle. When the invasion fleet anchored off Siboney, the Spanish garrison had withdrawn two and a half miles inland to set up defensive positions which overlooked the narrow road to Santiago. One primary mission of the cavalry was to reconnoiter ahead to find the enemy and, on the morning of June 24, although on foot, it was the cavalry which was sent to make contact with the Spaniards. Elements of the 10th Cavalry, consisting of 224 colored troopers, advanced along the narrow road, while 450 Rough Riders — most of the men of the unit which had not been left behind in Florida — supported by about 200 men of the 1st Cavalry of the Regulars, set out along a steep, narrow trail which ran parallel a half-mile to the west. The road and trail converged at Las Guasimas in the jungle, where Cuban scouts reported the Spaniards to be entrenched near the road and

139

on an overlooking hill, the entire area covered with thick foliage.

The advance of the 1st Volunteer Cavalry and the 1st Cavalry to their rear was to become steeped in controversy, as witnessed by Post: "We saw them as they passed through Siboney and started into the narrow jungle-bordered lane . . . (I) stopped near a Regular Army major who was also watching their column. He turned to me. He was exploding and he *had* to say something to someone. 'Goddamit — they haven't even got a point out!' The dismounted cavalry, headed by the Rough Riders, was in column of fours, solid, and only lacked a band at its head to give it a thoroughly festive and inconsequential air. It walked into an ambuscade at Las Guasimas." Richard Harding Davis, well known as an ardent admirer of Roosevelt, was one of two correspondents with the Lieutenant Colonel near the head of the column and he wrote: "I and Marshall were the only correspondents with Roosevelt. We were caught in a clear case of ambush." Indeed, when the Spanish volleys began suddenly to cut into the ranks of the Rough Riders and the Americans darted their eyes in vain into the jungle trying to locate the enemy, it would seem that they had been caught totally off guard. Were Wood, the experienced combat veteran who wore the Medal of Honor, and Roosevelt, the brilliant, fearless natural leader, really so careless as to have blundered into an obvious trap? Probably not.

The Regular Army major and Private Post, who had been appalled at the apparent lack of basic military precautions as the Rough Riders left Siboney, could not have been aware of the virtual impenetrable character of the foliage. Any unit advancing toward the enemy places a point — first, a single soldier, then several more some yards behind, then a platoon, followed by a company, as the lead element — before the main body moves on. Riflemen were also sent out to the right and left flanks, especially in the hilly country, to scout for any sign of hostile forces. All of those standard procedures were impossible to perform on the trail to Las Guasimas. Wood and Roosevelt were well aware of the presence of the enemy, but such a jungle fight belongs — at least initially — to the defenders, not to the attackers.

The point of the 1st Volunteer Cavalry, in this case, the first men silently stalking along the trail ahead of the rest of the single file column, consisted of Sergeant Hamilton Fish, the New York aristocrat, and Captain Allyn Capron, perhaps the most dashing officer in the entire cavalry division. In fact, Capron actually discovered the Spaniards before they saw him and sent word back, enabling the main body to drop into defensive positions. Hardly an ambush! The first Spaniard to rise up to fire was shot dead through the head by a sharpshooter in Capron's Troop L. Immediately, the Spanish force of over 2,000 men opened a furious fire from three sides, and Sergeant Fish was the first trooper killed. According to Edmund Morris, biographer of Roosevelt (and Ronald Reagan), in

The Rise of Theodore Roosevelt: "The first soldier to be killed by these first rifle shots of the Spanish-American War was Sergeant Hamilton Fish, who fell at the feet of Captain Capron. Then another Mauser took Capron in the heart." In this writing, Morris was wrong, apparently unaware of the four fatalities at Caimanera, almost two weeks earlier.

Whether or not the Rough Riders were ambushed, they immediately sprang into action, the smoky puffs from the muzzles of their rifles informing the enemy of their precise locations while the smokeless powder of the Spaniards' Mausers kept them virtually hidden. Wood and Roosevelt raced to the front, and, as exposed as any of their men, they led and encouraged them onward through the withering fire. The Lieutenant Colonel, armed with sword and revolver, also grabbed a Krag-Jorgensen rifle which had been dropped by a wounded man, enabling him to set a further example by shooting at the distant Spaniards who, once the cavalrymen ascertained their positions, began to flee their forward trenches. Roosevelt then led a charge up a clear slope where Spanish soldiers were defending a blockhouse with heavy rifle fire, his troopers screaming Indian war cries. Waving his sword, the bold commander started up, but his men briefly hesitated under the heavy fusillade. Suddenly, the black troopers of the 10th Cavalry charged from the valley road and along with the 1st Regulars, added their strong accurate fire to the fray and joined the Rough Riders, who were cheering their timely arrival. The Spaniards hastily fled the hill, the entire force in full retreat toward Santiago.

The savage skirmish had lasted two hours and cost the Americans 16 dead and 52 wounded, mostly Rough Riders. The enemy casualties were considerably less: ten killed and just eight wounded, but little over 900 Americans, at great disadvantage, had routed more than double — perhaps triple — their number from overwhelmingly superior positions. At Manila Bay, the Navy had proven itself; the Army did likewise at Las Guasimas. The performance of the 10th Cavalry was summed up by Watterson: "The courage of the black troops as they charged deliberately up the slope was everywhere applauded. There was no hurry, no hesitation but cool deliberation. When a man was struck, his comrade turned and called 'Hospital!' with as much presence of mind as if it were a sham battle. The black troops displayed fine courage and discipline." Private Post was among the reinforcements rushed along the trail the Rough Riders had taken and he passed the wounded straggling back from the fighting. "How'd you get yours?" he asked a trooper wounded in the thigh, who was riding a mule, his trouser leg blood soaked. "Damn near stepped on the sonofabitch," was the reply, "then he got me. But I got him. I got mine. Now you go an' git yours."

The road was now virtually clear leading to the San Juan Heights, where formidable Spanish defenses protected the hills overlooking Santiago and Cervera's fleet. The Spanish were massing concentrated forces and bringing in every available man, artillery piece and rifle. Both sides knew that the outcome of the battle for that ridge line would determine the course of the war — and of history. For almost a week, the Americans cautiously advanced into position and laboriously dragged their light artillery and siege guns along the jungle trails from Siboney. Climatic conditions were unbearable, as a reporter for the *New York Sun* related: "The heat is almost intolerable. The sun is like a great yellow furnace, torturing everything living and turning everything dead into a thousand mysterious forms of terror. The fierce light swims in waves before the eyes of the exhausted soldiers... Two hours later the first great tropical rainstorm we have encountered fell from the sky, not slantwise, but straight down... For three hours a great, cold torrent swept down from the clouds, drenching the soldiers to the skin, soaking blankets and carrying misery into our vast camp... extinguishing camp fires and sending rivers of mud and red water swirling along the narrow road..."

With such horrendous conditions of weather, fatigue and hardship, malaria, yellow fever and other tropical ailments began taking a toll throughout the ranks of the American expeditionary force, as Roosevelt wrote in *The Rough Riders*, concerning his promotion to full colonel just one day before the decisive battle: "General Young (the 2nd Cavalry Brigade commander) was struck down with the fever, and Wood took charge of the brigade. This left me in command of the regiment, of which I was very glad, for such experience as we had had is a quick teacher. By this time the men and I knew one another, and I felt able to make them do themselves justice in march or battle. They understood that I paid no heed to where they came from; no heed to their creed, politics or social standing; that I would care for them to the utmost of my power, but that I demanded the highest performance of duty; while in return I had seen them tested, and I knew I could depend absolutely on their courage, hardihood, obedience and individual initiative."

Even before the siege of Santiago de Cuba began in earnest, desperation within the city became pervasive, with famine rampant; even the Spanish military lacked subsistence rations. There was a scarcity of water once the Americans cut two of the aqueducts, but wells within the city alleviated part of the loss. Spanish forces continued preparing for a hopeless last stand, with elaborate earthworks, trenches and barbed wire obstacles, while the guns of Cervera's ships were trained on the approaches the U.S. Army would have to cross. Twelve thousand Spanish regulars, under the command of General Linares, garrisoned the defenses, one-third of whom were disabled or on sick call. Between 5,000 and 11,000 *soldados*, led by General Pando, were expected to break through to the city from Manzanillo, but General Pareja was unable to

help, being pinned down by the Marines and warships at Guantánamo Bay. A six-mile front line, from Aguadores on the Caribbean Sea south of Santiago, north to El Caney, was manned by 12,000 Americans and Cuban General Calixto García's force of more than 3,000 *insurgentes*, so both sides were comparable in terms of manpower and firepower, with the Spaniards having the advantage of the high ground, strong defensive positions and clear fields of fire on the San Juan Heights.

On June 30, the obese General Shafter, sweaty and miserable in the hellish heat, was carried on the back of the strongest mule in the Army to the front where he outlined his plan for the next day's assault on the San Juan Heights. Meanwhile, Admiral Sampson's fleet, now reinforced by the battleship *Oregon*, began pounding the coastal defenses of Santiago. Shafter's plan was simple and effective: General Henry Lawton's infantry division was positioned to the north, forming the right wing, and was assigned to take El Caney, a fortified town northeast of the main objective. General Wheeler's cavalry division, along with the command of General Kent, was positioned at El Pozo, four to five miles south, and would form the center, seizing the well-defended San Juan Hill. Down by the coast, General Duffield's Michigan Volunteers and Cuban units would attack Aguadores, where the Navy was centering its bombardment. The latter was just a feint to fool the Spaniards into thinking that

Captain Allyn K. Capron, commander of Troop L of the 1st Volunteer Cavalry, was the second Rough Rider killed, hit a few seconds after Sergeant Hamilton Fish was mortally shot. Capron's father, with the same name, commanded the artillery battery at El Caney, just one week later.

would be the main thrust, rather than San Juan, thereby pinning down a large enemy force. Two thousand Cubans, under General Garcia, moved around Lawton's right to interdict any Spanish reinforcements that might be headed for Santiago.

In the early dawn of July 1, 1898, Colonel Roosevelt, his new eagle epaulets on his shoulders, gazed intently as the mists rose above the lines of hills stretching in three directions to his front, moved by the vista which he described as "an amphitheater for the battle." He was also aware that Shafter had not noticed, or simply ignored as insignificant, another hill in the way of the Rough Riders' assault on San Juan. The colonel was planning how he would first have to take that obstacle, which was crowned with a block house. He would be leading not one, but two, furious charges this historic day.

The battle was joined at 6:30 a.m. as the mist cleared, when two batteries of American artillery, the first commanded by Captain Allyn Capron, the father of the Volunteer Cavalry officer killed at Las Guasimas a week earlier, opened fire. The Spanish guns responded belatedly, commencing

the action that would make this day the one which, for the rest of his career, Roosevelt would refer to as "the great day of my life." Leaving the Camino Real, the road across San Juan to Santiago, the Regulars started across San Juan Creek; while not deep, it was within clear view of the Spanish positions. Here the Americans suffered their greatest casualties of the war, as hundreds were hit, the red flowing of the creek earning the name "Bloody Ford." In order to reconnoiter an alternate crossing point, the Signal Corps sent up a tethered observation balloon which, after locating another ford, served only to pinpoint the exact location of the thickest concentration of American troops for the eager Spanish gunners! Roosevelt managed to get the 490 remaining men of his regiment across just before the enemy artillery zeroed in, and proceeded north toward the small hill, to await orders to attack.

After waiting for several hours, restlessly watching and feeling helpless, as the Regulars started up San Juan Hill, the 1st Volunteer Cavalry received its orders to take the intervening rise which, in addition to the block house, had several

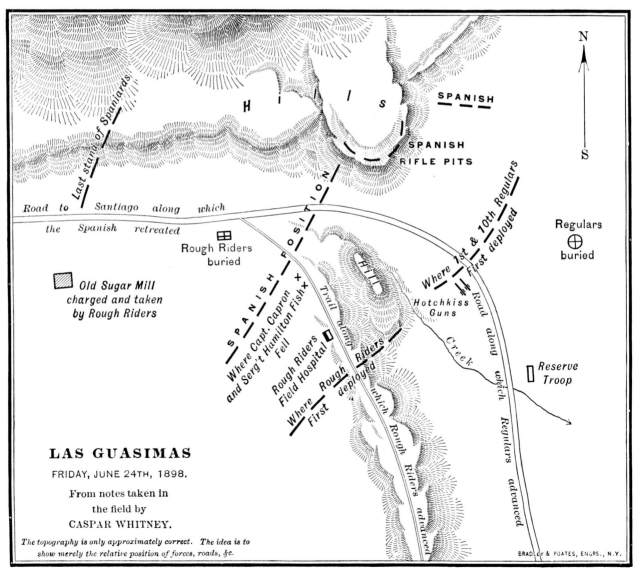

LAS GUASIMAS

FRIDAY, JUNE 24TH, 1898.

From notes taken in
the field by
CASPAR WHITNEY.

*The topography is only approximately correct. The idea is to
show merely the relative position of forces, roads, &c.*

BRADLEY & POATES, ENGRS., N.Y.

smaller structures and an enormous iron pot used in the sugar refining process. It was that sugar cane cooker that gave the knoll and the battle their American name, "Kettle Hill." Colonel Roosevelt mounted his horse, Texas, waved his hat straight to the front and started out into volleys of Mauser bullets, moving slowly to enable his dismounted troopers to keep up with him. After passing through the positions of the front line of regular cavalry, Roosevelt, the only man on horseback and in the lead, was obviously commanding, drawing intense fire. Many of his loyal troopers stayed close to him, purposely trying to draw the fire to themselves. A number succeeded and were killed or wounded. Still, the colonel rode steadily forward, brandishing his hat and his pistol, erect in the saddle, inspiring his men and no doubt impressing the Spaniards with his valor and his seeming invincibility. Once the Rough Riders fought their way to the summit of Kettle Hill, Roosevelt immediately regrouped his command and joined the main assault.

Henry Watterson's *History of the Spanish-American War,* published just months after the event, gives an excellent account of the fury and bloodiness of confusion and heroism on both sides at San Juan Hill:

"Immediately behind this regiment (the 71st New York Volunteers, Private Charles Johnson Post's unit), came the 3rd Brigade commanded by Colonel Wikoff. It consisted of the 9th, 13th and 24th Regulars. Moving into the open, it seemed to invite a concentration of all the ambuscaded Spanish hatred. Colonel Wikoff was killed a moment after he had reached the ford. Lieutenant Colonel Worth of the 13th succeeded him and in five minutes fell wounded. He was succeeded by Lieutenant Colonel Liscum of the 24th, who also fell in five minutes, badly shot. Lieutenant Colonel Ewers of the 9th then became commander. The brigade had had four commanders in 11 minutes!

"The three divisions of our army toiled and fought with dogged persistence for hours against

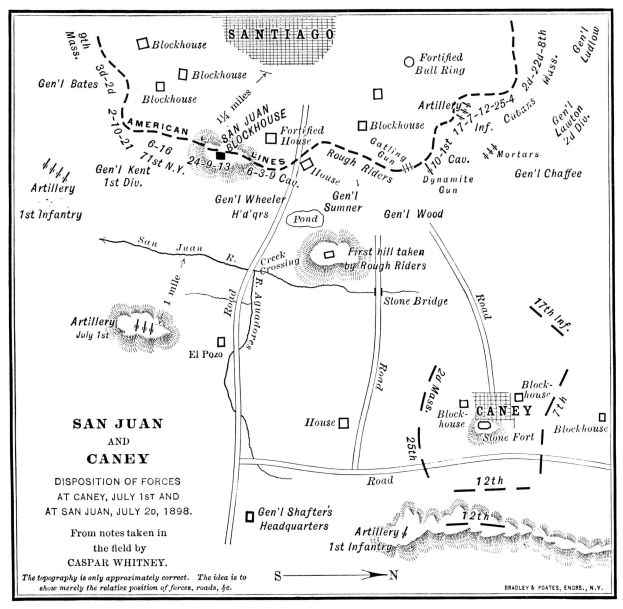

SAN JUAN
AND
CANEY

DISPOSITION OF FORCES
AT CANEY, JULY 1ST AND
AT SAN JUAN, JULY 2D, 1898.

From notes taken in
the field by
CASPAR WHITNEY.

The topography is only approximately correct. The idea is to show merely the relative position of forces, roads, &c.

BRADLEY & POATES, ENGRS., N.Y.

143

As the 71st Infantry stormed the crest of San Juan, Lieutenant Jules Ord, leading his men, was shot and killed.

continuous ambuscades, only less concentrated and dismaying than those at the 'Bloody Bend.' The cavalry in front, marching to get opposite the enemy's left, advanced the entire distance through this deadly fire, being torn by shrapnel from San Juan whenever they came into view in the flat and broadening valley, having continually to make detours to drive the enemy from the hills that rose on the sides, and which were defended by trenches, barbed wire, and trees concealing sharpshooters no eye could detect. With the cavalry, occasionally parallel, sometimes in advance, marched Hawkins' infantry, under the same force of resistance, while the brigades of Pearson and Ewers, detouring to the left, were passing hillside ambuscades.

"It is not wonderful, therefore, that — now advancing, now stopping to make a diversion against a hill — commands, regiments, battalions, and companies became confused, orders went astray, and the rear guard became the advance without knowing it. But not one body of these troops turned back ... No troops ever made better use of their advantages than the Spaniards did about San Juan. Ingenuity had seized upon every bush and

every weapon that could be brought into play. No place of concealment was neglected, no opening left unguarded. Knowing the range to every open spot through which our troops must pass, concealed by smokeless powder, they were spirits of air, terrible because unseen.

"After two or three hours of advance, the cavalry was on the east front of San Juan, Hawkins' brigade was on the southeast, and Pearson's and Ewers's brigades were on the south and southwest ... From this time, about two o'clock in the afternoon, all accounts of the battle that have been available are confused with respect to the general action and are based upon individual observations by officers of their own commands, unable to correctly perceive the forces supporting or operating at another part of the field. A halt was called. Nothing had been heard from Lawton's division at El Caney, except the booming of Capron's guns from time to time. To take San Juan without Lawton's assistance was not in orders, and yet there was nothing left but to take the hill, go into camp under the very muzzles of its artillery and rifles, or to retreat. Retreat was ignored as impossible and encampment under fire is absurd.

"It was a moment pregnant with heroism. It was delivered of thousands of heroes, one of whom by his conspicuous rank, his intrepid coolness and magnetic control of men, stood out among them all. This was Brigadier General Henry S. Hawkins, whose conduct in another part of the field was duplicated by Colonel Theodore Roosevelt, and on yet another side by regiments and battalions, with no orders or settled leadership, whose men acted upon the intelligence that perceived opportunity and seized it by common impulse... Yard by yard the cool regulars drove the enemy back from clumps of bushes and thickets until they found themselves over the last terrace, with the center of San Juan Hill rising in front of them, crowned with trenches in which the enemy was lying in force... General Hawkins, a magnificent soldierly figure, tall, stalwart, with a white moustache, pointed gray beard, and the eye of an eagle, rode out in front of his two regiments, the 6th and 16th, and scornfully turning his back to the Spanish line, every man in which marked him for death, cried: 'Boys, the time has come! Every man who loves his country, forward and follow me!' He turned his horse and with set face rode forward up the hill. Two thousand Americans leapt to their feet with a tremendous cheer in which the rebel yell and the Indian yell were mingled, and dashed up the hill after their fearless leader. Through volley after volley of withering fire, during which men reeled and fell out, while their unhurt comrades sprang to fill the gaps, the men, steadying down from the first rush, climbed and pulled themselves up the slope until they could see the strained and amazed eyes of Spaniards gazing at a spectacle never before witnessed in war — the dogged advance of those intrepid Americans who would not be denied by even the yawning hell that modern instruments of war could belch in their faces."

With a Gatling gun brought up to enfilade the Spanish trenches, in front of the 3rd Brigade, the U.S. forces made a final rush with fixed bayonets, finishing off any Spaniards who had not fled, to take up final defensive positions in trenches before the wall of Santiago. General Joseph Wheeler, the grizzled old Confederate cavalryman, was considering whether to directly assault his sector of the objective when Colonel Roosevelt earnestly announced: "If you will let me, I will lead the way!" When Wheeler agreed, he galloped to the head of his regiment, waved toward his front and shouted: "Forward! Charge the hill!" Joined by elements of the 21st Infantry and the 9th and 10th (colored) Cavalry, Roosevelt led the Rough Riders in a succession of advances until they attained the summit, as the last surviving Spaniards fled.

At El Caney, Capron's guns did a thorough job of softening up the fortified buildings — including the old church — and barbed wire obstacles, so that 3,500 men of Brigadier General Adna R. Chaffee's 7th, 12th and 17th Infantry and Colonel Miles' brigade consisting of the 1st, 4th and 25th Infantry, as well as Brigadier General Ludlow's 8th and 22nd Infantry and 2nd Massachusetts Volunteers could take the town. The bravest of the Spaniards along the six-mile front were the forward sharpshooters who hid in the trees and behind bushes and rocks well out into no-man's land. After picking off many Americans, they were invariably killed, for once their enemies had advanced to their hiding places, there was no escape for them. They were especially deadly at El Caney, accounting for many casualties. The advance of the U.S. forces was slow and prolonged by hours-long rifle exchanges as the Americans crept towards the fortifications.

The confusion and mistakes made by senior commanders were illustrated by an incident that could have turned El Caney into a disaster had not its commander indulged in flagrant insubordination, as told by Watterson: "At 10:30 we were just holding our advance in good safety, although losing more than the enemy, when an order arrived from Shafter to cease the assault and move to the assistance of Wheeler and Kent at San Juan. It was a serious interruption. As a military observer present pointed out, to comply with the order would have entailed a demoralizing defeat in the face of the enemy. General Lawton did not obey the order, but pressed the attack. The 4th and 25th Infantry joined in the attack." The stone fortress was captured by mid-afternoon; beyond it lay the town of El Caney. Soon American soldiers were advancing along the streets and experiencing a rarity for that time, but common in later wars: house-to-house fighting. The enemy was holed up all over the tightly packed buildings and inflicted heavy losses on the advancing troops. Finally the Spanish forces were driven out and the Stars and Stripes replaced the red and gold flag of Spain above the church. Belatedly that night, General Lawton tried to obey Shafter's order to relieve Wheeler, whose forces were firmly in position on top of San Juan, but there were still many Spanish snipers scattered about the battlefield, so that he did not link up with the cavalry division until noon on July 2.

The day after the decisive battle, which had accounted for half of the casualties of the war in one day, with almost 500 Americans killed and about 1,300 wounded, the Spaniards counterattacked, but the tired and hungry troops fought them off. In the field hospitals, the doctors and nurses were overwhelmed; some seriously wounded men had to wait up to eight hours with just rudimentary first aid treatment to sustain them. With the San Juan Heights affording a panorama of Santiago de Cuba and Admiral Cervera's fleet miles off in the distance, plans were being made to attack the city and capture or destroy the Spanish warships. The command decision carried out by Cervera the following day, July 3, would, fortunately for the Americans and inhabitants of the city, make a further assault by land unnecessary, but that would not be evident for days to come and forebodings of death and disaster hung heavy over Santiago and its besiegers.

At the time that the American army came ashore, Brigadier General Ludlow met and conferred at Cuban commanding General García's rugged mountain camp. Within hours, their two armies were fighting side by side on the road to the San Juan Heights above Santiago de Cuba.

The scene along the road taken by the 10th Cavalry shows the officers and men of the Hotchkiss battery firing their guns at the Spaniards pinning down the Rough Riders, while the black troopers are forming their skirmish line to begin their linkup with the besieged force. In the foreground, 10th Cavalry medics carry one of their wounded white officers to the rear. Within minutes, the two American thrusts at Las Guasimas had linked up and immediately drove the enemy forces from their dominant defensive positions.

Artwork by R. F. Zogbaum

Resting in a trench (above), the 71st New York Volunteer Regiment awaited their orders to begin the assault on San Juan Hill the morning of July 1, 1898. Private Charles Johnson Post of the 71st painted men of his regiment advancing towards the Spanish positions, while newspaper tycoon William Randolph Hearst (below) sat astride his horse, reviewing the troops going into battle, no doubt quite satisfied with his prominent role in instigating the war.

Two photos, National Archives

At the foot of San Juan Hill, the 9th U.S. Infantry (above) arranged their packs and bed rolls, preparatory to beginning their advance. When Best's artillery battery had to withdraw to a more secure position, troops from 71st Regiment Companies F and M were deployed in prone firing positions (opposite, top) to cover their movement. The notorious Signal Corps observation balloon (below) beginning its ascent above the creek that the advancing troops would soon be fording. Its lo- cation quickly alerted the Spanish commanders and they began pouring in a murderous fire from their high positions. The heavy casualties among the Americans at Bloody Ford (opposite, bottom) were the most severe of the entire war, as sharpshooters in the San Juan blockhouse and in other positions were able to pinpoint the exposed U.S. soldiers and mow many of them down.

Opposite, Charles Johnson Post, Smithsonian Institution

In the final assault, American soldiers charge towards the San Juan blockhouse.

At the foot of San Juan Hill, the 71st Regiment.

Grimes' light artillery battery moves up El Pozo Hill (left), with artillerymen riding the straining horses as they drag the gun carriages over the rough terrain. This battery provided valuable covering fire during the final assault. Hand-to-hand fighting (below) dislodged the last Spanish defenders of the San Juan blockhouse.

Above painting, Frederic Remington   Below, Howard Chandler Christy

Troop C, 9th U. S. Cavalry (Colored) leading the charge up San Juan Hill.

Artwork by Fletcher C. Ransom

Cutting through barbed-wire obstacles, U.S. 7th Infantry (above) advance elements charge towards the fortified village of El Caney, under the command of Major Corliss, shown urging his men forward at the moment that he was hit in the shoulder by a Mauser bullet. One of the guns of Captain Capron's battery (center) poured unrelenting fire into Spanish fortifications at El Caney, especially the stone fortress (below), which suffered heavy damage from American artillery.

Colonel Theodore Roosevelt, commanding officer, First Volunteer Cavalry Regiment, U.S. Army.

Major General William R. Shafter, because of his weight, had great difficulty in getting around within his command in Cuba, but being a decisive and courageous officer, he did his best. When Private Post sketched him riding alone on a buckboard as he inspected the lines at San Juan Hill the evening of the battle (above), the sagging of the frame seemed comical, yet Post insisted that his illustration was not exaggerated. At least one especially strong army horse (below), was capable of carrying the 300-pounds 5th Army Corps commander on the road between his headquarters and the forward positions three miles away.

Charles Johnson Post, Smithsonian Institution

Gatling guns, the first operational automatic arms employed by American forces in combat, proved decisive in the Battle of San Juan Hill, when they were positioned (above) to pour enfilading fire into the Spanish trenches, causing the initial rout of the defenders. The standard small arm of the U.S. Army, authorized in 1893, was the Norwegian Krag-Jorgensen rifle and the stubbier carbine version (below), the latter shown inside its cavalry saddle scabbard. The rifle has a fixed bayonet and between them is the standard 50-round waist belt of 30.40 calibre ammunition, worn by both infantry and cavalry soldiers. Although an excellent arm in its day, the "Krag" saw service with just the armies of Norway, Denmark, Venezuela and the U.S., unlike the Mauser, which was the standard arm of 16 countries, or the Mannlicher, used by ten of the leading armies. Issued in large numbers to U.S. units beginning in 1896, the Krag was used just nine years, when it was

supplanted by the Springfield 03 in 1905. As the main weapon of the Spanish-American War and the Philippine Insurrection, the Krag proved to be the tool that U.S. troops used to win the most one-sided conflict in their history. A century later, the five-round magazine weapon is still regarded as the smoothest-operating of all bolt-action military rifles. Although the regular army had been fully equipped with a total of 53,571 Krag rifles and 11,715 Krag carbines during the War with Spain, the older .45-calibre "Trapdoor" rifle was issued to volunteer units (except the Rough Riders, whose prominent and well-connected commanders used their influence to obtain Krag carbines). The volunteers were armed with 84,391 .45-calibre rifles and 3,276 .45-calibre carbines. Between them, regulars and volunteers also carried 9,515 .38-calibre revolvers and 13,363 .45s as well as 8,045 sabres.

Below, Ron Ziel; guns, collection of Richard G. Hendrickson

The Spaniards had ample opportunity to erect elaborate defensive works on the approaches to the San Juan Heights, including multi-layered barbed-wire obstacles (above), which impeded the advance of the Americans, increasing casualties as they paused to cut through the wire. Major General Adna R. Chaffee (lower left), saw service which was typical of the general officers of the Spanish-American War having served with distinction in the Union Army during the Civil War and in the Indian campaigns afterwards. Playing a leading role under General Lawton in the battle of El Caney, he was later appointed chief of staff of the military government of Cuba, serving until 1900. Then he was given the command of the American forces which sup-

pressed the Boxer Rebellion in China. Promoted to major general in the regular army for his meritorious service in China, Chaffee was sent to the Philippines as military governor and commander of American forces there, a post he held from February 1901 until October 1902. He then served as commander of the Department of the East until 1903, and promoted to lieutenant general, he was Army chief of staff for two years, until January 1906. Retiring the following month, Chaffee moved to Los Angeles where he died November 1, 1914, at the age of 72. Major Henry Carroll of the 1st Regular Cavalry (lower right) was among the many officers wounded at San Juan Hill.

Three photos, National Archives

Once the American positions on the San Juan Heights, overlooking Santiago de Cuba were secured, the generals began planning a final assault on the Spanish stronghold below. The Gatling guns (above), which had been so effective in taking the ridge line, were ready to advance on the city. In a warehouse converted to barracks, troops who had captured the crest lined up (center) for inspection. Typical of the forward American trenchline on San Juan was the sector (below) held by the 9th Infantry Regiment. Fortunately for both sides, Spanish General Toral, seeing the futility of further resistance, chose surrender over bloody extermination.

Above, National Archives   Center, collection of George H. Foster

Painting by R.F. Zogbaum

The *USS Indiana* under way, fires a starboard broadside from her main battery of 13-inch, 8-inch and 6-inch cannons.

Battle of Santiago Bay

For more than a month, Admiral Sampson's fleet had been positioned in an eight mile-long semicircle, from two to six miles offshore, blockading the entrance to the bay at Santiago de Cuba, where Admiral Cervera's ships lay anchored, protected by the fortress batteries of Socapa Point and Old Morro at the narrow entrance. Although the American ships had repeatedly shelled the fortifications, especially in preparation for the Battle of San Juan Hill, a formidable number of the modern long-range guns were still in action, making any attempt by the U.S. Navy to sail into the bay an unacceptable risk. The scuttling of the collier *Merrimac* had partially blocked the narrow channel, but the big warships of either side could still cautiously pass. The Spaniards continually watched for the Americans to come storming through the tight passage, while each night the American battleships would creep up to a point just beyond the range of the fortress guns to shine powerful searchlights onto the channel, expecting Cervera to make a dash for the open sea. It was a long, nerve-wracking standoff for both sides, most Spanish and American commanders believing that only if the U.S. Army assaulted the city would Cervera be forced to break out and challenge Sampson's squadron.

Two days after the great battle of San Juan Hill, with both sides peacefully recuperating and resting, many still asleep on the magnificent clear calm morning of Sunday, July 3, 1898, the Americans were totally unaware that Cervera's plans of using his powerful naval guns to beat back an invasion of Santiago had now become impracticable; the U.S. advance had been so fast and close to the Spanish forces that the notorious impreciseness of their gunners was bound to be as fatal to their own forces as to their enemies. Then, the Madrid government and Captain General Blanco were deeply concerned that the real American plan, now that Santiago was virtually lost, would be to assault Havana, so Admiral Cervera received orders to break the blockade and head for the capital. It seemed obvious to Admiral Sampson and Commodore Winfield Scott Schley that should Cervera attempt to break out, that it would be at night, but Cervera, very cognizant that the *Merrimac* made a full-steam exit hazardous, knew he would have to leave in daylight, thereby proving that Hobson's heroic mission had succeeded to a considerable degree. The bold Spanish admiral chose Sunday morning for his dash, hoping to surprise his adversaries when they would be "at church."

The five big American battleships, *Indiana, Iowa, Massachusetts, Oregon* and *Texas,* were slower than the Spanish cruisers, so Cervera believed that if he concentrated on outrunning the range of their guns quickly, he need fear just Schley's flagship, the *Brooklyn,* and Sampson's flagship *New York,* both fast cruisers capable of chasing down the Spaniards on the open sea. Spanish lookouts at the forts had reported that the battleship *Massachusetts* had sailed eastward out of sight (on a normal run to take coal at Guantánamo), then the encouraging news that the *New York* was also steaming away to the east; she was heading for Siboney, taking Sampson to a strategy meeting with General Shafter. Both of these favorable factors convinced Cervera to make his run that Sunday morning.

With Schley in command of the blockading squadron in Sampson's absence, the latter's standing orders were sufficient; a Spanish attempt to get through had been anticipated — and planned for — from the start. All of the American lookouts had noticed smoke rising above the hills, blocking the view of the harbor, alerting them, but such smoke was not unusual. This was different, as each sailor, including those on the *New York* seven miles away, seemed to sense that something unusual and exciting was about to occur. Then, above the lowest drop of the cliffs, the masts of a warship and thick smoke appeared moving at high speed. Signals that the enemy fleet was sailing forth went up on every American ship, with Commodore Schley ordering "Close and engage the enemy!" Because of the standing orders, the captains of the American ships hardly noticed the signal flags, instinctively sounding the orders to man battle stations and get underway at top speed to go into combat. But only half of their boilers were steamed up, so speed would be limited as the stokers furiously went to work below decks. At 9:35 a.m., the bow of *Infanta Maria Teresa*, the Spanish flagship, came into view, turning westward to engage the *Brooklyn*, her most dangerous adversary. Unfortunately for Cervera, his ship was within range of all four battleships, and they commenced firing with every gun that could be brought to bear. The first hit severed her vital water-supply pipe, knocking out the firefighting system, and the second exploded in the admiral's quarters, turning the stern into an inferno. One of the *Indiana*'s heavy guns lobbed a shell that killed 60 men in a gun room. Still bearing for the *Brooklyn,* Cervera's guns were not doing any more damage than Montejo's had done at Manila two months earlier.

The *Vizcaya,* the cruiser which had paid a visit to New York Harbor just after the *Maine* blew up, steamed out 800 yards behind the flagship, followed by *Cristobal Colón,* the fastest Spanish ship. Because of the utter predictability of where and when each vessel would appear, the U.S. battleships did not initially require a full head of steam; for them, it was a great opportunistic shooting gallery! Following the *Colón* closely came *Almirante Oquendo,* with the torpedo destroyers, *Plutón* and *Furor* bringing up the rear of the Spanish flotilla. All hell was rolling westward along the southern coast of Cuba! In cold, bloody, methodical precision, the U.S. Navy ships dispatched every Spanish vessel in showers of high explosive shells and shrapnel. To get steam up more rapidly, the American stokers were firing the boilers with oil-soaked coal, sending flames right out of their funnels, along with thick columns of black smoke. Adding to the boiler fireworks were clouds of gun smoke so heavy that, at times, even the massive battleships were totally enveloped, giving observers on land and distant ships the impression that the American vessels were also on fire; a supposition that ever so briefly boosted the morale of some forlornly hopeful Spanish sailors.

With uncontrolled fires and the murderous fusillade from the American battleships annihilating her gun crews, *Maria Teresa* was doomed, as all four battleships raked her from bow to stern. Her captain, Victor Concas, had just inquired of his second officer: "Shall we beach the ship for humanity's sake or fight longer, disabled as we are?," when, a split second later, he was hit by a shell and killed. It had taken just 20 minutes to destroy the flagship; her surviving crew, including Admiral Cervera, jumped into the surf and swam ashore. Cervera was old, but was saved largely through the efforts of his son, a lieutenant on the ship.

The *Vizcaya* at first sought to ram the *Brooklyn*, whose two hot boilers could initially only allow her a speed of eight knots, but when her captain saw the plight of the flagship, he steamed to her assistance in vain. She was pulverized by American gunners, but was able to continue onward, when the *Cristobal Colón* appeared and every operable gun on every ship on both sides opened up with the most furious display of firepower ever seen in warfare up to that time. The fast *Cristobal Colón*, named to honor the great navigator whose 15th Century discoveries were the birth of the Spanish Empire, that morning ironically through her demise would bring down the final glory of Spanish greatness. At strategic moments, almost hidden by the expanding clouds of stack, gun and fire smoke which hung low on the surface of the sea, she was the only ship after the *Vizcaya* to run the American gauntlet and do so relatively unscathed. Positioned at the east side of the narrow exit from Santiago Bay, the light gunboat *Gloucester*, a vessel of high pedigree, lay off Aquadores, blasting brazenly at each Spanish ship as it cleared the inlet. In their panicky haste to get past the big guns of the American battleships, the Spaniards had scant desire or opportunity to respond to the little pirate. And a pirate she was; just a few months previously, she had been perhaps the most lavish and famed of American yachts, financier J. P. Morgan's elegant *Corsair II*. With the outbreak of hostilities, the U.S. Navy began purchasing all classes of vessels at home and abroad, including modern, fast yachts which could be quickly converted into auxiliary craft, especially gunboats. The performance of the *Gloucester* at the Battle of Santiago Bay was to prove the wisdom of the policy of converting luxurious pleasure vessels into deadly gunboats.

To make the situation worse for Cervera's fleet, her skipper was none other than Lieutenant Commander Richard Wainwright, who had been the executive officer of the *Maine* when she blew up in Havana Harbor. Like virtually all other Americans, Wainwright probably blamed the Spaniards for the incident and was emboldened by a desire for revenge.

The perky, trim and fast *Gloucester* was well suited to do battle with the last pair of enemy craft to emerge from Santiago Bay, the small high-speed torpedo destroyers, *Furor* and *Plutón*, vessels more her equals. In a foray of valorous daring which brought cheers of admiration from the crews of the mighty American battleships, the small, unarmored *Gloucester*, her light batteries blazing away as she steamed in at a greater speed than any other vessel in the battle, cut right in front of the enemy destroyers, simultaneously firing her starboard guns at them while unleashing all of her port side rapid-fire guns at the pair of Goliaths *Almirante Oquendo* and *Vizcaya*. Then the *Texas* landed a shell right in *Plutón*'s boiler, while the *Gloucester* shot away her steering mechanism, which sent her drifting toward the shore. As a parting show of contempt of danger, Wainwright then cut between the pair of torpedo destroyers, hitting both with sustained broadsides. Suddenly, Admiral Sampson joined the fray, bringing in the *New York* at full steam as he chased after the escaping *Colón*, firing two shots at the *Furor* as he sped by. The *Gloucester* drove on into the fire of the shore guns and the remaining cannon of both destroyers, raking the dying ships with her accurate rapid-fire batteries; minutes later, both *Furor* and *Plutón*, burning and sinking, pulled down their flags and settled into the shallow surf.

Meanwhile, the *Almirante Oquendo* had been jumped by the quartet of battleships and the *Brooklyn*, one shell blowing up a torpedo compartment, causing an inferno which rapidly spread, as concentrated fire from a hundred guns pulverized her decks, killing the gunners and dismounting their weapons. In courageous desperation, her surviving crewmen fought a delaying action, drawing the fire of the Americans to gain time for *Cristobal Colón* and *Vizcaya* to achieve a lead in their run from certain death. The *Brooklyn* and *Texas* moved out in hot pursuit of the cruisers, every gun that could be pointed aft pouring unrelenting fire at the *Oquendo* until they were out of range. Scarcely a mile beyond the point where the flagship had careened ashore, *Almiralte Oquendo* used all of her diminishing steam supply to make for the beach. After striking her colors, Captain Juan Lazaga, in the conning tower, reportedly shot himself as his mortally wounded ship's hull began scraping the rocks. On board the *Texas*, the crew began cheering loudly, but Captain Phillip quickly admonished: "Don't cheer, boys! The poor devils are dying!" Respectfully, his sailors immediately fell silent. As soon as the wreckage began to cool, the American boarding party went to the conning tower and

ADMIRAL DEWEY: "Here, Sampson, Take Him Over to Your Ocean; I'm Finished with Him in Mine."

found ashes, charred bones, a sword with jewels on its hilt and a revolver; its cartridges had discharged from the heat, except the one aligned with the barrel, which had been fired by the hammer. There could be no doubt that the remains were those of Captain Lazaga and that he had indeed committed suicide rather than live out his life in self-imposed disgrace.

Now the chase was on! The *Vizcaya* and the *Cristobal Colón* strained to get every last pound per square inch of steam power from their boilers in their race to round the western end of Cuba and reach a mythical haven in Havana Harbor. *Brooklyn*, *Oregon* and *Texas* were right behind, with *Indiana* and *Iowa* further astern, but with all boilers firing, they began slowly gaining on their quarry. Among the horrendous stories of the last moments of the doomed Spanish men-of-war was a comparison published by Watterson. So terrible that it repels all belief, it is quoted here without further comment:

"Except the *Brooklyn*, it was heavy battleships against swift cruisers. Down in the furnace rooms on the battleships, stripped to the skin, dripping oily sweat from their shining bodies, the stokers — those obscure heroes, without the inspiration of scene or objective to encourage them — were true Americans. On the *Brooklyn*, when the chase began after the *Cristobal Colón*, Commodore Schley realized the position of the engine room and furnace men. He called his sailors, formed a line down the stairs and sent cool beer, kept for the officers, down the line to cheer the faithful workers. In addition, an ensign stood at the hatchway and described the chase, the shots and the results to the first man on the line. The message was thus carried down to the depths of the hold by human telegraph. Every point of our success was cheered by the gallant stokers, who worked on with renewed energy to send the great ship with greater speed than even her builders had expected.

"That was the American way.

"On board one of the Spanish vessels, it was told with horror that firemen and engineers who were unable to endure the heat, smoke and escaping steam, and who attempted to come up, were pushed back by the officers and the hatches fastened. Then, finally, in an insane fury, coal oil was poured over the hatches and ignited when the ship was about to drift ashore — and no man came out alive out of that hell under the water line.

"That was the Spanish way."

The speedy, relatively undamaged *Colón* soon began to outdistance the *Vizcaya*, and from long range, the Americans began to hit the hapless latter vessel; shortly she was burning and heading for the beach. As lifeboats were lowered and sailors jumped overboard to save themselves, Cuban insurgents on shore began firing at the survivors. Such callousness would not be tolerated by Captain Evans of the *Iowa*, who ordered the crew of one of the lighter guns to fire warning shots which had the desired effect, causing the confused allies to back off. With the *Vizcaya* beached at Aserraderos, 15 miles west of Santiago, the *Iowa* broke off the final chase after the *Cristobal Colón* and rescued the 38 officers and 240 sailors who were huddled in blood, fatigue and anxiety on the shore.

The *Colón*, steaming under forced draft close to the south coast of Cuba, was belching flames and heavy smoke from her funnels as she lengthened her lead from her pursuers, *Brooklyn*, *Texas*,

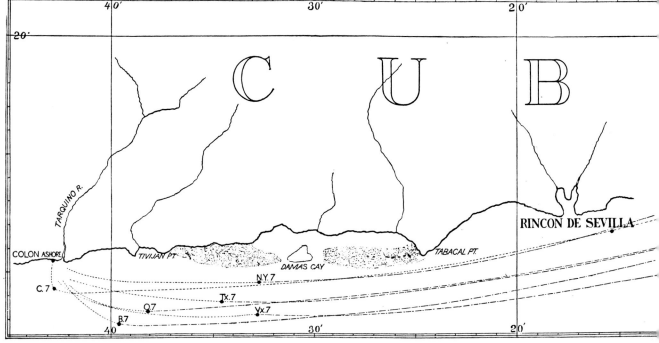

C U B

TARQUINO R.

RINCON DE SEVILLA

COLON ASHORE   TIVIJAN PT.   TABACAL PT.

DAMAS CAY

C.7
                NY.7
            Tx.7
Q.7   Vx.7
B.7

40'   30'   20'

ABBREVIATIONS:—N. Y., *New York*; B., *Brooklyn*; Tx., *Texas*; A., *Iowa*; I., *Indiana*; O., *Oregon*; G., *Gloucester*; Vx., *Vixen*; the ships at seven stages in the progress of the battle—9.35 A.M., 9.50 A.M., 10.15 A.M., 10.20 A.M., 10.30 A.M.,

Oregon and the gunboat *Vixen*, with the *New York* far astern, but rapidly closing. Unable to maintain the pace, the desperate Spaniard began to lose velocity as the four leading U.S. Navy warships, comprising an elliptical formation, prepared to close the pincers. Unexpectedly exceeding their known capabilities, both *Oregon* and *Texas* were up to a speed of 17 knots, actually keeping up with the *Brooklyn*. Awed by what they knew was impossible for their ships to do, the officers held their fire, intent instead to run their quarry down, like hounds after a fox. Finally, after 40 miles, Cape Cruz lay dead ahead, jutting out into the paths of the approaching vessels and heralding the immediate demise of the fast Spanish ship, which would have to circle the point, while the *Brooklyn* and *Oregon*, further offshore, would travel a straighter line, coming abreast of their target.

Knowing that the Spanish cruiser had been purchased from Italy, Captain Clark, on the bridge of the *Oregon*, signaled a message to Commodore Schley: "A strange ship, looking like an Italian, in the distance." Schley instructed his signalman, with a smile: "Tell the *Oregon* she can try one of those 13-inch railroad trains on her." The distance had closed to four miles as the first 13-inch shell exploded just astern of the *Cristobal Colón*. Knowing when to quit, the Spaniard took a direct hit on her bow, then fired one last shot and, missing the *Texas*, struck down her flag and steamed into the beach at Río Tarquino. Here the Battle of Santiago Bay ended at 1:15 p.m., 48 miles and less than four hours after it began. This location was especially poignant for the Americans; for it was right where *Cristobal Colón* surrendered that the men of the *Virginius* came ashore and many of its American crew and passengers were taken to be massacred a quarter century earlier.

As the first boarding party rowed up to the beached ship, her crewmen shouted "*Bravos Americanos!*" and the U.S. Navy sailors grinned and answered with a loud "*Bravos Españoles!*" Back where the other defeated vessels were ashore, the victorious commanders were dispatching boats, surgeons and food and medical supplies to aid the vanquished and bring them on board the battleships as prisoners of war. The *Vizcaya* was still burning fiercely, with many of her crew trapped on board. Rescue boats were launched quickly from the *Iowa* and, although sections of *Vizcaya's* hull were glowing red from the internal conflagration and her magazines could explode at any moment, scores of American sailors scrambled aboard to rescue the confused and the wounded survivors. Captain Antonio Eulate had brought his beloved *Vizcaya* into New York the previous February, and when the proud officer, tattered, exhausted and wounded, was piped aboard the *Iowa*, Captain Evans ordered up an honor guard. Carried into Evans' cabin, Eulate kissed his sword and offered it to the man who had defeated him. The American handed it back, saying: "Keep your sword, sir. You have fought like a brave and gallant officer." Such a magnanimous gesture was bound to have a profound effect on a proud man and Captain Eulate deeply appreciated it. Other emotions could not be suppressed; as he was carried to his stateroom, he was crying and repeating: "My poor *Vizcaya*—lost, lost!"

The furious naval battle of July 3, 1898, had cost the Americans one man killed and two wounded. Perhaps 500 Spaniards had died, hundreds wounded and 1,600 were taken prisoner. Unlike Manila Bay two months earlier, the two fleets were not equal in strength, the Americans at Santi-

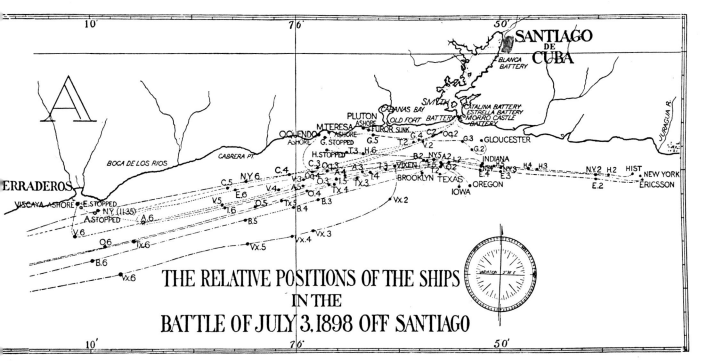

THE RELATIVE POSITIONS OF THE SHIPS
IN THE
BATTLE OF JULY 3, 1898 OFF SANTIAGO

H., Hist; E., Ericsson; T., Teresa; V., Vizcaya; C., Colon; Oq., Oquendo; P., Pluton; F., Furor. The chart shows the positions of 11.5 A.M., and 1.15 P.M. Chapman's drawings represent the battle from different points of view and at different times

ago Bay having greater advantage in almost every category: number and size of vessels, firepower, strategy and tactics. The superior gunnery of the U.S. fleet again was a deciding factor, as was the morale of all the men and the courageous initiative of officers such as Lieutenant Commander Wainwright of the *Gloucester*. Astute preparations and anticipation, as well as training and maintenance, also were salient aspects of the American triumph. Together, the two great sea battles of 1898 had destroyed two-thirds of the deep water naval forces of one of Europe's major powers — at a cost to the United States of one man killed and ten wounded. That American accomplishment stands unmatched in more than 3,000 years of warfare between ships at sea.

Admiral Sampson sent a message to Washington. It was given to President McKinley at noon on Independence Day. The first sentence of his dispatch electrified the whole country: "The fleet under my command offers the nation, as a Fourth of July present, the destruction of the whole of Cervera's fleet — not one escaped."

The reply from the commander-in-chief: "You have the gratitude and congratulations of the whole American people. Convey to your noble officers and crews, through whose valor new honors have been added to the American Navy, the grateful thanks and appreciation of the nation. William McKinley." The entire American people were truly grateful, for although U.S. arms had won the battles of San Juan and El Caney just two days before, the appalling casualties of more than ten percent had cast a despondent gloom across the country. July 4, 1898, suddenly became a day of raucous celebration all over the United States, with the names of Sampson and Schley on everyone's lips, as that of Dewey had been two months earlier. The

naval victories had come quicker and more dramatically than those of the Army, making the admirals and commodores instant heroes, while the generals eased into their valorous roles in slower fashion.

Admiral Cervera had been all too aware of the fate that lay lurking beyond the fortresses guarding the entrance to Santiago Bay, later stating: "There could be no doubt as to the outcome, but I should never have believed that our ships would be destroyed so rapidly." He ruefully observed that "the third day of July has been one of terrible disaster, as I had foreseen. Nevertheless, the number of dead is less than I had feared. The country has been defended with honor, and we have the consciousness of duty well done, but with the bitterness of knowing the losses suffered and our country's misfortunes." After being taken off the beach by a boat from the *Gloucester*, Cervera and his surviving senior officers were treated exceedingly well on board the former yacht, according to the admiral, and even more so when they were transferred to the *Iowa* and then to the cruiser *St. Louis*. His report to Madrid expounded on the concern of the Americans for him and his men and the chivalry and decency that the enemy exhibited: ". . . they suppressed their shouts of joy in order not to increase the suffering of the defeated, and all vied in making captivity as easy as possible."

Almost immediately after the battle, an unseemly and open dispute erupted concerning the question as to who should receive the primary credit for the stupendous victory, the absent Admiral Sampson or Commodore Schley, who was the commanding officer in the heat of action. Sampson's initial communiqué mentioned no officers or ships by name, crediting the success simply to "the fleet under my command," which unfortunately, dismayed many armchair admirals in government and the press, as well as the citizenry. At Manila Bay, there had been no question that Commodore Dewey had been the man who solely had made all of the decisions, but at Santiago, it was a clear case of divided command and the controversy was to drag on heatedly for four years, even delaying the promotions of both of the gallant and superb officers until March 1899. Most knowledgeable officials in and out of the Navy gave the ultimate responsibility to Sampson's detailed preparations, standing orders and strong discipline. The press and the public, regarding Sampson as aloof and enigmatic, believed that the more accessible Schley was the obvious victor, disregarding the facts that he had, early in the battle, turned his flagship *Brooklyn* away from the rest of the squadron, confusing his other captains and nearly colliding with the *Texas;* that Sampson's absence was due to his having to attend an important conference with General Shafter; and that once the Spanish ships had challenged the blockade, he immediately rushed to the fray with his flagship *New York* under a full head of steam.

Three years later, in July 1901, Schley was granted a court of inquiry to settle the dispute. Presided over by none other than Admiral Dewey, the court ruled that Schley was wrong, but the furor was intensified when Dewey issued his minority report which favored Schley. The official side of the controversy was finally settled in January, 1902, when former Assistant Navy Secretary Theodore Roosevelt, respected for his knowledge of the subject and, by then, President of the United States, gave his approval to the findings of the majority. It was indeed sad that two such respected, brave and heroic admirals had become engaged in such an egocentric melee.

The naval attaché of the Japanese embassy in Washington, D.C., Lieutenant Akijama, had been an observer of the Battle of Santiago Bay on board one of the American warships. His astute conclusions concerning command during the fighting were published in the *New York Sun,* on July 22, 1898. Asked if he had any opinions, he replied: "Many. First, the arrangement of the American fleet by Admiral Sampson. It was complete. It was without fault." When asked if he thought Sampson should have credit for the victory, Akijama was adamant: "Sincerely I do. The officers of other governments all agree with me that the greatest credit is for the admiral. He made the plans. He gave the orders. He said where each ship should

wait for the Spanish . . . The result was the most complete victory that ever was known. He was not there. He was unfortunate. But the fight showed by its complete victory that his plans were right . . . Commodore Schley fights well. He led the fleet with great dash…"

Aside from several warships in Puerto Rican waters and a few still remaining in Havana and Manzanillo, Cuba, Spain possessed just one formidable fleet after her disaster on July 3; the reserve or home fleet at Cádiz. Spanish authorities engaged in many feints and contortions with the squadron under the command of Admiral Cámara, to confuse the Americans concerning its destination. These were clever tactics; if it headed across the Atlantic Ocean to bombard the east coast, the U.S. ships besieging Cuba would have to be hastily withdrawn and sent north. If Cámara settled for the Caribbean, would it be to relieve Cuba or to defend Puerto Rico — or both? The suspense was draining on the Americans, until the Spanish fleet rounded Gibraltar and headed into the Mediterranean Sea. It seemed that it was bound for the Philippines to dislodge Dewey's squadron, which had been reinforced by several more vessels. The Americans waited until the entire Spanish flotilla passed through the Suez Canal, paying $260,000 in tolls, before virtually announcing that a powerful U.S. Navy squadron was being assembled to bombard the coast of Spain! In a comic circus of events, the Spanish fleet was quickly ordered back to defend the homeland, paying another round of tolls; the total of more than a half-million dollars spent in complete uselessness, further bankrupting the national treasury. Under the neutrality laws, Cámara could not buy government-owned coal to augment his dwindling supplies, then discovered that American agents had secretly purchased every lump of privately owned coal at Port Said!

Finally, Cámara returned to Cádiz by mid-July. By then, Cervera's ships had been destroyed and the U.S. government continued preparations of the squadron commanded by Rear Admiral John Crittenden Watson to hit the Spanish coast. This sent a wave of hysteria across the Iberian peninsula, with many coastal cities being virtually abandoned, their populations terrorized at the thought of being targets of the same Navy that had destroyed most of their armada without mentionable losses. Cámara's magnificent warships were back in home waters, but the Spanish populace had lost all faith in the ability of their government to protect them.

A sword salvaged from the *Viscaya* and a Filipino insurgent dagger were U.S. adversaries' edged weapons.

Ron Ziel photo; weapons collection of Richard G. Hendrickson

The *USS Brooklyn* was a twin-screw armored cruiser of impressive size, speed and armament. When Commodore Winfield Scott Schley was appointed commander of the flying squadron, based at Hampton Roads, Virginia, with the mission of intercepting any Spanish naval attack on the east coast of the U.S., the able *Brooklyn* was his flagship. On July 3, 1898, with Admiral Sampson seven miles away conferring with General Shafter, Schley was in command of the ships blockading Santiago Harbor, as the Spanish fleet made its desperate and hopeless dash for the open sea. The *Brooklyn* played a leading role in the destruction of Admiral Cervera's fleet along the south coast of Cuba that day.

The battleships *Indiana* and *Massachusetts*, moored stern to stern during one of their port visits just after the war.

Above, artwork by H. Reuterdahl

The three Spanish ships which put up the most spirited resistance to the U.S. Navy squadron awaiting their departure from Santiago Bay are shown here; they were the finest of the Spaniards' armored cruisers. *Almirante Oquendo* was under way in rough seas (above), escorted by a small torpedo boat; showing clearly is the single 11-inch gun protruding from her forward turret, hardly a match for the twin 13-inch guns mounted on American battleship turrets. The latest known photograph of

Cristobal Colón and *Viscaya* (below) show the two vessels in April 1898, at the Cape Verde Islands, prior to their desperate run into Santiago Harbor. The *Colón*, at left, was commissioned in 1896 and the *Vizcaya* dated from 1891. They were the only vessels of Cervera's fleet to get past the guns of the U.S. Navy battleships at Santiago, but despite their speed, they were run down at sea and both were steamed ashore as the American warships raked them with accurate cannon fire.

Below, U.S. Naval Historical Center

The Spanish admiral assigned the doomed mission of challenging the U.S. Navy in the Caribbean Sea, was Rear Admiral don Pasqual de Cervera y Topete, Count de Jerez, Marquis de Santa Ava (above), who was well aware that his fleet would lose any encounter with the Americans. Even so, he was later astounded at the rapidity of the destruction of his ships before the onslaught of the Yankee guns. His flagship was the *Infanta Maria Teresa* (below), shown in happier days flying an American flag while visiting a U.S. port. She was an armored cruiser, displacing 7,000 tons; length, 340 feet; breadth, 65 feet; maximum draught, 21 feet, 6 inches; 13,758 horsepower; armor plating, 3-12 inches. Her batteries consisted of two 11-inch and ten 5.5-inch (all Hontoria guns); eight 2.2-inch rapid-fire; eight 1.4-inch and two muzzle-loading rifle guns. She carried six torpedo tubes, was rated at a speed of 20.25 knots, and was manned by 500 officers and men. She cost just $600,000 — a mere one-fifth the money expended on her American counterpart, *USS Brooklyn*.

Above, Biblioteca Nacional, Madrid

William Thomas Sampson was born in Palmyra, New York, on February 9, 1840, and graduated first in his class at the U.S. Naval Academy in 1861. During much of the Civil War he was an Academy instructor and stationed at Newport, Rhode Island, but in the last year of hostilities he served on the monitor *Patapsco*, which blew up when hit by a Confederate torpedo in the harbor of Charleston, South Carolina, in January 1865. He saw several tours of duty in both the Atlantic and Pacific, as well as various shore station commands over the following 30 years, giving him a well-rounded career in all facets of naval operations. In the mid-1890s, as chief of the Bureau of Ordnance, Captain Sampson's leadership was responsible for much improved gunnery training and the introduction of smokeless powder. Taking command of the just-commissioned battleship *USS Iowa* in June 1897, he was senior captain of the North Atlantic Squadron, but was transferred in February 1898, to serve in the important and prestigious position of president of the court of inquiry which investigated the explosion of the *USS Maine* in Havana Harbor, after which he took command of the North Atlantic Squadron, being promoted to rear admiral. Joined by Commodore Schley's "Flying Squadron,"

Sampson established an iron-clad blockade of Cuba, after Admiral Cervera steamed his flotilla into the protected bay of Santiago. The role Sampson played in escorting the 5th Army Corps convoy to its beachhead in Cuba and in maintaining the blockade, while issuing standing orders which proved flawless during the great naval battle of July 3, was one of the most important and decisive of the war. Unfortunately, both Sampson's and Schley's stellar reputations were sullied by their dispute over credit for the victory at Santiago Bay, but Sampson went on to become one of three American commissioners governing Cuba during the final months of 1898, later resuming command of his squadron. His final assignment was to be in charge of the Boston Navy Yard, until his retirement in February 1902. He died just three months later, in Washington, D.C. [Admiral Sampson (above) as he looked in 1899 and on the bridge of his flagship *USS New York* (upper right) with that vessel's skipper, Captain French E. Chadwick.] The *New York* (right) was spotlessly maintained as she rode at anchor in New York harbor in September 1899, during the celebration of the return of Admiral Dewey from the Philippines.

Two photos, U.S. Naval Historical Center   Artwork by T. de Thulstrup

A native of Maryland, where he was born on October 9, 1839, Winfield Scott Schley graduated from the Naval Academy in 1860, and after a Pacific cruise he was assigned to the *Potomac*, blockading the Confederate Gulf coast, in 1861. He saw distinguished service in Mobile Bay and other Civil War naval operations, then, like Dewey and Sampson, Schley experienced more that three decades of various ship and shore commands, spending much time in the Pacific and the South Atlantic stations. In 1895-97 he was captain of the *New York*, which became Sampson's flagship during the Spanish-American War. In February 1898, Schley was promoted to commodore and given command of the "Flying Squadron," with the grave responsibility of defending the entire Atlantic coast of the U.S. against the then unknown capabilities of the Spanish Navy. Or-

dered to blockade the southern coast of Cuba, he was criticized for tardiness, resulting in Cervera's successful run into Santiago Bay; the Spanish Admiral proclaiming his fleet "safe" from the U.S. Navy and Schley declaring that the Spaniards were "bottled up" in the bay! It was Schley who had direct command of the blockading squadron, when Sampson steamed off to a meeting with General Shafter, just as the Spanish squadron made its disastrous run for the open sea. Executing Sampson's standing orders and fighting the battle with coolness, professionalism, and courage, Commodore Schley defeated Admiral Cervera in a virtual repeat of the U.S. victory at Manila Bay nine weeks earlier. In September and October 1898, Schley served on the Puerto Rico Evacuation Commission which repatriated the defeated Spaniards and turned the administration of the

172

island over to the Americans. The following year he took command of the South Atlantic Squadron, a position he held until retiring from the Navy in October 1901. Still feuding with Sampson over credit for the Santiago Bay victory, Admiral Schley outlived his adversary and died in 1909 at the age of 70. A water-level bow view of the *USS Brooklyn*, Schley's flagship (left) shows the steep inward slope of her hull above the waterline. While this configuration may have stabilized the ship, it also made for less deck space; after July 3, 1898, however, there could be no doubts concerning her capabilities as the finest of warships! Schley is shown with the *Brooklyn's* captain, F.A. Cook (upper right), on the bridge of the flagship and in a formal portrait (lower right) taken from an 1898 postcard.

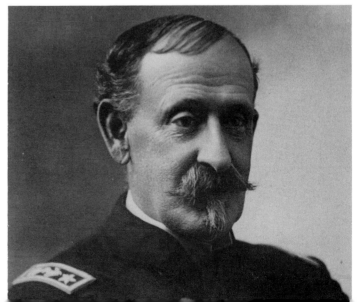

The *USS Gloucester,* the speedy and gutsy former yacht which wreaked such havoc upon Admiral Cervera's fleet during the Battle of Santiago Bay, is shown in her gray war paint in fore and aft views at the time of her legendary exploit in 1898. Although mounting light guns, she virtually darted through the Spanish squadron's positions, inflicting heavy damage at much closer range than the bigger battleships and cruisers. Her daring commander, Richard Wainwright, posed for his portrait a few years later, after he had attained the rank of captain. The Navy had to wage a bureaucratic battle just to acquire the vessel from J. P. Morgan, the financier who had become one of the richest men in America thanks to the opportunities offered by his country. Morgan was incapable of displaying a fraction of the courage and patriotism of the poor farm boys and city lads who were going off to lay down their lives as he resisted the government's offer of $225,000 for the *Corsair II,* which would be returned after the war was over. He did not even consider the money, but under mounting pressure he released his plaything against his will, and not wanting to wait for the return of the yacht, he promptly ordered a larger, even more elegant *Corsair III.* As the *USS Gloucester,* the vessel was to remain on active duty until she sank in the Gulf of Mexico in 1919 while charting those waters.

American gunners had no trouble repulsing the attack.

Above, artwork by H. Reuterdahl

Captain John W. Philip, commanding officer, Battleship *USS Texas*

With the *USS Texas* close behind, the *Oregon*, belching flames and black smoke from her funnels, cuts loose with what Commodore Schley called "one of those 13-inch railroad trains," as she zeroes in on the doomed *Vizcaya*.

Artwork by Carlton T. Chapman

Shortly after the Battle of Santiago Bay, still wearing her gray coat of warpaint, the *USS Iowa* (above) steams back into U.S. waters, with many of her officers and men standing on deck, forward of the 13-inch gun turret. During the battle, crewmen of the *Iowa* stand on deck beneath the big guns, watching as a burning enemy ship in the distance (below) takes a severe pounding as it made a vain attempt to outrun the American pursuers.

With the *Cristobal Colón* squeezing every possible pound-per-square-inch of steam out of her boilers as she flees under forced draft (above), the *USS Brooklyn* and behind her, the *USS Oregon*, have closed to zero in their guns on the doomed quarry. Within minutes, she struck her colors and headed for shore. At the moment of the surrender of the *Colón*, the crew of the *Oregon* (below) raised a rousing cheer.

An aft view of the *USS Oregon* accents the immense size of the 13-inch gun turret and to a lesser extent, the 8-inchers, as she heads into an unidentified port, returning from Cuban waters.

Admiral Sampson's flagship *USS New York* has slowed to a virtual halt (above), with her signal flags displaying the order "Cease Firing," as the *Cristobal Colón* signaled that she was surrendering. The *New York's* little steam launch, mounting a small-calibre rapid-fire gun on her bow, is already under way, bound for the beached *Colón*, to begin the evacuation of the crew. Admiral Sampson, through no fault of his own, had missed the battle, but had the satisfaction of being able to accept the final surrender of his enemies' fastest ship.

The crew of one of the rapid-fire guns of the *USS Hist* is shown in action on July 3, 1898, in a photograph taken by Navy Lieutenant F.H. Hunicke. Such gunners had no protection from shells or shrapnel, not even a steel-plate shield in front of the mount, as was often used on crew-served weapons.

Racked by shells from the American battleships, burned out and run onto the Cuban coast, the *Viscaya* was a total loss, resting in the shallow water.

Two photos, U.S. Naval Historical Center

The hero of the *USS Merrimac* scuttling, Lieutenant Richmond P. Hobson, and Captain C.F. Goodrich of the *USS Newark*, were sitting on the deck of the wreck of Cervera's flagship *Infanta Maria Teresa*. The Spanish warship was being salvaged, with the tugboat *I.J. Merritt* tied alongside; the date was September 14, 1898.

Once the Spaniards surrendered Santiago de Cuba in mid-July, the U.S. Army finally took over the forts guarding the narrow entrance to the bay. Part of the defenses at Punta Gorda included two big modern 16 cm guns (above) here being inspected by American troops. At the strategic Socapa hillside, right at the entrance, with the Morro fortress on the opposite shore, U.S. artillerymen (below) manned a battery of Hotchkiss rapid-fire guns.

Spanish Vice-Admiral Cámara, commanding officer of the Reserve Fleet which made the useless and expensive round-trip through the Suez Canal.

Although Commodore John Crittenden Watson did not fight any naval battles during the Spanish-American War, his planned mission — already in its final development stage — had much to do with having Spain sue for peace. He was to command the squadron consisting of the battleships *Iowa* and *Oregon*, plus the *Yankee*, *Yosemite* and *Dixie*, which would cross the At-

lantic to bombard the coast of Spain itself, probably to destroy the Spanish home fleet in the process. Promoted to rear admiral, Watson was ordered — on May 8, 1899, a year and a week after the Battle of Manila Bay — to succeed Admiral Dewey in command of the Asiatic Squadron, enabling Dewey to come home at last, for his hero's welcome!

The Spanish home fleet, led by the *Pelayo*, the sole first-class battleship in the Spanish Navy, crossing the Mediterranean Sea, on its ill-conceived journey to Port Said and the Suez Canal.

Painting by L.A. Shafer

183

With other officers behind them, the three most legendary cavalry leaders of the American Army during the Cuban campaign met to plan tactics at field headquarters. Standing, left to right, are Major General Joseph Wheeler, Brigadier General Leonard Wood, and Colonel Theodore Roosevelt; a trio that will always be respected and admired in the annals of American military history.

Cuba Libre

With financial ruin imminent, two-thirds of its warships gone and future military engagements promising further disaster, the government of Spain began to realize the utter futility of trying to salvage its empire. The demoralized Spaniards could only see the daily increase of the industrial and military might of the United States and its war-making power on land and sea; they were, however, unaware of the rapid deterioration of the U.S. 5th Army Corps which was preparing to lay siege to Santiago de Cuba. It was the horrendous conditions and lack of provisions within the city that most affected the judgments of General José Toral, the commander of the besieged defenders; he was ignorant of alarm spreading among the American field-grade officers on the San Juan Heights. The deadly combination of battle fatigue, climate and disease, abetted by the ineptitude and unpreparedness of the War Department which allowed the front line soldiers to suffer from lack of food, tents, medicine and other vital supplies while transport ships crammed with all of the indispensable necessities lay offshore requiring only the orders to be unloaded, were already devastating the ranks by Independence Day of 1898.

Malaria was the main culprit, but a few cases of yellow fever, deadlier and contagious, were also attacking the soldiers, and, by the second week of July, some units reported 20 percent of their men on sick call. Fearing a Spanish counterattack, General Shafter summoned his division and brigade commanders to a strategy session at El Pozo, midway between his headquarters and San Juan. Shafter was in a difficult position: General Kent recommended a withdrawal from the forward line, while the other senior officers wanted to stay put. From Washington, D.C., he was under direct pressure from Secretary of War Alger and President McKinley to achieve a final victory in the Cuban campaign. Suffering from gout, the obese commanding officer had great difficulty contending with the oppressive heat. Torrential downpours added to the problems of supplying the troops from the dock at Siboney along the vulnerable road. The historic morning of July 3 saw Shafter trying to settle his dispute with Admiral Sampson, insisting that the fleet must forge into the bay and destroy the enemy ships before he could consider storming Santiago. It was a classic chicken-and-egg situation, with Sampson reiterating that until the Army captured the fortress guns at the entrance and the mines were cleared, the risk to the American ships was insurmountable.

Then the Spanish squadron emerged and Sampson broke off the meeting, got back to the *New York* in great haste and headed west to the blockade station. The sea battle of July 3 changed the situation, but did not solve Shafter's dilemma. His message to Alger of the previous day was still valid: "We have town well invested on the north and east, but with a very thin line. (Enemy defenses) so strong it will be impossible to carry it by storm with my present force and I am seriously considering withdrawing about five miles and taking up a new position." Alger, after discussing the grave situation with the President, gave Shafter a free hand but requested that if at all possible, he should hold the line on San Juan. Military commanders interpret such a request to be an order, so the troops remained. While Theodore Roosevelt had played leading roles in preparing the Navy and in the capture of San Juan, his pugnacious personality and disregard for adverse reactions to anything outlandish or controversial that he might say or do if he believed himself in the right, now surfaced to make him the truly pivotal man of the Spanish-American War. Although just an assistant secretary in government and a colonel in the field, his service was to have a greater influence on events than most cabinet secretaries and generals. It began with a letter to his powerful friend, Senator Henry Cabot Lodge, of Massachusetts:

"Tell the President for heaven's sake to send us every regiment and above all, every battery possible. We have won so far at heavy cost; but the Spaniards fight very hard and charging these entrenchments against modern rifles is terrible. We are within measurable distance of a terrible military disaster; we *must* have help — thousands of men, batteries and food and ammunition. The other volunteers are at a hideous disadvantage owing to their not having smokeless powder. Our general is poor; he is too unwieldy to get to the front."

The colonel was well aware that this letter and his writings and actions immediately following could get him court-martialed for insubordination, but he knew that what he was doing was right, for the lives of thousands of men and their mission were in grave jeopardy, and being a volunteer officer soon to be mustered out of the service, he could speak out, whereas the regular Army generals would end their careers by doing so. Then Colonel Edward McClernand, an officer on Shafter's staff, suggested that he demand that Toral surrender Santiago. Shafter quickly accepted the idea; an audacious bluff might just turn the trick! The American commander sent a message demanding that unless the Spaniards surrendered, he would order that Santiago be subject to an all-out bombardment and that all foreign nationals and women and children be evacuated immediately.

General Toral was a commander who was more interested in the preservation of lives and property than in futile resistance, but he was also a man of honor — both to himself and his beleaguered country — so he agreed to a meeting beneath a flag of truce, which took place on July 10.

Toral's suggestion was a brilliant means of his forces giving up Santiago without a fight, yet saving face for his command and for Spain: the U.S. artillery batteries and big naval guns should launch an impressive display of firepower over the city, the shells actually landing where they would do little harm. Under such circumstances — the city and his command threatened with annihilation under the heavy barrage and the infantry and cavalry attack sure to follow — he would have no prudent choice but to withdraw. Shafter's affirmative decision was equally visionary, humane and personally heroic, for he could perceive the horrendous casualties to be suffered on both sides, should he refuse and give Toral no alternative but to stand firm in Santiago, fighting house-to-house to a bloody conclusion.

Colonel Roosevelt's reaction to this scheme was not his finest moment, as he indignantly wrote to Lodge on the same day: ". . . General Shafter is tacking and veering as to whether or not he will close with the Spaniard's request to allow them to walk out unmolested. It will be a great misfortune to accept less than unconditional surrender. We can surely get the whole Spanish Army now, at a cost of probably not more than a couple days' fighting, chiefly bombardment." The colonel's casually dismissed "couple days' fighting" could result in casualties far greater than those of July 1, but incredibly, he either did not realize that or he was so disgusted with any plans to allow the enemy to "escape" that he simply ignored the rapidly worsening situation, which his journalistic admirer, Richard Harding Davis, had already observed was becoming so tenuous that "one smelt disaster in the air."

The reaction of President McKinley was similar to that of his former Assistant Navy Secretary and he denied approval to Shafter. The big guns of Sampson's battleships then opened fire on Santiago, giving Toral a prelude of what to expect if he refused to give up. Meanwhile, Roosevelt continued to view the situation in ambivalent terms; as an uneasy truce followed the American bombardment, the hiatus seemed to him ". . . a further cessation of hostilities by tacit agreement." Although seeming to be desirous of nothing less than an all-out attack, he feared it would result in casualties of at least one in four and ardently told his officers that he was hoping than an assault would not be necessary. Fortunately for the Americans, the Spaniards and the Cubans, his latter desire prevailed, when the commanding general of the U.S. Army, Nelson A. Miles, arrived to join Shafter in the next meeting with Toral on July 14.

With the imposing figure of Miles added to the sheer bulk of Shafter at the negotiating table, the hapless Spanish general must have indeed felt that he was defeated, as he was presented with stern surrender demands directly from the American President and the Secretary of War. Three days later, on Sunday, July 17, a ceremony in which the documents ending the land fighting in Cuba were signed, was held in the central plaza of Santiago de Cuba. Toral surrendered and his force of 22,000 men was disarmed to be returned to Spain, finally ending nearly 400 years of tyranny and religiously sanctioned genocide. Shafter's grand bluff had worked, for had his sick and malnourished regiments been ordered to assault the city, they might well have been repulsed with great losses in the field and vast political repercussions for the McKinley administration back home. With Puerto Rico remaining as the final objective, American arms were — on land and sea — victorious in every engagement large and small, a record unequalled since the Old Testament accomplishments of the ancient Israelites, only their commander held higher rank and was by far more experienced than were the 19th century Americans!

With the ground fighting in Cuba terminated, Theodore Roosevelt was to seize an initiative which may well have been the finest act of his fateful and illustrious career, when just one month after his great military victory at San Juan Hill, he took upon himself the responsibility of saving the 5th Army Corps from almost certain liquidation by disease and malnutrition. Even as late as the turn of the 20th century, soldiers in the field often feared microbes far more than they feared Mausers or mortars; it was not unusual for ten times as many soldiers to be felled by bacteria as were struck by bullets. Indeed, the conflict of 1898 saw close to 5,000 U.S. servicemen killed by disease, with fewer than 1,000 dead from enemy fire. Colonel Roosevelt and other senior officers were well aware of these disheartening statistics, and sanitary methods for fending off fatal diseases were most difficult to observe in combat zones, much more so in a tropical climate in mid-summer! Humanitarian concerns further weakened the debilitated American soldiers when more than 20,000 starving, disease-infected women and children left Santiago under the demand of General Shafter's ultimatum to Toral: most of them headed straight for the U.S. front. Sympathetic American troops were quick to share their scarce rations, blankets and other supplies, while doctors tried to save as many civilian lives as possible, often leaving their severely wounded and ill military patients. Noble and commendable as it was, this effort further wreaked havoc among the American ranks. An appreciable number of the starving refugees carried yellow fever which began to infect a few Americans — but not many; the psychological effect of the fever cases on the rest of the men was a problem, as was the rocketing incidence of malaria, with 1,500 men already infected.

Realizing that the health crisis had become by far the number one threat to his command, General Shafter, at the end of July, called a meeting of his senior officers, which included Colonel Roosevelt, who, through attrition of the higher ranks, had been promoted to command the 2nd Brigade. By this time, according to Roosevelt, over half of his 1st Volunteer Cavalry Regiment had wound up

Black troopers of the 9th Cavalry at Santiago, doing what soldiers always do: shooting craps.

"... dead or disabled by wounds and sickness." Yet the seemingly invincible Roosevelt appeared as a towering hulk of robust health; the more the situation deteriorated, the more he thrived. Despite the intense discomforts suffered by Shafter, he too had benefitted, the campaign had reduced his weight of more than 300 pounds to about 250. At the conference of brigade and division commanders, the colonels and generals agreed that the vacillation of the War Department on the question of immediately evacuating the combat troops and replacing them with the freshly arriving occupation army would soon cause the deaths of hundreds — then thousands — of America's finest soldiers. They all agreed that a formal message, couched in the strongest and most unambiguous terms, must be sent immediately to Washington, D.C., or the 5th Corps was doomed to a needless and horrible demise.

Of course, this situation trapped all of the regular officers, whose careers could be destroyed by what would probably be construed as mass insubordination by the administration in Washington, D.C. Although national publicity may have been a factor in the decision that the most junior officer at the meeting, Roosevelt, then made, that consideration would only be of peripheral interest to him. His great concern was for the welfare of his beloved troopers, whom he saw wasting away and dying before him. As their commander, he was responsible for their welfare, as were the other field-grade officers present duty-bound to the ranks under their commands. The 39-year-old colonel suggested that he be the composer of what was to become one of the most famous messages of the 19th century: a "round-robin" letter, to be signed by all of the men at the meeting and sent to the War Department. Devastatingly short and curt, but overflowing with knowledge and perception, it read:

"We, the undersigned officers . . . are of the unanimous opinion that this Army should be at once taken out of the island of Cuba and sent to some point on the northern seacoast of the United States . . . that the Army is disabled by malarial fever to the extent that its efficiency is destroyed, and that it is in a position to be practically entirely destroyed by an epidemic of yellow fever, which is sure to come in the near future . . .

"This Army must be moved at once or perish. As the Army can be safely moved now, the persons responsible for preventing such a move will be responsible for the unnecessary loss of many thousands of lives."

The "round-robin" letter was not really insubordinate, but added to it was a much stronger missive, which was signed only by Roosevelt. Shafter had discreetly allowed an Associated Press reporter to be present, and once all of the officers — Bates, Chaffee, Ludlow, Sumner, Wood (who had been appointed military governor of Santiago) and lastly, Roosevelt (the only one below the rank of

Brigadier General) — signed it as a letter to Shafter, the commander refused to accept it, then brushed it aside leaving it on the table right in front of the AP correspondent who incredulously realizing that he had just been given the "scoop" of his career, turned toward Roosevelt, who also saw to it that he had the colonel's flaming condemnation note. One noteworthy sidelight: General Wheeler's signature was not on the letter and his attendance at the meeting is not known.

Theodore Roosevelt stood at the most critical crossroad of his career on the date of the passing of the letter to the AP correspondent. He had taken on all responsibility, including actually allowing the reporter to pick up the documents; Shafter had merely (although obviously) shoved them in his direction. Once published, all those at the meeting that August 3, knew that a national commotion of monumental magnitude would ensue and that the McKinley administration would suffer deep mortification. The petty bureaucrats, most notably, Secretary of War Alger, of course failed to acknowledge that had the "round-robin" not been released and the sure-to-occur predictions come true, the McKinley administration would have, politically, followed the hapless soldiers in Cuba to certain death. Already Roosevelt knew of the movement to run him as the Republican candidate for governor of New York. There was a strong possibility that he faced a court-martial, demotion in rank, or worse. Of course, already a hero and the best known man in the United States, he could be consoled by the sure knowledge that public opinion would be overwhelmingly on his side. Still, what he had done was every bit as heroic as his charges at the enemy just weeks previously.

President William McKinley was particularly incensed when he learned of the two letters by reading the bold headlines of the morning newspapers. Alger decided to give Roosevelt a double stab in the back: he released a personal letter, in which the colonel, exuding boyish pride in the exploits of his Rough Riders, had written that they were the equal of the best regular army units and worth three National Guard regiments. Alger must have known that the large number of voters serving in New York National Guard units would not be happy about what he had written, although many mature men were to dismiss it for what it was: pride in his own command, not meant as a slur of other soldiers. Far more hurtful to the colonel was that, although General Wood, after receiving strong endorsements from other officers (including two generals) and numerous enlisted men who had witnessed him in action on San Juan, had recommended him for the Congressional Medal of Honor, Alger was never to act upon the request. Ironically, 46 years would pass before one of his sons, Brigadier General Theodore Roosevelt, Jr., would receive the nation's highest decoration, posthumously, for his gallantry during the first day of the Normandy invasion. At last, a Theodore Roosevelt received the Medal of Honor; many his-

torians feel there should have been two.

Alger was attacked by the press for releasing a private letter as much as or more than Roosevelt had been taken to task for embarrassing his civilian superiors, but the colonel was soon to be vindicated when the decrepit, ghostly troops returned. The nation realized then that the risky and draconian move had saved the brave veteran Army which did not deserve to survive one of the most grueling campaigns to perish due to bureaucratic malfeasance. As Congress flew into an uproar, the press and population across the country demanded immediate action and the administration quivered, with McKinley furious at not having been informed of the medical plight of the Army, the War Department suddenly — for the first time — swung into vigorous and immediate action, taking just a few days to send the transports and to establish a recuperation camp. Most of the Army was saved but with scant time to spare.

The war had begun with the U.S. Navy establishing a blockade of Cuba in April. The last fighting to occur against the Spaniards in the country that was the cause of the United States going to war, was also to be fought in Cuban waters: the Battle of Manzanillo, on July 18, one day after the surrender of Santiago. Technically, General Toral had only relinquished the eastern tenth of Cuba to the conquerors. With communications between various sections of the island and Havana tenuous at best and contact between Havana and Madrid even more problematical, confusion among the Spanish commands as to what was going on was rampant. Indeed, Toral's forces, which had been outside of Santiago at the time of their giving up, scarcely knew of the loss of Cervera's fleet and some still thought that Dewey had been defeated at Manila Bay, eleven weeks earlier. Under such circumstances, further skirmishes — even major battles — were to be expected until a formal cease-fire could be negotiated and made known to the scattered forces. There was still remaining, at the port of Manzanillo on the eastern shore of the Gulf of Guacanayabo beyond Cape Cruz, almost 100 miles west of Santiago, a few Spanish cargo ships guarded by an unknown number of gunboats, the latter fully ready for an attack by the U.S. Navy.

In late June, Admiral Sampson decided that the gunboats at Manzanillo should be disposed of and ordered the Navy auxiliary vessels *Hist, Hornet* and *Wompatuck* into the Gulf of Guacanayabo to attack them. *Wompatuck's* draught was too deep for her to maneuver in close enough to engage the enemy with her light guns, so she remained in the channel to cut off the escape route, while the pair of smaller gunboats moved in, engaging an enemy vessel which was able to effectively move near land in the shallow water, close enough to bring a rain of small-arms fire from hundreds of soldiers on shore upon the *Hist.* As the two American boats closed in, the Spanish gunboat tried to speed across the harbor, but was hit by the three- and six-pounder guns of both and suddenly exploded. Despite the intense rifle fire from land, there were no American injuries. When the three American boats steamed into the harbor at Manzanillo, they confronted not four more enemy craft, as mentioned in Sampson's orders, but nine gunboats in a crescent formation spread across the harbor. Undaunted, the outnumbered U.S. Navy flotilla moved in, and — after a furious fight lasting an hour and 40 minutes, in which all three vessels were hit numerous times and the *Hornet* was disabled when a shell severed her main steam pipe — inflicted considerable damage. The *Wompatuck* towed the *Hornet* to safety for repairs and there were no American casualties.

The next day, July 1, the naval exploit at Manzanillo was totally obscured by the events at San Juan Hill, 100 miles to the east, when the U.S. gunboats *Osceola* and *Scorpion* steamed into the port of Manzanillo to take on the four remaining Spanish gunboats known to be waiting for them. There were five, plus the shore guns and the infantrymen on the beach, all laying down an intense barrage of fire. The Spanish vessels were positioned with their bows pointed at the Americans, presenting minimal targets. With no updated depth charts, the latter could not maneuver much beyond the known channels. Apparently, the U.S. boats in-

flicted considerable damage, but nothing decisive, and they withdrew, having suffered few hits, only to return for a final killing engagement less than three weeks later.

Admiral Sampson ordered a task force of seven gunboats, *Hist, Helena, Hornet, Osceola, Scorpion, Wampatuck* and *Wilmington*, under the command of Captain C. C. Todd, into Manzanillo Harbor, and they arrived at 7:00 on the morning of July 18. Watterson related the almost forgotten last naval battle of the war: "At 7:30 o'clock the *Wilmington* and *Helena* entered the northern channel toward the city, the *Scorpion* and *Osceola* the mid channel, and the *Hist, Hornet* and *Wampatuck* the south channel, the movements of the vessels being so timed as to bring them within effective range of the shipping at about the same moment.

"At 7:50 fire was reopened on the shipping, and, after a deliberate fire lasting about two and a half hours, three Spanish transports . . . were burned and destroyed. The pontoon, which was the harbor guard and store ship, probably for ammunition, was burned and blown up. Three gunboats were destroyed. One other was driven ashore and sunk, and a fifth was driven ashore and believed to be disabled.

"The firing was maintained at a range beyond that of the shore artillery. It was continued until,

The *USS Scorpion* began the work carried on by the *Gloucester* at Santiago Bay, when she joined in the attack on the Spanish gunboats at Manzanillo on July 1, proving that luxurious yachts could be simply converted into deadly swift gunboats. With shallow draught, and high speed and agile maneuverability, *Scorpion* and her once-posh sisters overcame the Spanish gunboats in every engagement. U.S. Naval Historical Center

after a gradual closing in, the shore batteries opened fire at a comparatively short range, when one of our ships was recalled, the object of the expedition having been accomplished. No casualties occurred on board any of our vessels. Great care was taken in directing the fire that as little damage as possible should be done to the city itself. The gunboats destroyed or driven ashore helpless, were the *Delgado, Guantánamo, Ostralia, Continola,* and *Guardian.*

"If the Manzanillo engagement had occurred at the outset of war, it would have taken a great place in history. It is only smaller in size than the other great engagements and the result was exactly the same — the enemy's ships annihilated, not one of our vessels injured and not one American sailor injured.

"The achievements of the Navy up to July 19 were extraordinary. The two squadrons under Dewey and Sampson had destroyed, of Spanish war vessels, four armored cruisers, three torpedo boats, 17 unprotected cruisers and gunboats, and four transports, and had captured nearly 30 merchant prizes of considerable value. Our only loss was the damaged *Winslow,* six men killed and seven men wounded. The Spaniards had lost about 1,200 killed, 600 wounded, and 2,000 prisoners.

"Commander Todd's triumph at Manzanillo was in keeping with the glory of this unparalleled naval record."

Once the elaborate ceremonies marking the surrender of more than 22,000 troops, thousands of rifles and more than 10 million rounds of ammunition and the city of Santiago to General Shafter were over, plans were immediately made to send the Spanish soldiers home. The prospect of returning to Spain was the only good news that many of the *soldados* had heard in months; they were thoroughly demoralized by hunger, disease, fatigue and defeat, plus the shock of learning the truth of the events of the past 11 weeks, revelations which totally contradicted the propaganda and lies of great Spanish triumphs they had received from Madrid. Even as the prisoners were being marched to nearby internment camps, General Shafter ordered that 45 tons of foodstuffs be immediately issued to them, an act that brought forth great feelings of gratitude from the famished, vanquished officers and enlisted men.

Perhaps never before in the history of warfare had defeated prisoners of war been as well treated by the victors as had been the astonished Spaniards in Cuba. On August 21, as half their number — 11,000 — were about to sail home, they published the results of a unanimous plebiscite they had taken, which authorized a common soldier — obviously educated and intelligent — to compose a letter to the commandant of their recent adversaries:

"Major General Shafter, Commanding the American Army in Cuba:

Sir: The Spanish soldiers who capitulated in this place on the 16th of July last, recognizing your high and just position, pray that through you all the courageous and noble soldiers under your command may receive our good wishes and farewell, which we send them on embarking for our beloved Spain. For this favor, which we have no doubt you will grant, you will gain the everlasting gratitude and consideration of 11,000 Spanish soldiers, who are your most humble servants. (Signed) Pedro Lopez de Castillo, Private of Infantry."

There followed a much longer letter for Shafter to relay to the men of his command. A few excerpts: "Soldiers of the American Army: We would not be fulfilling our duty as well-born men in whose breasts there live gratitude and courtesy, should we embark for our beloved Spain without sending you our most cordial and sincere good wishes and farewell. We fought you with ardor, and with all our strength, endeavoring to gain the victory, but without the slightest rancor or hate toward the American nation. We have been vanquished by you . . . but our surrender and the bloody battles preceding it have left in our souls no place for resentment against the men who fought us nobly and valiantly . . . You fought us as men, face-to-face, with great courage . . . You have . . . given honorable burial to the dead of the vanquished, have cured their wounded with great humanity, have respected and cared for your prisoners and their comfort, and lastly, to us, whose condition was terrible, you have given freely of food, of your stock of medicines, and you have honored us with distinguished courtesy, for after the fighting, the two armies mingled with the utmost harmony. With this high sentiment of appreciation from us all, there remains but to express our farewell and with the greatest sincerity we wish you all happiness and health in this land which will no longer belong to our dear Spain, but will be yours . . ." Interspersed were strong condemnations of the Cubans: ". . . the descendants of the Congo and of Guinea, mingled with the blood of unscrupulous Spaniards and of traitors and adventurers, these people are not able to exercise or enjoy their liberty, for they will find it a burden to comply with the laws which govern civilized communities."

The fighting between the Spaniards and the Cubans had been of a particularly bestial nature, with little quarter given on both sides, so the battles with the Americans, although hard fought, had come as a pleasant revelation to Private de Castillo and his comrades. Of course, he had failed to mention that it was the genocide, the deception, the duplicity and cruelty that had been official Iberian policy for four centuries, that had turned the peaceful natives who had met Columbus into vicious warriors who executed prisoners, sometimes utilizing their severed heads as soccer balls, because they knew that they would receive even worse treatment from the *peninsulares.* The Spaniards, in 1898, were the first to learn that if a country was going to be defeated, the wisest move was to assure that the United States was the power that achieved victory over them!

Spanish prisoners of war, most of them barefoot (above), are guarded by American soldiers at Siboney on July 8, 1898. A map of eastern Cuba (below) shows the disposition of Cuban, Spanish, and American forces in mid-July, just prior to the Spanish surrender.

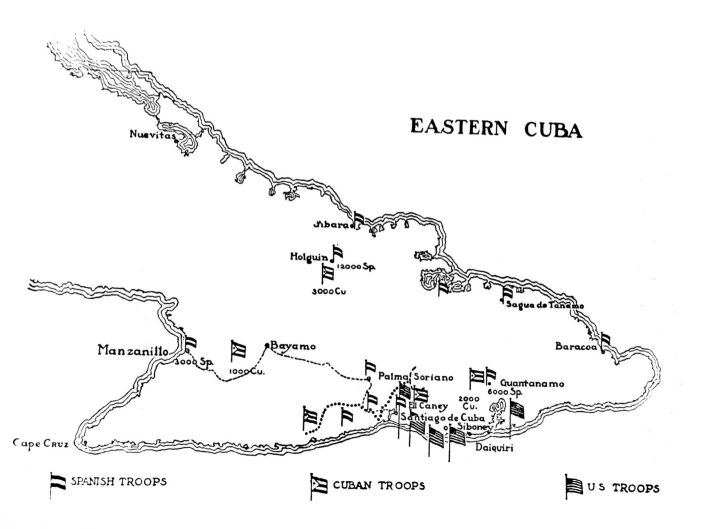

EASTERN CUBA

Nuevitas

Jibara

Holguin   12000 Sp.
            3000 Cu

Sagua de Tanamo

Baracoa

Manzanillo
        3000 Sp.   1000 Cu.   Bayamo

Palma Soriano   Guantanamo
                                6000 Sp.
            El Caney   2000
            Santiago de Cuba   Cu.
Cape Cruz   o Siboney
                    Daiquiri

SPANISH TROOPS   CUBAN TROOPS   US TROOPS

When Spanish General Toral realized that his only remaining options by mid-July were a bloody losing defense of Santiago de Cuba or surrender, he reluctantly conveyed to the American commanders, Generals Miles and Shafter, that he would agree to the latter. Officers of both armies shook hands in a field (above) as they assembled to discuss the details of the cessation of hostilities in eastern Cuba. General Miles, on horseback (below) was briefed by a junior officer during the negotiations. The end of the fighting had come just in time — for both sides.

American troops at the front cheering the news of Toral's surrender.

NOT THE KIND OF BULL THEY WERE LOOKING FOR!

American soldiers bivouacked on Misery Hill, on the heights overlooking Santiago, awaiting
orders to assault the city or an attack of tropical disease; whichever deadly prospect came first.

The U.S. Army hospital ship *Relief* (above), as she appeared during the Spanish-American War when she served in Cuban waters. The most severely wounded and the sickest soldiers were brought aboard the ship for treatment. A view of one of the wards of the *Relief* shows that the vessel was well-equipped and layed out (below) for her mission of mercy, including double-tier beds and electric fans and lighting.

Two photos, U.S. Naval Historical Center

The three gunboats which wreaked havoc on the Spanish vessels in the Gulf of Guacanayabo on June 30 and which played major roles in the final naval engagement of the war on July 18, are shown here. The *USS Hist* was a sleek converted yacht (opposite), shown on June 7, bound for the Cuban theater of operations. Close-up, a chief petty officer is shown operating a 37 mm Maxim machine gun onboard the *Hist,* with the *USS Topeka* in the background. The *USS Hornet* (above) was one of the few U.S. Navy ships to suffer serious combat damage during the war when, during the first Battle of Manzanillo on June 30 with all three gunboats receiving numerous hits, the *Hornet* was disabled by a shell which severed her main steam pipe. Under fire, the *Wompatuck* (below) steamed up to the *Hornet* and towed her out of range where she was quickly made fit again. Even a seagoing tugboat, a vessel of a low and rather peaceful calling such as *Wompatuck,* when armed with light rapid-fire batteries and manned by competent officers and men, could turn in a devastating battle performance!

U.S. Naval Historical Center

During the first six months of the American occupation of Cuba (July 1898-January 1899), the U.S. Army Signal Corps did much work to improve communications, mostly by establishing new telegraph and telephone lines and rebuilding the telegraph facilities that had been damaged in the revolutionary fighting. At Pinar del Rio, in far western Cuba, the Signal Corps telegraph office (above) was well established and staffed in January 1899. The tent of a Signal Corps company-grade officer (below) in the same area was spartan in its accruements, but adequate, with its raised wooden floor, porch-like platform, and the mandatory mosquito netting around the cot. Also in Pinar del Rio, several Signal Corps wagons (opposite, top) were loaded with supplies as they were ready to leave camp and go to work along a telegraph line. A vintage train of 1860s equipment (opposite, bottom), under the command of Lieutenant Chandler, was used to erect a telegraph line along the Nuevitas-Puerto Principe Railway in central Cuba.

Four photos, National Archives

physician of President Grover Cleveland, retaining the post under President McKinley. Wood's raising of the 1st Volunteer Cavalry Regiment, along with his second in command Theodore Roosevelt, is covered elsewhere in this volume, as is his other distinguished service in the Spanish-American War. As military governor of Santiago de Cuba and later of the entire country, he turned in a stellar performance through his reforms in all matters of civil administration, including public order, but especially in the medical and sanitation fields, where the abysmal conditions, exacerbated by decades of warfare, had proven to be a most daunting challenge. By then a major general of volunteers, Wood aggressively tackled every problem in the former Spanish colony, including communications, transportation, education, police, the Cuban Army, and the legal system. He worked closely with Major William Gorgas to eradicate Yellow Fever, and under his administration the mortality rate from many causes in Cuba drastically declined. After supervising the creation of a constitution and new legal code for Cuba, Wood was sent as an observer of German Army maneuvers in 1902, and in March 1903, he was posted to the Philippines where he was soon appointed governor of the rebellious Moro Province. He received his regular army rank of major general in August 1903, which caused some controversy, since he had been just a captain less than six years previously; the fact that his longtime confidant, friend, political ally, and fellow officer in Cuba, Theodore Roosevelt, was then President of the U.S., surely did not impede his rapid advance in rank and responsibility! He was given command of the Department of the Philippines in April 1906, a post he held until returning stateside in November 1908. Until World War I began, General Wood held various top-level army commands, including chief of staff, and it was widely assumed that should the U.S. enter the conflict, he would lead the expeditionary forces. But political intrigue and vindictiveness and the fact that he was a "Roosevelt Man" were to shoot down Wood's rapidly rising star. Like T.R., he was openly and vociferously in favor of military preparedness and his civilian superiors in Woodrow Wilson's pacifist administration soon began taking notice. He went well beyond administration policy when he established training camps for civilians at several locations in 1915, and by April 1917, when the U.S. declared war on Germany, more than 40,000 volunteers had trained at 16 camps, providing a much-needed cadre. Like the Washington bureaucrats who were too petty to see the importance of Roosevelt's "insubordination" in 1898, men in the same positions were to treat Wood just as shabbily 19 years later, especially after Roosevelt made speeches to the volunteers at the camp in Plattsburg, New York, which severely criticized President Wilson's peace policies, as though Wood was expected to edit and muzzle a former President of the United States! So it was, that General John J. Pershing was selected to command the American Army in France despite the fact that Wood was the senior officer. He spent the war training divisions to fight in France, and in 1920, he forged into the lead for the Republican nomination for President (a role that may have fallen to Roosevelt, had he not died the previous year), but he lost to Warren G. Harding on the tenth ballot. In 1921, President Harding sent Wood on a mission to the Philippines, then appointed him governor-general of the colony, a post he held until his death on August 7, 1927, after surgery for a brain tumor in Boston.

When Secretary of War Russell Alger visited Cuba on a tour of inspection, he was guided by Brigadier General Leonard Wood (left) and Colonel Mann (right). Wood was appointed military governor of Santiago Province and was the official host for Alger in that region. Wood was born in Winchester, New Hampshire, on October 9, 1860, and enrolled in the Harvard Medical School in 1880, earning an M.D. degree in 1884. Two years later he received an appointment as an army assistant surgeon with the rank of first lieutenant, being assigned to Arizona Territory where he served under Captain Henry W. Lawton, whom he would work closely with, when both held general rank in the Cuban campaign. Although a medical officer, Wood soon blossomed as a bold and courageous line officer and was awarded the Medal of Honor for bravery in the campaign against the Apaches. He held down rather routine medical assignments until 1895, when he became the personal

The administration of Cuba officially passed from Spain to the U.S. on January 1, 1899, with elaborate flag-raising ceremonies, parades, and meetings in several large cities. In the plaza in Pinar del Río (above), American Army officers accepted the transfer of authority from Spanish civil officials, in the midst of a large crowd of onlookers. Havana saw the biggest celebration, with the U.S. Army occupation troops marching in snappy formation. The 1st battalion of the 2nd Regiment of Volunteer Engineers (below) were the only unit of engineers that had served at the front in Cuba.

End of the Spanish Empire

The commanding general of the U.S. Army, Major General Nelson A. Miles, had lost his brief lobbying effort to invade Puerto Rico before Cuba was taken, but once the surrender of Santiago de Cuba was accomplished, he was given the task of leading the assault on the last Spanish possession in the Western Hemisphere. Even before Admiral Cervera had sailed his fleet into Santiago Bay in May, Admiral Sampson brought his squadron to Puerto Rican waters and began to bombard the harbor and the forts at the capital, San Juan. His first day's efforts did little damage, and before he could resume firing, the Spanish fleet was sighted off Martinique, prompting the Naval War Board in Washington, D.C. to order him to head for Cuba, and to order Commodore Schley to rush his flotilla from Hampton Roads, Virginia, to set up the blockade of the main objective of the American war effort. Once Santiago was occupied by the U.S. Army on July 17, Miles dashed into action, landing the invasion force of fresh troops that he had gathered at Guantánamo Bay, Cuba, in Guanica, on the southwest coast of Puerto Rico, just eight days later. His initial expedition consisted of infantry and artillery units totaling 3,415 men, plus two companies of Engineers and a Signal Corps company. Waiting in the fortified cities and the forests and the mountains of the island were more than 17,000 Spanish troops — 8,233 regulars and 9,107 volunteers.

With nine transports crammed with troops, supplies and equipment, convoyed by the gunboats *Columbia, Dixie, Gloucester* and *Yale*, with the battleship *Massachusetts* — which had missed the Battle of Santiago Bay while she was coaling — as the flagship, the port of Guanica was attained with little resistance. The light auxiliary gunboats *Annapolis* and *Wasp* arrived shortly, while the *Amphitrite* and the *Puritan* joined the *New Orleans* which was blockading San Juan. Soon, Major General Brooke came ashore, leading a portion of his corps, as well as Major General John M. Wilson with elements of a division and Brigadier General Theodore Schwan's 3rd Army Corps brigade, bringing the total to nearly 17,000 troops, just 350 men fewer than the Spanish army. Although virtually equal in numbers, weaponry and firepower, the campaign for Puerto Rico was just like the previous engagements, with the Spaniards defeated at every turn, as American forces rapidly spearheaded inland, occupying important towns and commandeering the railroad line and key roads.

The field artillery in action (opposite) during the American advance in Puerto Rico. This painting, by T. de Thulstrup, shows typical Caribbean weather, with the artillerymen bathed in bright sunlight while a few hundred yards away over the next hill, a tropical downpour is soaking the landscape — and probably American soldiers as well.

As the American troops marched eastward toward Ponce, 30 miles down the coast, they engaged and routed Spanish defenders at Yauco on July 26. The next day, the Navy escorted transport ships into Ponce harbor and, within 24 hours, the U.S. Army had taken the city, immediately advancing north and east along the main road to San Juan in hot pursuit of the retreating enemy. Thirty miles east of Ponce on August 5, General Brooke's forces seized Guayama and pushed the Spaniards further inland, toward Cayey. Four days later, U.S. forces broke out of Yauco, striking due north where they captured San Germán, Sábana Grande, Lares, and Arecibo in rapid succession. With the occupation of Mayaguez the following day, August 10, the American Army had control of virtually the entire southwestern quadrant of the island. The fighting at Coamo resulted in the capture of 167 Spanish *soldados,* and by August 12, U.S. artillery was laying siege to Asomanteo. On August 13, as the Army was about to move into Asomanteo and toward the opposite end of Puerto Rico, General Brooke was just commanding a battery to open fire on his next objective, Aibonito when Signal Corps messengers came galloping up to the various field commanders with urgent despatches from Washington, D.C.: cease firing, a truce had been signed the previous day, suspending all hostilities.

Of this final action in the war against Spain, President McKinley reported to the American people: "This campaign was prosecuted with great vigor, and by the 12th of August much of the island was in our possession and the acquisition of the remainder was only a matter of a short time. At most of the points in the island our troops were enthusiastically welcomed. Protestations of loyalty to the flag and gratitude for delivery from Spanish rule met our commanders at every stage. As a potent influence towards peace the outcome of the Puerto Rican expedition was of great consequence, and generous commendation is due to those who participated in it."

Because of the demoralization of the Spanish forces, the skirmishes and battles in less than three weeks of fighting, although at times moderate in intensity, nevertheless resulted in far fewer casualties than the Cuban campaign. After firing a few half-hearted volleys, the Spaniards would quickly withdraw. The hottest firefight, involving artillery, infantry and cavalry, occurred near Hormigueros, as the Americans advanced on Mayaguez, dislodging a firmly entrenched enemy force of equal strength. The Spaniards suffered heavy casualties, but just one American died and 16 were wounded. The incredibly low cost to the United States of the 19-day campaign for Puerto Rico was three killed and 40 wounded, while the Spanish losses were more than ten times that toll. Defeated on sea and land at every turn, its treasury depleted and a shocked and angry population seething on the brink of revolt, the government in Madrid had sued for peace, ready to accept the severe terms of the United States, conditions that would permanently terminate its four-century reign as a significant world power.

In addition to the campaigns which had been waged over Cuba and Puerto Rico and the ongoing fluidity of the conflict in the Philippines, the United States had also acquired several strategic islands — both Spanish-held and unclaimed — stretching like a pearl necklace across the Pacific Ocean, a necklace that would be used to supply gems far more valuable than pearls to the U.S. Navy. The treasure so desperately coveted by the captains of American warships were the black diamonds of the mountains of Appalachia — common coal. Even before the end of the war with Spain, Navy strategists had been quick to realize that the United States would shortly become the major power in the Pacific, and would require an enormous fleet to not only uphold its interests but to counter the expanding strength of the Imperial Japanese Navy. Bases and coaling stations would be an absolute necessity to reinforce this role, giving the little islands an importance far out of proportion to their size and meager resources. The Spanish possessions of Guam and the Philippines, as well as Hawaii and Midway and Wake islands, could host the bases to enable the Navy to operate unimpeded across the entire Pacific Basin far into the future.

In 1890, an obscure U.S. Navy officer, who ironically detested sea duty, had published a book, *The Influence of Sea Power Upon History*, which was to profoundly motivate the thinking of American and foreign naval strategists, including future Assistant Secretary of the Navy Theodore Roosevelt. Actually the author, Alfred Thayer Mahan, had himself been influenced by Roosevelt's definitive work, *The Naval War of 1812*, produced when Roosevelt was just 22 years old, so they were already well acquainted and shared the same strategic vision of a modern U.S. Navy entrusted to a new and vastly upgraded mission. For more than 100 years, the role of the Navy had been to defend the coast of the United States and to protect merchant ships, while occasionally going into action overseas, as in the suppression of the Barbary Pirates in the Mediterranean Sea in the early 1800s. Now Mahan advocated construction of large fleets of swift, modern cruisers and floating fortress battleships as essential to maintaining a robust, accelerating economy and accumulating national wealth, security and prestige in the Industrial Age. Long-range ships which mounted long-range guns and rapid-fire batteries were the only means by which a modern nation could grow, prosper — and survive, according to Mahan and Roosevelt.

Mahan also felt that such wide-ranging squadrons of ships should greatly increase their effectiveness by being available to control the strategic "pressure points" of international shipping lanes, such as Gibraltar, the Straits of Malacca and the Straits of Magellan, a policy which Great Britain was already pursuing. These theories cannot be overrated for their importance in forming the philosophical keel for naval construction and tactics in the 20th century. They rapidly evolved into hard policy when Theodore Roosevelt — first as Assistant Navy Secretary, later as President — became the father of the modern American sea juggernaut that, beginning with the great victories of 1898, was to dominate the oceans of the world through the 1900s, and in all probability, far into the 2000s as well.

The taking of Guam, the Spanish island in the archipelago known as the Ladrones or Marianas, was another of the comical respites of the Spanish-American War. Guam lay 1,200 miles east of the Philippines, a lonely outpost, with no contact with the outside world except for ships which would arrive every two months to deliver mail and provisions. On June 20, while escorting a convoy which carried part of General Merritt's army to the Philippines, the U.S. Navy cruiser *Charleston* steamed into Umata Harbor, intent on defeating the small Spanish garrison and raising the Stars and Stripes over the fortresses of Santa Cruz and Santiago. On that rainy, misty morning, the *Charleston*'s skipper, Captain Henry Glass, discovered that Fort Santiago was not manned and, assuming that the Santa Cruz facility was active, he opened fire with his five-inch guns, blasting the tower and walls. There was no return fire, indeed no indications of any activity at the fortress. Puzzled by the total lack of any sign of life, Glass ceased firing and began planning what to do next. Presently a rowboat came around the small island upon which Fort Santa Cruz was perched. The boat carried the Spanish naval captain in command of the port of San Luis d'Apra, a Spanish army surgeon and an English-speaking merchant. Once aboard the American warship, the Spaniards began to humbly apologize for not being able to return the impressive salute that had been fired in their honor! From their location in the town behind the fort, they had not seen that the "salute" had consisted of high-explosive shells, rather than blanks.

They could not return the courtesy, they explained, since there no longer was any powder or cannon at San Luís and they were not used to having the honor of a salute bestowed upon them. Captain Glass then politely informed them that their country and his were now at war and that he had not been saluting their flag and honor but was bombarding the fortifications. The Spaniards were incredulous, for they had not received any messages since April and the June steamer — perhaps seized on the high seas as a prize by the American Navy — was several weeks overdue. Learning of the defeat and destruction of their fleet at Manila Bay, their amazement was complete and they left the *Charleston* with Captain Glass's orders to go to Governor Marina to make surrender arrangements. The following day the governor, his officers, 54 Spanish soldiers and an equal

Few photographs survive of Spanish *soldados* on duty in Puerto Rico; this one, being one of the best, is a studio shot. With an "out of focus" background painting of trees, a stretched piece of canvas representing a tent, and seated on a mat of artificial grass, five officers of the Hunters Battalion posed at mess (one with a parrot on his shoulder) about 1890.

numbers of native troops turned in their weapons; the disarmed natives were released and the Spaniards were brought aboard ship as prisoners of war and taken to be interned with the survivors of Montejo's flotilla at Cavite, in the Philippines. The English-speaking merchant was a Spaniard who happened to be a naturalized American citizen, so in the informality of 19th century warfare, Captain Glass left him in charge of the new possession, after the merchant, Francisco Portusac, assured him that it was not necessary to station a garrison there, as he had complete confidence in the orderliness of the natives.

The taking of Wake Island on Independence Day 1898 was even easier than the seizure of Guam just two weeks earlier, as related in *Harper's:* "Down on the horizon a long white line pops up, and the shouts of 'Land! Land' break from our ship-weary hearts. 'Wake Island, a coral atoll 19° 11' north by 166° 33' east,' shouts down the captain from the bridge. As we draw near, two open boats are lowered, and General Greene celebrates the Fourth in earnest by raising the American flag on the island. A dreary sun-beaten spot we find it, glistening with white coral and shells, and covered with a sickly growth of low shrubs. This barren waste stretches along for 20 miles. An oblong lagoon, cut from the sea by shallow reefs, over which the waves constantly break, eats its way into the heart of the island. Perhaps this heretofore unclaimed island may someday be used as a telegraph post, or even a coaling station. It lies well on the way to Manila..." Like Guam, Wake Island was just another piece of strategic real estate seized as a diversion by American forces on the way to occupy the Philippines!

Meanwhile, in the Philippines, General Merritt, working closely with Admiral Dewey, was consolidating his forces at Cavite, just south of Manila, in preparation for seizure of the capital city. By early August, American troops had advanced to the edge of the city and Dewey called for it to be surrendered by the Spanish garrison or it would be bombarded. By this time, the last hope of the Spanish Captain General and his troops, that the German fleet would intervene on behalf of the defenders, had proven hopeless; while Admiral von Diedrichs had been aggressively carrying out the Kaiser's policy of favoring Spain, Dewey's earlier displays of "Gunboat Diplomacy" had kept the Germans at bay. Although never acknowledged publicly, there seems to have been a surreptitious agreement between Berlin and Madrid, that if the Germans succeeded in driving Dewey out of the Philippines, part — or even all — of the colony would have been turned over to Germany. That seemed plausible; it would have been far better for Spain to have a friendly power in charge, rather than a despised conquering enemy.

Negotiations between the American and Spanish commanders were held the second week in August, and a version of the "Shafter-Toral" plan at Santiago de Cuba, overruled by President McKinley, was carried out at Manila to placate Spanish honor by staging a halfhearted bombardment to impress the residents and the press corps. Apparently, some Spanish officers either were not informed of the tacit agreement or they did not agree with it; for in occupying Manila on August 16, 12 Americans were killed and 39 wounded in the last act which pitted the fighting spirit of Spain against the determination of the United States. Unfortunately, the fighting for Manila had occurred after the cease-fire agreed to by the warring governments; news of it arriving just after the surrender. As part of the fall of Manila, the American commanders made the decision that their forces alone would occupy the city, as they forcibly excluded the armed Filipino insurgents from even entering, much less giving them any role in the transfer of administration or governing their capital. This situation convinced Aguinaldo that his people appeared to be merely trading the rule of one foreign power for another. After the brief, heady exultation at being freed from Spanish tyranny, the natives soon turned to the serious business of confronting the newly arrived replacement occupiers. Their attitude was understandable, for while American policy had clearly called for Cuba to be turned over to its own people, no such declarations had been stated for the Philippines; even the peace protocols, quoted below, were vague on the subject.

The powerful senator from Massachusetts, Henry Cabot Lodge, succinctly described the war situation which, by mid-August, had forced the Spanish government to capitulate: ". . . Admiral Dewey and General Merritt, thanks to distance and a severed cable, were able to complete their work and set the final crown upon their labors by taking Manila before the order reached them to cease hostilities. That order, when it came, found them masters of the great Eastern city they had fought to win. In Puerto Rico, the news stayed Schwan's cavalry in pursuit of the Spaniards, Brooke's gunners with the lanyards in their hands, and halted the other columns in their march over the island. In Cuba, it saved Manzanillo, just falling before the guns of Goodrich and his little squadron, and checked the movements which were bringing port after port into American possession. It stopped also the departure of a fleet which, by its existence and intention, was a potent cause of the coming of peace. Even before the battle of the 3rd of July, the department at Washington was making ready to send a fleet consisting of the *Iowa*, *Oregon*, *Yankee*, *Yosemite* and *Dixie*, under Commodore Watson, in the flagship *Newark*, direct to Spain, primarily to

fight the fleet of Admiral Camara, which had wandered helplessly across the Mediterranean with vague outgivings about going to Manila, but which merely went through the Suez Canal, and then turned around and came back again. But after the battle of July 3, the preparations of Commodore Watson's squadron were pushed more energetically than ever, reinforcements were prepared, and it was known that it was to cross the Atlantic in any event, and carry war to the very doors of Spain's coast cities. This fact was soon as well known in Europe as in America. Presently it became clear that Watson's fleet was no pretense, but a very grim reality; that it was nearly in readiness; and finally, that it was on the very eve of departure . . . Spain did not like the prospect, and some of her neighbors were as averse as she to the sound of American guns in the Mediterranean, not heard in those waters now for nearly a century. It would be something new, something which might disturb concerts and *Bundes* and other excellent arrangements, and must not be permitted. It became clear to the diplomatic mind that Spain must make peace, and make it at once, on any terms. Hence arose what is politely called pressure, although poor Spain did not need much pressing . . ."

President McKinley, after giving his own account of events leading to cessation of hostilities, gave credit for victory to the same power that had been claimed by Spain during its ruthless 400 years of colonial mayhem: "In tracing these events we are constantly reminded of our obligations to the Divine Master for His watchful care over us and His safe guidance, for which the nation made reverent acknowledgment and offered humble prayer for the continuance of His favor." Christian rulers and soldiers freely have sought the assistance of God as they slaughter other Christians, then humbly credit Him for defeating their enemies, but rarely seem to wonder why the Almighty would favor one population of His followers over another!

Perhaps on a firmer foundation politically than he was theologically, McKinley also related how the peace negotiations were conducted: "The Spanish government . . . made overtures of peace through the French Ambassador, who with the assent of his government had acted as the friendly representative of Spanish interests during the war. On the 26th of July, M. Jules Cambon presented a communication signed by the Duke of Almodóvar, the Spanish Minister of State, inviting the United States to state the terms upon which it would be willing to make peace. On the 30th of July, by a communication addressed to the Duke of Almodóvar and handed to M. Cambon, the terms of the United States government were announced, substantially as in the protocol afterwards signed. On the 10th of August, the Spanish reply, dated August 7, was handed by M. Cambon to the Secretary of State. It accepted unconditionally the terms imposed as to Cuba, Puerto Rico and an island of the Ladrones group, but appeared to seek to introduce inadmissable reservations in regard to the demand of the United States as to the Philippine Islands. Conceiving that discussion on this point could be neither practical nor profitable, I directed that in order to avoid misunderstanding, the matter should forthwith be closed by proposing the embodiment in a formal protocol of the terms upon which the negotiations for peace were to be undertaken. The vague and inexplicit suggestions of the Spanish note could not be accepted, the only reply being to present as a virtual ultimatum a draft of protocol embodying the precise terms tendered to Spain in the note of the United States of July 30, with added stipulations of detail as to the appointment of commissioners to arrange for the evacuation of the Spanish Antilles. On August 12, M. Cambon announced his receipt of full powers to sign the protocol so submitted. Accordingly, on the afternoon of August 12, M. Cambon, as the Plenipotentiary of Spain, and the Secretary of State, as the Plenipotentiary of the United States, signed a protocol providing that Spain relinquish all claim of sovereignty over and title to Cuba; that Spain cede to the United States the island of Puerto Rico and other islands under Spanish sovereignty in the West Indies, and also an island in the Ladrones to be selected by the United States; and that the United States occupy and hold the city, bay, and harbor of Manila pending the conclusion of a treaty of peace which should determine the control, disposition and government of the Philippines.

"The protocol provided also for the appointment of joint commissions on the part of the United States and Spain, to meet in Havana and San Juan, respectively, for the purpose of arranging and carrying out the details of the stipulated evacuation of Cuba, Puerto Rico, and other Spanish islands in the West Indies; for the appointment of not more than five commissioners on each side, to meet at Paris not later than October 1, and to proceed to the negotiation and conclusion of a treaty of peace, subject to ratification according to the respective constitutional forms of the two countries. It also provided that upon the signature of the protocol, hostilities between the two countries should be suspended, and that notice to that effect should be given as soon as possible by each government to the commanders of its military and naval forces."

That was on August 12, 1898; the cease-fire orders were immediately sent by telegraph and cable around the world. Due to the isolation from communications by some units — especially those of Spain — and the fact that Dewey had cut the international cables in Manila Bay at the time of his attack on May 1, post-protocol battles continued for several days. As far as Spain was concerned, *la Guerra Españolamericana* was over and the terms for withdrawal from the relinquished territories generous. Spain did not have to evacuate San Juan, Puerto Rico until October 18; it was at the stroke of noon on New Year's Day of 1899 that the Spanish

Captain General of Cuba, in an elaborate ceremony, turned over the government of Cuba to Major General Brooke, who had been appointed military governor of the island by McKinley. General Fitzhugh Lee, prior to being called to active duty in 1898, had been the American Consul to Havana, so it was no surprise that he was immediately made the governor of the capital city, a move loudly celebrated by the joyful inhabitants who had known him as a sympathetic friend and welcomed him and his troops as liberators. Spain also received a $20 million gesture from the U.S.

Sick and weak, the American Army which had freed Cuba was already rapidly recuperating back in the United States; Sampson's squadron was preparing for a grand victory welcome home at east coast ports and the demobilization of 100,000 volunteers began before the end of August. That was in the Atlantic theatre of operations. In the Pacific, Admiral Dewey would not be able to leave to sail into New York Harbor for more than a year, for his great hero's welcome there. The Philippines situation would embroil the United States in a controversy of colonialism and imperialism for years, as well as fighting the native insurgents — a series of events inseparable from the war just concluded. In Washington, D.C., serious debate in the administration and Congress was ongoing concerning the size of the U.S. Army and Navy, so recently saddled with a worldwide role in protecting the interests and projecting the power of the United States. The 18,000-man Army and three-squadron Navy of just six months earlier had become as outdated as the Civil War muskets still used by some Cuban rebels. The finality of the short war with Spain left no doubt that the armed might of America — on sea and land — must be geometrically enlarged at a rapid pace. President William McKinley and his successor, Theodore Roosevelt, were most attuned to what must be done, and the jingoes in Congress, joined by many moderates, became quickly aware of the costs that came with the assumption of world power.

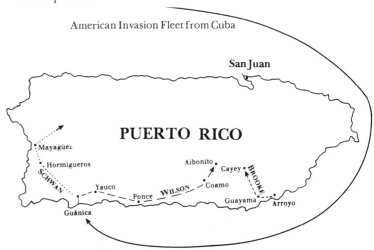

The brief American campaign in Puerto Rico, showing the three main thrusts toward San Juan by Generals Brooke, Schwan and Wilson.

Once the initial landings at Guanica, Puerto Rico, were successful, the Army quickly advanced 30 miles eastward to Ponce, a deep harbor capable of handling a large number of transport ships (above) as well as men-of-war. The bulk of the American invasion force came ashore at Ponce (below and upper right), and soon struck inland, clearing the southwest quadrant of the island, routing the Spaniards in every engagement. Shortly after coming ashore, the 3rd Artillery (lower right) was leaving Ponce for the front, where they provided heavy covering fire for the advancing infantry forces.

Four photos, National Archives

The *USS Massachusetts* is shown arriving at New York Harbor in August 1898, when she and the other ships of Admiral Sampson's fleet toured east coast ports in a series of victory reviews. While the ship is gray and weathered, the sailors standing on the 13-inch gun turrets and on deck, are dressed in spotless white uniforms, for shortly they will be facing a cheering, welcoming crowd along the waterfront.

The captain of the destroyed battleship *USS Maine,* Charles D. Sigsbee, was assigned to command the *USS St. Paul,* just converted into an armed merchant cruiser. Armed with a main battery of 5-inch deck guns (above), the former Atlantic passenger steamer was built in Philadelphia in 1895, was 535- feet, 5-inches long, and had a gross tonnage of 11,629. A sister ship of the *St. Louis,* both vessels were identical, including being built the same year. Because of their speed, the two ships could outrun anything that they could not outshoot and were well-suited for running down blockade violators. The *St. Paul,* several of her 5-inch guns barely discernible (opposite, top), as she looked somewhat worse for wear at the end of the war. On June 22, the Spanish torpedo boat destroyer *Terror* made a high-speed run at her right off San Juan, Puerto Rico (left), but her gunners had no trouble repulsing the attack. This painting, by the prominent illustrator M. Reuterdahl, was based on sketches and a detailed description given by Captain Sigsbee.

Three photos, U.S. Naval Historical Center

Of course, the U.S. Navy just had to have a warship named for the location of the Naval Academy at Annapolis, Maryland! Although powered by both steam and sail, the keel of *USS Annapolis* was not laid down until April 18, 1896 — a late date for sails on a gunboat. She had six 4-inch rapid-fire guns, four 6-pounders, and two 1-pounders. Trim and sleek, the vessel played an important role in both the Cuban and Puerto Rican campaigns in 1898. She joined the small blockading flotilla outside of Havana Harbor on May 2, assisting in the capture of several blockade-violating vessels there and later on the south side of Cuba. She then joined *USS Marblehead* and *USS Ericsson,* covering the position held by the New York Volunteer Marines and the coaling operation at Guantanamo Bay, and set out along the coast, where she established contact with Cuban forces and indulged in a firefight with a Spanish shore battery. After that mission, she joined three other gunboats in the capture of Nipe Bay, where they found an enemy gunboat, *Don Jorge Juan,* which they de-

stroyed after a brisk exchange of fire on July 18. Four days later, *Annapolis* sailed for action in the invasion of Puerto Rico, where she assisted the Army capture of Ponce on July 30; she remained active in that area of operations until the end of the war. After the turn of the century, she served three years in the Philippines, China, and Japan, carrying out various assignments. After spending most of ten years on duty in the Pacific Ocean, *Annapolis* was assigned to gunboat diplomacy missions to Nicaragua and Mexico, and before the end of World War I, she had sailed through the Panama Canal to take up patrolling duties in the Gulf of Mexico. In 1920, out of commission, she was towed to Philadelphia and loaned to the Pennsylvania State Nautical School as a training ship, where she served for 20 years, then she was presumably scrapped in 1940. She is shown in 1899, back in her white hull and beige superstructure peacetime livery, anchored at Greenport, on eastern Long Island.

Suffolk County Historical Society

Battery B of the 4th U.S. Artillery (above) was shelling a Spanish blockhouse during the advance on Coame on August 9, 1898, just three days before the cessations of hostilities. During the U.S. Army advance on Lares and Arecibo (below), the lead platoon of the 11th Infantry swept out of the thick forest to attack a Spanish position, in this painting by R.F. Zogbaum. A dead Spanish soldier, still holding his rifle, lies in the foreground.

Just as General Brooke was about to loose an artillery barrage on Aibonito,
a messenger trotted up with the order to end hostilities immediately.

Artwork by T. Dart Walker

On August 10, smartly decked-out Spanish soldiers (above) were assembled at Mayaguez to go into battle against the oncoming American juggernaut. Just four days later, after U.S. forces seized the city, bedraggled, dirty, and defeated (below), the Spanish *soldados* returned — as prisoners of war.

American soldiers, armed with Krag-Jorgensen rifles, guarding an old siege gun overlooking Luneta and Manila Bay.

A group of Spanish prisoners of war recuperated from their ordeal were resting in Manila, awaiting repatriation home.

Above, National Archives

Opposite, T. de Thulstrup

One of the few photographs taken during the fighting between Spanish and U.S. forces in the Philippines shows an artillery position (above), where a signal is being sent, ordering the reserves to advance after the retreating enemy. The picture was made at Malate, just outside of Manila, on August 13, 1898. By the end of this last day of fighting, American troops occupied Manila; the truce had been signed the previous day, but because of the severed cables leading to Manila, the cease fire orders were delayed. Major General Wesley Merritt, commanding U.S. Army forces in the Philippines, met regularly with Admiral George Dewey to coordinate strategy and to plan the capture of Manila; the two highest-ranking American officers in the Philippine theater are shown (opposite) conferring in Dewey's cabin on board the flagship *USS Olympia.* Merritt was the commander of the 8th Corps which was sent to occupy the Philippines, and when Spain capitulated, he was appointed military governor of the new American colony. Apparently, his diplomatic prowess was even better known than Dewey's, for after just two weeks of administrating the archipelago, he was ordered to serve as an American commissioner to negotiate a final peace treaty in Paris.

The steel protected cruiser *USS Charleston*, shown in her gray warpaint (above) at Hong Kong after one of her trips escorting convoys to the Philippines, was to be the only major American warship to be lost during the brief period of the emergence of the U.S. as a world power. Her captain had seized Guam on June 20, after informing the Spanish commander of the state of war between their respective countries, continuing service with the fleet in the Pacific Ocean. The *Charleston* displaced 4,040 tons, was 312-feet long, and of a breadth of 46 feet. Her main battery consisted of two 8-inch and six 6-inch guns; the secondary battery, four 6-pounders and two 3-pounders, as well as two 1-pounders — all rapid-fire. She also deployed four 37 mm Hotchkiss revolving cannons and a pair of Gatling guns. With a rating of 6,666 horsepower, she could steam at more than 18 knots, carried a crew of 20 officers and 280 men, and cost $1,164,504.10. On November 2, 1899, while on patrol along the coast of Luzon in the Philippines, the *Charleston* was wrecked on a reef, ending her useful life. Even as Admiral Sampson destroyed the Spanish squadron as it steamed out of Santiago de Cuba, as a "a Fourth of July present" to the American people, the Army celebrated Independence Day of 1898, when General Greene mounted a small American flag on Wake Island (below) in mid-Pacific. Nobody else had apparently bothered to claim the coral atoll, but it was to form an important link in the defense chain that the U.S. was forging between the west coast and the Philippines.

Above, U.S. Naval Historical Center

M. Jules Cambon (above) was the astute French diplomat who negotiated the end of the fighting, and although he represented Spanish interests in Washington, D.C., he also had the complete trust of the Americans. With President McKinley and his cabinet looking on in the right background and diplomats to the left, Secretary of State John Hay (below) signed the Memorandum of Ratification of the cease-fire for the U.S. Hay's "Splendid Little War" was history; the world order profoundly changed.

As part of the Dewey welcoming celebration in New York City in September 1899, the battleships *Massachusetts* and *Indiana* were decked out like Christmas trees, with hundreds of electric lights illuminating them in the harbor at night

Celebrations and Scandals

Once Colonel Roosevelt's "round-robin" letter had finally broken through the indecisiveness and lassitude of the Washington, D.C. bureaucracy, ships quickly took on the sick and hungry American Army which had defeated the Spaniards at Santiago, while trains were loaded with the thousands of their comrades who had been left behind in Tampa. Fearing yellow fever, which few of the men had contracted, the War Department had but hours to decide where to establish a recuperation camp for 25,000 troops, thousands of horses and mules, and all of their weapons and equipment. To guard against an epidemic of the dreaded yellow fever and to speed healing with the aid of cool ocean air in the tepid summer, government officials sought out the most isolated peninsula on the northeast coast of the United States which had both railroad service and a dock capable of handling the returning transport ships. Montauk, on the far eastern end of Long Island, 115 miles from Manhattan, was the perfect spot. Just three years previously, the Long Island Rail Road (L.I.R.R.) had laid its tracks over the sandy spit and had built a small — but usable — dock. There was trepidation, however, with nightmares of Tampa all over, since the railroad line was single-track. With most of the men arriving by sea, the railroad was able to handle its tasks, and when the units were mustered out, they would be leaving piecemeal, so few serious tie-ups occurred, but that was despite, not because of, government planning.

As the convoy carrying the returning army steamed northward, the War Department finally decided to inform the L.I.R.R. officials that Montauk, which had been chosen as the site of Camp Wikoff named for the colonel killed at Bloody Ford, must be ready to receive the army within a week! Montauk was virtually devoid of any structures except the diminutive station shanty and a few houses mostly occupied by shepherds who tended herds at summer pasture. Despite the impossibly short notice, the railroad actually managed to construct a 12-track terminal, erect immense warehouses, and deliver hundreds of tons of lumber, tents, food, medicines and supplies before the deadline. The troops left at Port Tampa — some as sick as those who had gone to Cuba — preceded the ships carrying the veterans into Fort Pond Bay. Just 12 days after the orders had been issued to move the army out of Cuba, the ships began arriving at the new camp. The disembarking veterans were greeted by a panorama of frenetic activity as soldiers and civilian laborers strained to unload the ships and lines of freight cars, a steady procession of mule-drawn army wagons shuttled between the terminal and the continually expanding tent city over the dunes, while water pipes were being laid, and telegraph, telephone and electric lines were going up. Not only were the yellow journalists downplaying the incredible efforts of the railroad, but without a shred of proof, some of them accused its president, William Baldwin, of using his political influence to bring the camp to the farthest terminal to enrich the company! The truth was that the whole debacle had frazzled the nerves of the entire management, overworked the employees and cost the L.I.R.R. more than it earned.

General Wheeler and Colonel Roosevelt came down the gangplank from the transport *Miami* and were greeted by a large contingent of civilians shouting "Fighting Joe! Hurrah for Wheeler!" and "Teddy! Teddy!," followed by "Roosevelt for Governor!" Newspaper reporters immediately thronged about the robust Rough Rider commander, pressing him to reveal his political plans, especially his availability for the New York State gubernatorial nomination of the Republican Party. His reply was to praise the men of his regiment, expressing his pride in their courage and historic accomplishments. Playing coy, Roosevelt was clearly letting the nomination pursue him, rather than vice-versa. Major General Joseph Wheeler was given command of Camp Wikoff, during which assignment he passed his 62nd birthday. Although slender and grey, "Fighting Joe" carried on in the tradition of his bold and courageous service in both the Civil War and the Cuban campaign, and in 1899 he was sent to the Philippines to briefly command a brigade.

The first days at Montauk were chaotic as thousands of sick and wounded soldiers arrived at the unfinished business of the establishment of the recuperation camp. Food and medicine were in short supply; despite the heroic efforts of the Red Cross and other volunteer service societies, hospital facilities were inadequate and there was a severe shortage of doctors and nurses. When word of this latest of War Department fiascos quickly reached New York, the situation changed rapidly, from the extreme of want to one of plenty. So many gourmet chefs and carloads of delicacies were despatched by wealthy New Yorkers that many of the malnourished troopers developed stomach ailments from overeating. Civilian doctors and nurses rode out to Montauk on trains whose baggage cars were loaded with the finest instruments and medicines. Local citizens of eastern Long Island began arriving by rail and wagon, laden with food and gifts.

While the majority of the veterans quarantined at Montauk were enjoying a rapid recovery, more than 250 died and were interred in a temporary cemetery in the ocean sand at the edge of the camp. The fatalities, roughly 1 percent of the total military personnel, were not of an unusually high number, considering the time period and the state of medical and sanitary technology, but they were, nevertheless, depressing for soldiers and civilians alike. Given the primitive location, the distance

223

from sources of supply and the season, the recuperation at Camp Wikoff went reasonably well, again because of the efforts of the field commanders, such as Major Generals Wheeler and Young, and despite the idiocies of the Washington, D.C. bureaucracy. Conditions and life at Montauk during the late summer of 1898 were of great fascination to the entire country, and the fine harbor, decades before it was to become the most renowned of ocean sport fishing centers on the eastern seaboard, enjoyed two months of fame, the intensity of which it would never experience again.

Typical of the notoriety bestowed upon the sandy, desolate and wind-swept peninsula was a front-page article in the August 21 edition of the Illustrated Supplement of the *New-York Tribune:*

SCENES AT MONTAUK CAMP.
A COLONY OF SICK SOLDIERS IT IS.
PRIMARILY A HOSPITAL CAMP — THE
TRANSFORMATION OF THE REGION SINCE
THE ARRIVAL OF THE TROOPS.

"Three weeks ago Montauk was not a thriving place. The little railroad station with the mainline of single track and a siding, a little fisherman's house back on the sloping shore where the bay curves outward toward the east, a few cottages three and four miles away on the other side of the island near the ocean shore were all there was of it. Few people went there except to fish and hunt, and two or three trains a day sufficed... Now all that is changed. The sand dunes are being covered with canvas tents; cavalry horses and army mules graze on the grassy slopes; mounted men come and go over the roads that wind in and out among the sand dunes to the camps so far away; lumbering prarie schooners follow their tortuous windings; shacks

and new buildings lately erected around the station, a dozen sidetracks filled with cars, and the hustle and bustle of active life mark what was peace, quietness and lonesomeness so short a time ago ... the congestion of cars upon the tracks and the transports that ride at anchor in Fort Pond Bay and around Colloden Point.

"One of the interesting and picturesque sights is the colored teamster driving two, four, or six mules hitched to a canvas-topped wagon. He has a peculiar way of whistling at his teams to guide them on the road, and if he happens to be following you, you will turn several times to see who is signaling to you before you discover that the whistling is for the mules... In the earlier stages of the camp there were deep mud holes here and there and occasional boulders. But it was all the same with the colored driver. He slopped through the one almost up to the hubs of the wagon and jolted over the other. If an amateur were on the seat he would tumble off, but the colored driver never. He seems glued fast. Perhaps he is, for he never gets off to unload a wagon, except on rare occasions. He sits there on the seat silent, without a smile, but with a look that seems to say — particu-

One by one the transports returning from Cuba tied up at the small railroad dock at Fort Pond Bay, Montauk, Long Island, to disembark the returning veterans; the larger ships anchoring off shore with their passengers brought in by smaller craft. An officer seated on a rock in the foreground watches as soldiers in khaki uniforms — perhaps Rough Riders — march at right shoulder arms from the ship that carried them more than 1,000 miles along the eastern seaboard.

Suffolk County Historical Society

larly if you saw him make the trip: 'I almost broke my neck getting here. Now you do the rest.'

"In fair weather the canvas coverings and the hoop supports are taken off. The wagon loses its picturesqueness then until an empty one takes on a load of colored soldiers and teamsters, and they get to singing. Then it all comes back in a different way.

"But with all the beauty and picturesqueness of Camp Wikoff about you there is a feeling of sadness that keeps tugging at your heart strings. It is not a joyous camp of summer instruction, where the wives and mothers and sweethearts of the Boys in Blue can come and rejoice with them in their summer outing. It is not the glad camp of a victorious army flushed with victory. The troops, many of them at least, have won battles and performed deeds of valor and bravery in conquering a foreign nation and compelling her to sue for peace, but they have come to Camp Wikoff weakened and exhausted by malarial fevers and disorders engendered by exposure to semi-tropical storms and heat. The camp is one for a sick army. Turn where you will, this fact is ever before you. Ambulances are everywhere present . . . Climb Observatory Hill to the east of the station and you look down upon the plain of the detention camp, where the troops from Santiago are detained until the surgeons think they will develop no cases of an infectious nature. You can go no further, for no one is admitted near the camp, and the mounted cavalry guard warns you to keep on the crest of the hill. But you have a fine extended view from this elevation, the highest on Montauk Point, and you can see to the southeast, over the rolling sandhills, the white canvas of the general hospital, where there is room for several hundred sick, while more to the south, almost hidden by the rolling ground, is the yellow fever camp. Almost behind you, back down the hill on the shores of Fort Pond Bay, is the quarantine station, the entrance to the detention camp and yellow fever hospital. It is a short mile away, but its yellow flag easily marks it out. At this pier troops from infected ships are landed by barges and the *Vigilant*, an excursion boat of the propellor type, and all the sick come here to be transported in ambulances to the hospitals. A double chain of sentinels guards this part of the island, and no one is allowed to pass in or out. So on all sides of you you are impressed with the fact that this is a hospital camp."

Although much was being done to nurse the sick troopers back to health, most of the credit was due the Red Cross, more than 100 volunteer nurses and many other patriotic civilian organizations. The main work, policy-making and distribution of supplies, was still the jealously guarded prerogative of the War Department, which did its utmost to discourage the willing civilian helpers from even coming out to Montauk, and once there, they were even harassed by the government bureaucrats, while the disabled (and in many instances, dying) soldiers continued to suffer, as related in *The Little*

War Of Private Post, when the man ultimately responsible for official policy and actions inspected Camp Wikoff: "Secretary of War Alger came to the camp; everything had been slicked. Surgeon General Sternberg had ordered that everything must be a model for the Secretary. And it was, except for the men in camp. The Secretary walked through each street in a frock coat and a silk hat; slightly behind him was his staff; golden and immaculate. He was a small man, and slight, with a gray mustache and a goatee. He stopped at a tent and asked pleasantly how everything was. He was told bluntly that everything was rotten. A few said everything was alright, thank you, and were given hell by their squad. He talked to more tents, and kept his staff at a respectful distance. In the street of tents next beyond that he was then inspecting, men went ahead and passed the word: 'Have someone speak — give 'em hell — he wants to know. He's asking.' The street I was in was next. Back of my tent a voice was whispering: 'Get up, get up and tell — Alger's asking questions — have a man speak . . . we'll die if we stay here!'

"I was hastily picked to speak for us.

"The Secretary stopped and looked through the open tent flap.

"'Attention!' someone called. Men rose from their cots.

"'At ease,' said the Secretary. 'How are you men? Can we do anything for you?' His voice was pleasant. It may have been only the ordinary routine question. From the rear of the tent I could hear a tense whisper: 'Go on — get going!' I saluted. I have never forgotten that moment.

"'Mr. Secretary,' I said, 'I am speaking for this tent and many other tents. We are dying here without attention, without rations or medicines. Five men were picked up yesterday morning, dead. For two days men have been washing the grass with brooms so that you would not see the blood and dysentery or know the facts. Latrine boxes were in the streets; they have been removed. Every effort has been made to make this place nice for your inspection. And it's a lie; we're dying of neglect.'

"I was conscious of an audience behind me; men were pressing against the rear wall of the tent. There was another hoarse whisper; 'Go on — give it to him straight.'

"I could see the official staff, two paces beyond, stiffen; one of them, I knew, must be the surgeon-commander of this camp. Maybe they could shoot a sick man at sunrise, but not in front of the Secretary of War. I did not care.

"'You have been lied to in this inspection, Mr. Secretary,' I went on, 'this hospital is a lie. Anyone who tells you different is a liar . . . I have had five quinine and one blue mass since the transport landed. We will die if we are kept here.'"

While most of the spokesmen in the other tents were not as eloquent as Private Post, their point was made. Passes were issued for well soldiers to take the train to New York. The mustering-out process accelerated. But that was small comfort to the immobilized sick and quarantined men. After a century, the haze of time and the passing of the last veterans obscures the facts. If trainloads of food, medicine, volunteers, medical personnel and dignitaries were despatched to Camp Wikoff and so experienced and conscientious an officer as General Wheeler was in command, how could such appalling conditions as Post complained of be possible? Was part of the camp living luxuriously while a half-mile away, misery prevailed? While Charles Johnson Post was certainly an astute participant as well as chronicler of the soldiers' view of the war, he was not beyond engaging in yellow journalism himself, parroting the ridiculous charges against the railroad in his book.

A highlight of the eight-week existence of Camp Wikoff was a visit by the commander-in-chief, President William McKinley, on a clear Sunday, September 4, 1898. Leading the honor guard of mounted cavalry assigned to escort the President's horse-drawn coach from the railroad station was the commander of the 1st Volunteer Cavalry. The reaction of the Chief Executive to seeing his former Assistant Secretary of the Navy for the first time since before the fighting began, was a wonderful breach of protocol possible only in a fully flowering democracy. The incident was related in *The Rise Of Theodore Roosevelt:* "President McKinley . . . arrived on a mission of thanks to Shafter's victorious army. As he settled into his carriage with Secretary Alger, he caught sight of a mounted man grinning at him some twenty yards away. 'Why, there's Colonel Roosevelt,' exclaimed McKinley, and called out, 'Colonel! I'm glad to see you!'

"Secretary Alger manifestly was not, but this did not prevent the President from making an extraordinary public gesture. He jumped out of the carriage and walked toward Roosevelt, who simultaneously tumbled off his horse with the ease of a cowboy. In the words of one observer: The President held out his hand: Colonel Roosevelt struggled to pull off his right glove. He yanked at it desperately and finally inserted the ends of his fingers in his teeth and gave a mighty tug. Off came the glove and a beatific smile came over the Colonel's face as he grasped the President's hand. The crowd which had watched the performance tittered audibly. Nothing more cordial than the greeting between the President and Colonel Roosevelt could be imagined. The President just grinned all over. "Colonel Roosevelt,' he said, 'I'm glad to see you looking so well.'"

This was hardly six weeks after Roosevelt's "round robin" letter had so mortified the McKinley administration. But the President, great leader and understanding man that he was, harbored no animosity toward Roosevelt, as did Alger and many lesser officials. He must have already realized the risk and correctness of the letter and its release for publication and its importance in saving the army. He may also have realized that it could have saved him politically. Any remaining doubts about McKinley's feelings toward Roosevelt were dispelled less than two years later, when running successfully for re-election, the Colonel was his vice presidential running mate.

McKinley's handling of the scandals which hung over his subordinates' prosecution of the war with Spain may not have been quite as laudatory, but as Congress and the public clamored for investigations (and administration heads), the President found himself in an awkward and embarrassing position. Although the term "America the Unready" was applicable to the handling of Army affairs, virtually everything concerning the Navy had gone along beyond expectations (the President also must have been aware that the primary cause of the Navy's high state of preparedness had been his brash young naval undersecretary), but the Chief Executive had to address the issue, which he halfheartedly did. Perhaps it was loyalty to the subordinate officials to whom he had entrusted the prosecution of the war which, after all consideration, was perhaps the most one-sided conflict in history. Or McKinley may have felt that long investigations could destroy the careers of loyal and patriotic public servants, souring the great victory. Of course, such congressional and blue-ribbon commission probes which found evidence of ineptitude — perhaps even criminal corruption — could only do grave political damage to the man ultimately responsible — William McKinley! In addition to the day-to-day horror stories brought back by the mustered-out soldiers concerning lack of plentiful necessities stored nearby, the rejection of desperately needed civilian assistance and other shortcomings, there were the acts of criminal malfeasance: issuing rotten cast-off beef and other rations; soldiers being charged high prices for items that were either government property or for which the government had already paid the vendors; and bunks on the troop ships in which contractors had charged full price, then made big profits by not living up to specifications. Another traumatic thought must have scared the administration: how would Hearst's and Pulitzer's newspapers handle the investigations?

By February 1899, a presidentially appointed commission reported that Secretary Alger should be exonerated of responsibility, but the foul rations scandal was so incriminating that Commissary General Egan, a visible scapegoat, was forced to retire; he then chose to go far from the inquiring press and furious public to Honolulu. McKinley then put an abrupt end to any further investigations, but that did nothing to quell the resentment in the Army or the further questioning by Congress and the citizenry. Finally, after Alger took on General Miles one last time, by trying to strip him of his command of the Army and failing to do so, he resigned as Secretary of War, to be succeeded by the highly respected Elihu H. Root. That proved to be the sop that the people wanted and the scandals slowly receded.

Meanwhile, in Madrid, the Queen Regent was advised by her Cabinet to accept the treaty of peace

Your Uncle Samuel is speechless in the presence of such modest young men.

with the United States. In addition to relinquishing much of Spain's colonial empire to the Americans, the U.S. agreed to pay the bankrupt Spanish government $20 million — ostensibly to help it cover costs of evacuating the Philippines. The money was actually an inducement to accept the American peace terms, reminiscent of the Gadsden Purchase of 1853, when, just a few years after seizing all of northern Mexico, the United States paid the then astronomical sum of $10 million to acquire the portions of what was to become the territories of Arizona and New Mexico south of the Gila River, mainly to provide a future route for the Southern Pacific Railroad. Adding to the American suspicions about the relationships Spain enjoyed with Germany concerning the rapid advance of the United States across the Pacific Ocean, Madrid ceded to Berlin the Caroline Islands and the Ladrones (except Guam) for the sum of $4,375,000 (25,000,000 pesetas).

No sooner had the peace treaty been ratified when the Spanish government sought to punish those responsible for the humiliating loss of *la Guerra Españolamericana*. In their court-martials, Admirals Montejo and Cervera successfully were able to lay the responsibility for their defeats on

the Ministry for Marine — Spain's navy department. The Minister of Marine, Ramón D'Aunon, resigned, and all of the generals and admirals were acquitted.

Although the year 1898 was long before the equality of women began to achieve reality in the United States, the war and the service that the ladies of the country rendered earned them renewed respect and helped lay the foundation for their more substantial advances in the 20th century. Led by Clara Barton, who had been to Cuba to assist the *reconcentrados* before the war broke out, the Red Cross Society raised funds, gathered vast supplies of food, medicine, hospital pajamas, underwear, and other nonuniform items, and recruited nurses — many as volunteers — for the great effort. Most of these hard-laboring and patriotic workers were women. Wealthy women contributed large sums of money and Mrs. Helen Miller Gould not only donated freely, but at Camp Wikoff she personally sought out sick soldiers who had no families to turn to and had them transported to her magnificent mansion overlooking the Hudson River which had been converted into a hospital at her expense. There many otherwise hopeless troopers regained their health — and their morale —

through her generosity. Fully aware of what could happen to young soldiers, she performed another most practical service, according to *Harper's:* "When the soldiers at Montauk Point were mustered out or furloughed they usually went directly to New York, where they often fell victim to the snares of the metropolis and were soon penniless in some low lodging-house. Miss Gould, learning these facts, hired the Salvation Army headquarters and fitted them up as a hotel, where all soldiers were kept without charge. The Salvation Army people were placed in charge; agents were placed on all the trains running to the city from Montauk Point to notify the soldier where a good bed and wholesome food awaited him. The police were requested to take all drunken soldiers and sailors to 'Fort Gould', as they called it, rather than to the police station. The hospitality was accepted by hundreds, and when the soldier was ready to leave, if he had no money, his railroad ticket was purchased for him. And not only this, but headquarters were opened to all who wished to find employment."

Another socially prominent woman who gave selflessly of her time and expertise was General Wheeler's daughter, Anna, a southern lady who came prepared to work relentlessly, as related in *Harper's:* "When General Wheeler announced his determination to go to the war, his daughter Anna applied to the War Department for a commission as nurse, but was notified that none but trained nurses were accepted. Nothing daunted, she managed to enroll with the Red Cross nurses. Her youth, beauty, and social position made conspicuous the service which was gladly performed by a thousand others. Of her five months' hard work she said, in an interview, that for the first time she knew what it was to be perfectly satisfied. Her work engrossed every thought; she was never tired or conscious of heat or discomfort, being so profoundly possessed by a sense of the need there was of help and joy that she could give it."

The accomplishments of female nurses were well documented in an article in the November-December 1975 issue of *Nursing Research,* by Philip A. Kalisch, entitled "Heroines of '98": "At the beginning of the war with Spain, the Medical Department had been reluctant to use female nurses; by the end of the war, the nurses had so demonstrated their value that Congress established a permanent Army Reserve Nurse Corps." While many women nurses had worked in recuperation hospitals during the Civil War, few, if any, were at the front lines and they were only utilized because of the manpower shortage with no consideration being given to making them part of the permanent military establishment. That same attitude prevailed in 1898.

It had only been in 1887 that Congress authorized an Army Hospital Corps to serve in both the rear and front-line areas of operations, to be staffed just by males. At the start of the war, the corps comprised 192 officers and 823 enlisted men, which was hardly adequate for the peacetime regular Army on the eve of a planned ten-fold increase in personnel strength. The Surgeon General, Dr. George M. Sternberg, was opposed to admitting women nurses to military hospitals, insisting that the men of the Hospital Corps would suffice, but did relent concerning certain special cases and dietary work. He also authorized the Daughters of the American Revolution to respond to all inquiries and to maintain a list of eligible applicants, in the event that they may be needed. His response to a bill pending in Congress to authorize female nurses at Army facilities crystallized his bias: "Trained female nurses are out of place as regular attendants of sick and wounded soldiers in the wards of a general hospital."

Kalisch reported the results of denying qualified women the chance to serve: "Strenuous efforts to attract civilian (male) recruits and to persuade medically qualified volunteers to transfer from line regiments resulted in frustration. By August 31 . . . the corps still had barely half the number required for the Army of 275,000, and most of the recruits lacked training and experience. In their search for nurses for the camp hospitals, commanders temporarily detailed squads of infantrymen for ward duty. These detail men, usually the dregs of their units, were worse than useless in caring for patients, and their neglect of elementary sanitary precautions helped spread diseases such as typhoid through the camps." Even trained male nurses lacked in the necessary qualifications so abundant in females: "The male . . . with his inadequate pay and no rank, had little to expect but a full dose of ingratitude. His utmost devotion and best efforts were generally never realized and appreciated. . . . his duties were more arduous and taxing than those of his comrades on the line. Being constantly in contact with infectious diseases, he exposed himself to more danger than on the battlefield. *Most male nurses lacked the gentleness of manner and touch which soothed fretful patients*" (emphasis added). Clearly, the presence of qualified, caring and duty-bound patriotic women was desperately needed, but the bureaucrats of the War Department were bent on upholding their magnificent legacy of policies which had bordered on criminal incompetence!

When Sternberg finally relented and agreed to allow the trickle of female nurses to become a flood necessitated by his own prejudiced ineptitude, the women were thrust into such an abominable morass of unsanitary filth, lack of supplies and assistance, and demoralization that a high percentage of the nurses themselves were to succumb due to the inadequacies, long hours and exposure to typhoid and other bacteria. Chickamauga Park, Georgia was the largest Army base (War Department policy was to place the biggest facilities in the Deep South, logically assuming that their location would help to acclimate the troops to the tropical atmosphere where they would be fighting, but the heat and the humidity made sanitary and disease conditions worse), so sickness was particularly serious there. A totally inadequate and primitive hospital without windows — just holes in the rough-hewn plank walls for ventilation and the admission of millions of flies and mosquitos — was rapidly slammed together in the form of 13 shacks to house the geometrically expanding sick-call soldiers. Most appropriately, it was named Sternberg Hospital, probably by a sarcastic officer with a sardonically witty sense of humor! In the hospital, the heat was described as "tropical . . . a suffocating pressure of steamy, smelly, deadening matter, that passed for air. The flies and mosquitos multiplied by the millions and alternated their feeding between the sickbeds and the mess kitchens." One of the newly arrived female nurses described a typical night: "Two hundred suffering patients, mostly all delirious, were brought to the hospital . . . There was not a bed 'utensil' to be found and we, the nurses, suffered the consequences. The soiled clothing and bedding had to be taken care of and we had no way or equipment to handle it, so as to reduce to a minimum the danger of infection to us. We had no disinfectant whatsoever to use. There was not even one wash basin in these wards for the nurses to wash their hands. At one time, when there was a shortage of water for several days, we were requested 'not to wash at all.'

"The three toilets which were supposed to be adequate for the needs of the 200 nurses, were over 500 feet away from their sleeping quarters. Every one of the nurses had contracted dysentery and under these fearfully unsanitary conditions, consider how inevitable it was, that the majority of the nurses left the Sternberg Hospital service with an intestinal condition which soon became chronic..."

Barbara U. Austin, one of the 166 nurses at Sternberg Hospital, who often labored 12 and 14 hours a day in the stifling Georgia heat of August 1898, related the heroic selflessness of the nurses and the appreciation of their patients: "Our beds were filled with typhoid cases, and all desperately sick. Carrying ice and nourishment up and down the hillside. Rain failed to dampen our ardor as it did our uniforms and frequently left us soaked for the day. How grateful the boys were for these services. It made no difference to us that we were 40 to 50 in a shack when off duty, just room enough to stand between the cots. One lantern hanging in the middle of the building for light." Barbara Austin was to serve 20 years later in the Army Nurse Corps during World War I, where she reported that "conditions were sumptuous as compared with 1898."

It would seem that medical science would have advanced at least as much as other disciplines in the third-century which spanned the war between the states and the Spanish-American War and perhaps it did, but the difference in typhoid fever rates was startling: in the U.S. Army of 1861-1865, it was less than 30 per 1,000 soldiers; in 1898, the rate was more than 141 — almost a five-fold increase! Obviously this was not a case of medical shortcomings; rather the fault lay with the lack of prepared-

ness, supply and personnel in the War Department, the shortcomings resulting in 20,926 cases of typhoid, 2,192 of which were fatal.

President McKinley appointed the renowned retired Civil War Major General Grenville M. Dodge who, just after that conflict, had been responsible for building the Union Pacific portion of the first transcontinental railroad, to lead a commission to investigate the performance of the War Department during the 1898 war. Depositions taken from witnesses at Dodge Commission hearings were, without exception, laudatory of the services of female nurses, compared to the work of males. In one exchange, a major who was a volunteer brigade surgeon gave an answer that would have raised eyebrows a century later, illustrating how word meanings change over time. When asked a question concerning whether female nurses ate separately, or "Do they mess with the men?," he answered that they usually dined at separate tables, but sometimes they were known to mess with surgeons! Despite this messing, the Dodge Commission strongly recommended the creation of a female reserve corps of nurses "ready to serve when necessity shall arise." This recommendation, plus other advice from military commanders and leading nurses, resulted in the establishment of the female Army Nurse Corps by Congress on February 2, 1901.

The value of the women nurses in military hospitals was summed up in a report from Fortress Monroe, referring to their work, which ". . . surprised not only the War Department, but even the physicians themselves in charge of the hospital. Out of 1,572 cases brought to this point, but 34 deaths (of which three were non-medical) occurred. This record is the best of any hospital during the war, and it is a question if a better record has ever been made considering the condition of the patients, and the difficulties encountered . . . the physicians themselves have said that without the nurses, the record would have contained many more fatalities, and the mortality might have reached as high as 30 or 40 percent. This seems almost incredible, but it is true..."

The women of the old Confederacy worked as hard and with as much devotion to the cause and the servicemen as did their Northern and Western sisters, often more so, since the largest Army camps were in the South. Prominent women's organizations exerted monumental efforts: the Daughters of the American Revolution Hospital Corps contracted more than half (approximately 1,000) of the 1,700-plus nurses who saw wartime service; and the Women's Christian Temperance Union, as well as women of many church congregations, maintained rest homes for military personnel. The stories of the fine work done and the appreciation of the soldier recipients are long and honorable, and just as the circumstances of Yankees and Rebels fighting side by side in 1898 did so much to end Civil War animosities, so did the self-sacrificing efforts of American women, who for the first time, had come out of their houses and the shadows of their husbands.

With the quarantine lifted, all of the volunteers were mustered out of the service at Camp Wikoff and the regulars returned to their permanent garrisons by the end of September; many of the career soldiers were to find themselves on occupation duty in the far-off new possessions in the Caribbean Sea and the Pacific Ocean, as Army and Navy engineering units began constructing permanent bases and renovating the abandoned Spanish installations. Now a great world power, the United States fortunately could not only field competent and experienced soldiers and sailors to take on the vast new responsibilities, but the civilian population was enthusiastically quite prepared to back them solidly and the elected leaders possessed the fortitude and the vision to proceed with the right mix of caution and aggressiveness to make clear to the other Powers that the changes were indeed permanent. Less than two months af-

ter the disbanding of the Rough Riders, Theodore Roosevelt was elected governor of New York State, the first big step on his rapid ascendancy to the presidency of the nation. Many thought that would occur in 1904 — after the completion of a second term by McKinley — but just three years after the end of the war, an assassin's bullets speeded up the process.

Many of the victorious sailors and soldiers returned home to joyous parades and receptions, for they had won a "Splendid Little War" which even civilians not well versed in politics and foreign affairs could see had broad implications far into the looming 20th century. Sampson and Schley sailed their squadrons into east coast ports which welcomed them with celebrations befitting their great victories, but Dewey was still tied down in the western Pacific and would not return for a year. When at last he sailed USS *Olympia* into New York Harbor, "Dewey Day" — September 26, 1899 — became a citywide commotion to be long remembered.

The United States quickly pressed every type of vessel which it could acquire into service for the 1898 war, including ferry boats, which, of course, were never intended to venture out into the open sea. Yet the *USS Governor Russell* (named for a recently-deceased governor of Massachusetts), a wooden bridge ferry, was converted into an auxiliary gunboat almost immediately after her 1898 launching. She was first sent to New York, then to Port Royal, South Carolina, then up and down the coast, sometimes carrying ammunition.

Blundering into severe storms on at least two occasions in July and September, the ferry fortunately made it to a harbor each time. A dramatic photograph shows her deck awash and one of her guns securely wrapped in waterproof canvas during one of the storms which battered her. Because of the damage caused by weather of a severity she was not designed to endure, *Governor Russell* was ruled unfit for service and decommissioned on September 28, 1898, when hardly six months old.

As in all conflicts in modern American history — beginning with the Civil War — the domestic railroads were the backbone of transport of military supplies and organized troop movements, as well as the assemblyline of production and distribution of everything from rations to 67-ton 13-inch battleship guns in the Spanish-American War. The small, local Long Island Rail Road played a prominent role in the conflict by serving Camps Black and Wikoff. The 12-track terminal at Montauk (above), with its warehouses, was built by the L.I.R.R. in just six days; a century later it would have taken six months for the management to decide who the multimillion dollar contract outside consultants would be! The Camp Wikoff railroad timetable (below) showed an average of five round-trips per day, including "Special Fast Express" trains which brought visitors to the camp and carried soldiers out on furlough or after discharge from service. Although the yellow fever section of the rambling post was heavily guarded by mounted cavalry and nobody was allowed to enter that area, the entire facility was considered to be a quarantine camp (the main purpose of locating it at isolated Montauk), yet the railroad was permitted to bring thousands of visitors — many from the heart of New York City — each week, raising the question of exactly what was the definition of a "quarantine camp!"

Above, Theodore Roosevelt Collection, Harvard College Library

Below, Ron Ziel collection

LONG ISLAND RAILROAD.

Taking effect August 28th, 1898.

SCHEDULE OF TRAINS TO

MONTAUK

(CAMP WIKOFF.)

FROM NEW YORK, L. I. CITY AND BROOKLYN FOR MONTAUK.

Leave NEW YORK (foot of 34th St. E. R.), Week Days, 8.25 a.m. (8.50 a.m., Special Fast Express), (1.20 p.m. Saturdays only), 3.20 p. m. (and 4.50 p. m., Special Fast Express). Sundays, (8.50 a. m., Special Fast Express) and 9.00 a. m.

Leave LONG ISLAND CITY, Week Days, 8.36 a. m. (9.00 a. m., Special Fast Express), (1.32 p.m. Saturdays only), 3.33 p. m. (and 5.00 p. m., Special Fast Express). Sundays, (9.00 a. m., Special Fast Express) and 9.10 a. m.

Leave BROOKLYN (Flatbush Avenue), Week Days, 8.30 a m. (8.54 a.m., Special Fast Express), (1.40 p.m. Saturdays only), 3.24 p.m. (and 4.54 p. m., Special Fast Express). Sundays, (8.53 a. m., Special Fast Express) and 9.03 a. m.

FROM MONTAUK FOR NEW YORK AND BROOKLYN.

Leave MONTAUK, Week Days, 5.50 a. m., for Brooklyn and New York, making all way stops to Patchogue.

"   "   9.00 a. m., (Special Fast Express,) for New York only.

"   "   2.00 p. m., for Brooklyn and New York, making all way stops to Babylon.

"   "   5.00 p. m., (Special Fast Express,) for Brooklyn and New York.

"   "   7.30 p. m., for Brooklyn and New York, making all way stops to Babylon: also stopping at Amityville, Massapequa, Freeport and Rockville Centre.

Leave MONTAUK, Sundays, 6.30 a. m., for Brooklyn and New York, making all way stops to Babylon.

"   "   3.55 p. m., for Brooklyn and New York making all way stops to Babylon, excepting Bayport and Great River.

"   "   5.00 p. m., (Special Fast Express) for Brooklyn and New York.

"   "   7.48 p. m., for Brooklyn and New York, making all way stops to Babylon, excepting Mastic, Brookhaven and Bellport; also stopping at Amityville, Massapequa, Freeport and Rockville Centre.

☞ **SPECIAL EXCURSION TICKETS** At One-Way Fare for the Round Trip, **$3.50** VALID FOR THREE DAYS,

Will be sold between New York, Long Island City and Brooklyn and Montauk for trains marked "Special Fast Express." These tickets will not be honored on any other train.

W. F. POTTER,   H. M. SMITH,
General Superintendent.   Traffic Manager.

Long Island City, 9-10-98—2 M.

The lookout at the signal station observation tower at Montauk (left), peering through his two feet-long spyglass, was the first to sight the ships coming in from Cuba in early August. Disembarking from their transport at the railroad dock on Fort Pond Bay, the returning troops (below) were double-time marching down the embankment to report to their designated bivouac area. Red Cross volunteers were on hand with biscuits and hot coffee for the hungry soldiers. One of the Red Cross women, Mrs. Mott (upper right), was pouring coffee for battle-and disease-worn soldiers, many of whom carried a popular war souvenir — the Cuban machete; the man at the right with a drum had two of the cane-cutting knives. The picturesque army wagons — pulled by four mules or horses — then carried men and equipment through the dunes and over the hills (lower right) to the tent city rising in the background.

One of the oldest buildings at Montauk, Long Island, which survives at this writing is Third House, photographed in 1898(above), when it was the headquarters of the army command at Camp Wikoff. In her book, *Montauk, Three Centuries of Romance, Sport and Adventure*, dating from 1938, Jeanette Edwards Rattray, the late publisher of the weekly *East Hampton Star* newspaper, related some of Colonel Roosevelt's adventures at Third House. "Some of the officers stayed at Third House. Colonel Theodore Roosevelt was there with his famous Rough Riders. He lived in camp with his men; but Mrs. Roosevelt came on to visit him, bringing Alice (Mrs. Nicholas Longworth, then in her teens) and Theodore Jr., a boy of twelve; they stayed at Third House. "Everybody adored the Colonel; both his men and the Long Islanders who came to know him at this time ... There was a time, right after the Spanish-American War, when commissions were dealt out pretty freely; sons of congressmen and senators became captains and majors overnight, regardless of feelings of officers in the regular army. These youngsters would come down to Montauk with their valets and fancy clothes to stay at Third House; a simple old farmhouse without even running water. Good, substantial country food was served hot from four a.m. (when gunning parties would start out) until eleven p.m. Then Mrs. Conklin and her helpers had to stop. One night a frightened servant girl woke her about midnight, whispering; 'Young Captain M. is in the dining room swearing something awful! I've brought out everything in the pantry, cold meat and cake and milk, but he says he's got to have a hot supper!' Dressing softly not to waken her husband, Mrs. Conklin tiptoed downstairs. There sat the young captain, roaring hungry after an evening ride in the moonlight, probably with one of the sixty-five pretty nurses looking after the sick soldiers. Suddenly the door of a little office off the dining room filled up — there stood Colonel Roosevelt. He stepped over to the table: 'I am very sorry, Mrs. Conklin, that you have been disturbed; what you have here is good enough for the President of the United States. Please go and get your rest.' Third House never saw young Captain M. again. In the morning he was gone; some stranger came and got his things. Mr. Conklin asked after him, he liked him, he was such a 'witchcat.' Mrs. Conklin said, 'Oh he's gone.' That was all." A general view of the tents (right) of the 2nd, 8th and 10th infantry regiments. A trio of Rough Riders (upper right) enjoying the camaraderie of a coffee break.

Above, upper right, Suffolk County Historical Society

Lower right, Theodore Roosevelt Collection, Harvard College Library

234

During the long summer days at Montauk, with little in the way of duties to perform, the recuperating soldiers – including the 1st Volunteer Cavalry Regiment – fought boredom as they looked forward to returning home. Although Colonel Theodore Roosevelt was busy with the paperwork of mustering out his men and perhaps concentrating even more on the imminent political campaign for the governorship of the state of New York, he found time to mingle with his men. The Rough Riders had three mascots: a little dog named "Cuba," a bobcat known as "Josephine," and "Teddy," a full-grown eagle. Roosevelt is shown petting the eagle (opposite, top) while a few of his troopers play with the cat and the dog, as others look on. These veterans, about to leave the service, have discarded their military bearing, even though they were members of the most elite unit of the war. Their boots covered with dust, some unbloused, with hats askew, most not wearing belts, and one man with his hat brass pinned to his shirt, they all just want to go home! Roosevelt was always ready to oblige photographers, as the famous pose of him writing a letter in his tent (right) shows. It is highly doubtful that he would actually be handling a pen on a summer day while wearing his heavy cavalry gloves! It was on September 13th, 1898, that the Rough Riders began to deactivate – with a deeply emotional ceremony. The commander had announced his intention to bid a personal farewell to every surviving man in the regiment, but before the hundreds of his troopers lined up, he was confronted with a large object on a table covered with a shroud. When it was unveiled, there stood a sculpture by Frederic Remington, commissioned by the enlisted men. Roosevelt was deeply moved, especially since it had been the rank and file and not the officers who made the gesture. With "The Bronco Buster" statue behind him (opposite bottom), he then shook hands with and spoke to each man. So devoted were the troopers to their commander that one man later commented that a handshake seemed too little and that it had been the only time that he had wanted to hug another man! It seems almost incredible that this 1st Volunteer Cavalry Regiment, arguably the most famous and legendary Army unit in American history, had

been in a combat zone just three weeks, had seen heavy fighting for five days and had been in existence for merely 133 days! It was only six weeks later that Roosevelt was winding up his lightning campaign for governor of the Empire State as he addressed an enthusiastic crowd from the back of his whistle-stop train (below) at Greenport, Long Island, just a few miles from Montauk Point. Being an early devotee of public relations and realizing the influence of first-time perceptions, the candidate wore a hat and clothing of a military cut to constantly remind the voters of his recent heroic exploits; they responded by giving him a large majority on Election Day.

Three photos, Theodore Roosevelt Collection, Harvard College Library

Below, Suffolk County Historical Society

Two photos, Theodore Roosevelt Collection, Harvard College Library

Lower right, Suffolk Country Historical Society

The 24th Infantry (Colored) marching to their bivouac area (above), on the desolate, rolling hill country of Montauk. There were four Negro regiments that fought in the Spanish-American War: the 9th and the 10th Cavalry and the 24th and 25th Infantry. It is noteworthy that six Medals of Honor were won by blacks in the 1898 war (out of a total of 109), which was double the number given to blacks in the two world wars and Korea combined! It was not until more than a half-century after World War II that seven additional medals from that conflict went to blacks. Had the colored regiments been led by black rather than white officers, there would probably have been a higher proportion of Medals of Honor bestowed upon them, since officers are awarded the nation's highest military honor to a greater degree than enlisted men. Considering the statistics, blacks were the recipients of the award in by far the greatest proportion in the Spanish-American War than in any other conflict. Even Vietnam, which saw them receive 20 (of a total of 239), does not match the 1898 proportion, for the number of black American

fighting men in the latter conflict was about 40 percent, compared to just 10 percent in the war with Spain.

When President McKinley paid a visit of appreciation to the soldiers at Camp Wikoff on September 4, 1898, it was quite a media event. He is shown (upper right), waving his hat from his carriage, with Secretary of War Alger alongside him. The man in the foreground is easily identified as a Rough Rider — wearing the regimental polka-dot bandanna. The photo of a cavalry formation at the Southampton station of the Long Island Rail Road (lower right) is difficult to identify, since the information on the original negative envelope referred to them as "Rough Riders" and the date was 1899 — a full year after the 1st Volunteer Cavalry had been disbanded! Probably the date was 1898, with photographer Fullerton making a mistake later. Why these cavalrymen were posted at a station 25 miles west of Camp Wikoff is not known; possibly they were participating in a local victory celebration.

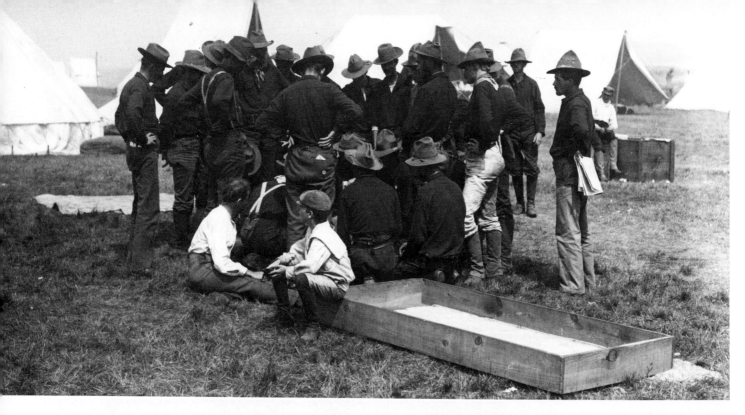

Camp life at Montauk was boring — especially for infantrymen who didn't have horses to exercise and care for — so the troops entertained themselves in various ways. Crap shooting was a much preferred pastime, as the two civilians — a man and a young boy — seated in the foreground are learning from the troopers in the huddle behind them.

Theodore Roosevelt Collection, Harvard College Library

Mustered out of active duty Army service by the end of August 1898, the 33rd Michigan Regiment is boarding the ferryboat *Newburgh* at Long Island City, bound for New York and a train ride home. All of the photos credited to the Suffolk County Historical Society were 5x 7-inch glass-plates made by the renowned photographer, agronomist, publicist and Long Island Rail Road special agent, Hal B. Fullerton.

Suffolk County Historical Society

The American Red Cross acquired, among other vessels, a sleek yacht which was quickly converted into a medical supply boat named *The Red Cross* (below), shown tied up idle in Florida in June 1898, because the War Department had refused the offer of her services. As reported by *Harper's*: "The reason given for its refusal is a good illustration of the technicalities by which military authorities are governed, and which strictly construed, often prove a rule 'how not to do it.' A government, under the Geneva Constitution, could accept a hospital-ship built and fitted out under its supervision, and to be used for no other purpose. But this boat contained also medical supplies, and this prevented it coming under the rule. Permission for *The Red Cross* to take coal from any naval coaling-station or boat, receipts to be given by the Red Cross representative, and bills to be paid by the committee was refused, and in various ways the Red Cross was made to feel that its assistance was not desired." Because of such bureaucratic nincompoopery, American soldiers severely wounded at San Juan were laid out on bare floors at Siboney, without even the rudimentaries of blankets and cots, much less medicine and trained medical personnel, while the War Department claimed that it had all that was necessary and outside help was neither required nor wanted.

National Archives

Although in her mid-70s during the Spanish-American War, Clara Barton (upper left), who had organized the American Red Cross in 1881, played a leading role in aiding the victims of Weyler's *Reconcentracion* policy in Cuba and coordinating civilian relief efforts to assist the U.S. Army and Navy during the conflict. She was to remain active until her death, at age 91, in 1912. Many high-ranking women in medical professions took leading roles in relieving the overwhelmed War Department in 1898, including Anne Caroline Maxwell (upper right, in later years), who was Superintendent of Nurses at the Presbyterian Hospital Training School for Nurses in New York City. She led the nurses at the Sternberg Field Hospital, where she never ceased reminding them that the nation was watching and that American women would be judged by their performance of duty. Strong discipline was stressed by Nurse Maxwell and her women never failed her. While her father led the Cavalry Division in Cuba, Anna Wheeler (below) worked long days under trying circumstances to alleviate the suffering of wounded and sick soldiers and return them to good health. Her devoted concern and demeanor, plus her social status, did much to emphasize the important work of the women nurses, accenting the need for their services on a permanent basis. The war artists of 1898 created excellent renderings which captured well the atmosphere and the emotions of camp life and operations in the Spanish-American War. The drawing "A Box from Home" (opposite) shows a nurse sitting in a tent with a recuperating soldier so recently aged beyond his years. His expression of admiration and gratitude is evident in this fine work by W. A. Rogers, one of the most notable turn-of-the-century illustrators.

Above, Library of Congress

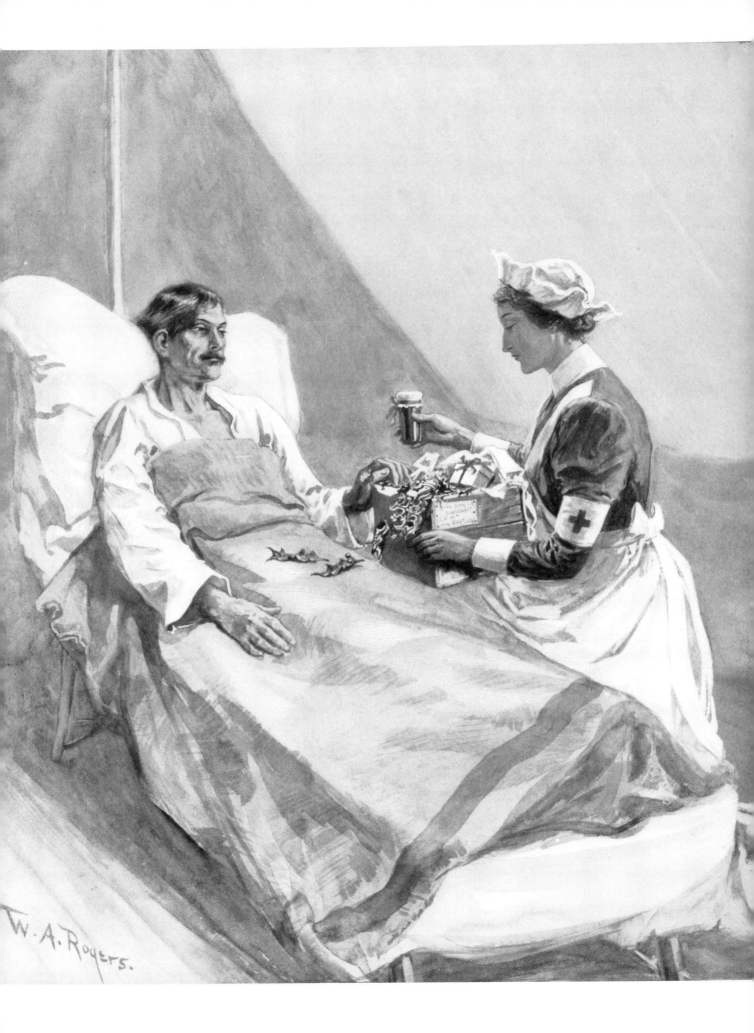

The American people were longing for the return of their greatest hero of the Spanish-American War, Admiral George Dewey, but he was to remain on board his flagship *USS Olympia*, helping govern the new possession of the Philippines until May of 1899. He then headed west, through the Indian Ocean, the Suez Canal and the Mediterranean Sea, stopping at various ports where he was welcomed with the respect and honor accorded a conquering hero. The most elaborate outpouring of affection and welcome upon Dewey's return was bestowed upon him in New York City; the metropolis eagerly awaiting *Olympia's* arrival in the harbor. Ready for the flagship were the cruisers and battleships of the North Atlantic fleet, including *USS Indiana* shown arriving at an east coast port (left) still wearing her gray warpaint, after returning from Cuba. The host ship of the fleet was the cruiser *USS Chicago*, a magnificent vessel (opposite), which had missed action in the war, spending the whole period in dry dock being refitted at the Brooklyn Navy Yard. When *Olympia* dropped anchor in New York Harbor (below), she was attended by little steam launches while many other craft — from tugboats to passenger steamers — circled around, their occupants admiring the symbol of victory and hoping perhaps to get a glimpse of the admiral on the bridge.

Above, collection of George H. Foster

Below, opposite, Suffolk County Historical Society

On Manhattan's Fifth Avenue, between 23rd and 24th streets, a magnificent victory arch had been erected for the parade to pass under the impressive and short-lived structure. The *New York Journal* newspaper was housed adjacent to the arch and an illuminated sign (below) in the right background reads: *N.Y. Journal* Dewey Celebration. The inscription on the pediment above the arch way (upper right) proclaims: TO THE GLORY OF THE AMERICAN NAVY AND IN GREETING TO OUR ADMIRAL, A GRATEFUL CITY RELYING ON THEIR VALOR HAS BUILT THIS ARCH. MDCCCXCIX. Although the greatest of all American band leaders, John Philip Sousa, was renowned as "the march king" for the rousing compositions he gave to the American people and the world, his band rarely marched! During the 40 years (1892-1932) that his band played almost 15,000 concerts, a mere seven occasions of great importance were to turn Sousa's concert band into a marching band. One of those significant events to be graced with the marching Sousa Band was Dewey Day in New York. Marching along the west side of Manhattan (lower right) with warships at anchor in the Hudson River and the hills of New Jersey behind, Sousa's musicians proclaimed the welcome home for the most beloved hero of the Spanish-American War. Still heavily booked for future engagements, the band master died at age 78, in 1932. During the year following the war, many major celebrations were held in cities around the United States. The great victory revue in Philadelphia featured an arch and sculpture as impressive as the Dewey welcome in New York.

Below, The New-York Historical Society

September 26, 1899 was a day long to be remembered in New York, and the parade for Admiral Dewey marched in bright sunlight, the Hero of Manila Bay riding in a carriage drawn by four horses (left) driven by a coachman with a sailor from the *Olympia* seated next to him. This angle obscures the silk-hatted man next to Dewey; he was President William McKinley. During their first meeting after Dewey's return the commander in chief mentioned that although he had the White House naval files scrutinized, there was no paperwork concerning the very touchy and volatile face-off between Dewey and the German Admiral Von Diedrichs in Manila Bay. In his own humble yet authoritative way,

the admiral replied: "You had enough on your mind, Mr. President, so I handled it." At the start of the parade, Marines from Dewey's squadron (above) are waiting to step off on the line of march. That night saw a grandiose light show supplied by electricity and gunpowder (below), in a panoramic photograph of lower Manhattan taken from Brooklyn Heights. To the far left of the picture, beneath exploding fireworks, the battleships *Indiana* and *Massachusetts* are firing salutes; in the center a barge load of flares and rockets ignites, and at the right, with floodlights mounted on its towers, the Brooklyn Bridge span displays a huge electric sign — probably the first of its kind — WELCOME DEWEY.

At a U.S. Army Signal Corps field telegraph station, the telegrapher hands a message to a mounted courier, to be delivered to the headquarters of one of the divisions advancing north of Manila.

The Philippine Insurrection

The question of what the United States should do with the Philippines became a burning topic of national debate even before the Spanish-American War had ended. The anti-imperialists were appalled that idealistic America, which had set the example for so many subjugated colonial people in casting off foreign domination and establishing self-government, was joining in the mad scramble to divide much of the world into empires and spheres of influence. The jingoes felt that if the imperialistic Europeans and the Japanese were seizing every piece of real estate in sight, the United States could find itself threatened by powerful fleets other than its own controlling the sea lanes, and besides, American rule would be far more democratic and reasonable than that of the arrogant Europeans. Hadn't the populations long dominated by Spain just raucously welcomed the Americans as liberators wherever U.S. soldiers showed their flag? The McKinley administration was under pressure from the left to issue a proclamation of policy similar to that concerning Cuba: that once order was established and native government functioning, the newly acquired colonies would be set free. The powerful warhawks who were flushed with the vindication of their views which had caused the recent war, pushed harder for an expanding American world role, and they were already planning for global dominance by the United States in the approaching 20th century. Led by rapidly ascending leaders like Theodore Roosevelt, the Social Darwinists passionately believed that the superior evolution of the Caucasian race (epitomized by the American nation) conferred both the opportunity and the awesome responsibility to lead (by force, if necessary) the unenlightened and less advanced races to the democratic and Christian western ideals.

There was justification for the United States taking over the Philippines, since the final defeat of its Spanish rulers had left the island country totally exposed to any and every expansionist power that might covet its riches and its strategic location. Because of centuries of harsh and dictatorial Spanish colonial rule whose policies kept the native population dependent, subservient, uneducated, and fearful, there was no civil service, ruling class or military hierarchy to govern and defend the country. With German and Japanese intentions in the Pacific abundantly clear and the British and French also active, with the Dutch controlling nearby Indonesia, it would take just months — perhaps weeks — for a half-dozen imperial powers to sail their formidable fleets into Filipino waters and begin fighting over, or more likely merely dividing up, the vast archipelago. Under U.S. control, the Philippines would remain united and the two-generations process of educating and training a civil service and military officer corps could pro-

ceed peacefully and effectively. Emilio Aguinaldo and his supporters, disgusted with hundreds of years of Spanish tyranny and naive concerning their vulnerability, disagreed — their opposing views soon taking forms of expression which were both disconcerting and deadly to their American rulers. Actually, in the long term, the policies of benevolent imperialism instituted by the United States were in the best interests of the Filipinos. When granted independence following World War II after nearly a half-century of American governance and tutelage, the Philippines was a nation of educated and democratically instilled people, ready to live in democracy and economic advancement. A Filipino official who had dealt with both Spanish and American overlords summed up his experience by remarking that a Filipino was regarded as totally inferior by the Spaniards and was never allowed to express opinions or make suggestions regarding government policies. The Americans, to his pleasant surprise, not only listened and often accepted native ideas, but Filipinos "could argue with the Americans and win . . ." Forty-eight years of American rule, interrupted only by three years of brutal and bloody Japanese occupation during World War II, left the Philippines with strong traditions of democracy and capitalism as it matured into a regional power in the western Pacific Basin.

But before this peaceful evolution of the Philippines could take place, a vicious and bloody conflict between the native insurgents and the occupying American forces, lasting for more than a year, with sporadic flare-ups into the early years of the 20th century, was waged as virtually a continuation of the Spanish-American War. Once the combined Army and Navy forces under General Merritt and Admiral Dewey forced the Spaniards to surrender Manila, within six months Aguinaldo's ragtag but often well-disciplined and motivated rebels, finding the hated Spaniards out of action, turned their guns on the victorious Yankees. Embarrassed and defensive concerning Philippine policy, the American government reluctantly ordered the Army and Navy to suppress Aguinaldo's forces, as the opposition at home was gaining support. The opponents soon organized the Anti-Imperialist League and attracted many prominent supporters, including Grover Cleveland, John Sherman (McKinley's former Secretary of State), Mark Twain, Andrew Carnegie, and Samuel Gompers — a politically and socially diverse group which ran the gamut from left to right. Those among the racially conscious anti-imperialists feared that black- and brown-skinned nonwhites would become a divisive and troublesome responsibility, never to be released from American parentage and emigrating to the United States to take jobs from American workers. A century later, that very issue had returned to a dominant role in domestic political discourse in the United States. The victory over Spain had left the Americans no choice but to assume the responsibility for the liberated former Spanish possessions, and the support for the imperialists in Washington was far stronger than for their opponents, as was expressed by a New England clergyman: "I'm proud of my country in Cuba and Puerto Rico . . . teaching the people to govern themselves and to enjoy the blessings of Christian civilization . . . this Spanish war has not been a grab for empire, but an heroic effort to free the oppressed, and to teach the millions of ignorant, debased human beings thus freed how to live." A mythical first-generation Irish saloon proprietor and creation of a Chicago newspaper writer, Finley Peter Dunne, was the most popular political and social satirist in the United States in the 1890s. As the famed "Mr. Dooley," he was quoted on every issue, including imperialism: ". . . if th' American people can govern thimsilves, they can govern anything that walks."

Emilio Aguinaldo restrained his Tagalog army for six months, while awaiting the wording of the final peace treaty with Spain and the votes of Congress on the matter, all the while building elaborate fortifications around towns such as Iloilo, just beyond Manila. As expected, the treaty unconditionally ceded control of the Philippines to the United States, but the vagueness of a resolution of the U.S. Senate, which declared that the U.S. had not actually annexed the Philippines but that it would be just protecting and governing the archipelago until they attained the political stability and experience to be self-governing, perplexed Aguinaldo's representatives in Washington, D.C., led by Felipe Agoncello. President McKinley forwarded the peace treaty to the Senate after much personal soul-searching over the Philippines: "I walked the floor of the White House night after night until midnight; and I am not ashamed to tell you gentlemen, that I went down on my knees and prayed Almighty God for light and guidance more than one night. And one night it came to me this way — I don't know how it was, but it came: (1) That we could not give them back to Spain — that would be cowardly and dishonorable; (2) That we would not turn them over to France or Germany — our commercial rivals in the Orient — that would be bad business and discreditable; (3) That we could not leave them to themselves — they were unfit for self-government — and they would soon have anarchy and misrule over there worse than Spain's was; and (4) That there was nothing left for us to do but to take them all, and to educate the Filipinos, and uplift and civilize and Christianize them, and by God's grace do the best we could by them . . . I went to bed and went to sleep and slept soundly . . ."

Thus had William McKinley, in less than a year, put his anti-war feelings, based on his Civil War experiences, where he had seen "the bodies piled high" and his belief that the United States had realized its Manifest Destiny with the closing of the Western frontier in 1890, behind him and had realistically — even courageously — confronted the new reality of global power. Supported by majorities in Congress and the population, the President forwarded the peace treaty to Capitol Hill, where, after spirited debate, it became law in February 1899. William Jennings Bryan, the candidate of the Democratic Party whom McKinley had defeated in 1896 and who had served as a colonel of volunteers in the recent war, was an anti-imperialist, and using that as a major issue he was beaten even more decisively in their rematch in the election of 1900. Still, McKinley's reasons for retaining the Philippines included protecting America's business interests and "Christianizing" a native population which had been incessantly given the message by zealous Spanish priests for nearly 400 years! No sooner had the deliberations of Congress concerning the Philippines been completed, when Agoncello despatched his dismay to Aguinaldo and left the United States. Whether or not the charismatic Filipino leader wanted to further pursue negotiations was rendered moot by what his followers perceived as the same old foreign domination — including their soldiers being banned from their capital — so during the night of February 4, 1899, a Nebraska regiment sentry fired at a group of natives who were running across the military cordon around Manila. Suddenly, fire erupted along the cordon boundary, and the next day, almost 20,000 Filipinos attacked the U.S. front, commencing a fierce series of battlefield and guerilla engagements which, over three years, would cause more American casualties than did the war with Spain.

On August 6, 1898, while the Americans and Spaniards were fighting on the outskirts of Manila, a week before the peace protocols and the surrender of the capital, Aguinaldo issued a proclamation addressed to foreign governments, including the United States, outlining the policies and intentions of his government: "The revolutionary government of the Philippines on its establishment explained through the messages dated the 23rd of June last the true causes of the Philippine revolution, showing according to the evidence that this popular movement is a result of the laws which regulate the life of a people which aspire to progress and to perfection by the sole road to liberty.

"In (the 15 provinces ruled by the revolutionary government) complete order and perfect tranquility reign, administered by the authorities elected by the provinces in accordance with the organic decrees dated 18th and 23rd of June last. The revolution holds . . . about 9,000 prisoners of war . . . and at the end of the war (against Spanish rule) it has more than 30,000 combatants *organized in the form of a regular army.* (Emphasis added.)

"In this situation the chiefs of the towns comprised in the above-mentioned provinces, interpreting the sentiments which animate those who have elected them, have *proclaimed the independence of the Philippines* (emphasis added) petitioning the

revolutionary government that it will entreat and obtain from foreign governments recognition of its belligerency and its independence, in the firm belief that the Philippine people have already arrived at that state at which they can and ought to govern themselves."

That proclamation, coming six months before the outbreak of hostilities between the Filipino and American armies, should have left little doubt in the minds of American officials and military officers that if the U.S. forces remained to occupy the Philippines, war was inevitable, for the natives considered their country to be independent and free. Once the Agoncello mission had failed to gain that recognition from Washington, D.C., Filipino fighters merely transferred their hatred from Spain to America. Knowing the terrain and supported by the native population, while fortified with revolutionary ideals (Americans called it drug-inspired fanaticism), the insurgents soon gave the U.S. forces a much tougher fight than ever the Spaniards did — with the exception of San Juan Hill.

The week during the general commencement of hostilities on February 4th, the Filipinos had begun firing sporadically at American outposts and tensions were exacerbated. U.S. troop movements were intensified on February 6 and the following day skirmishing began; on February 8, orders were issued to prepare to attack Iloilo, as the main Filipino force was being entrenched at Caloocan. Meanwhile, at Manila on that same day, Admiral Dewey informed the insurgents holding San Roque, adjacent to Cavite and the strategic causeway connected to it, that they must withdraw by 9:00 the next morning, or he would bombard that town. The rebels fired the town, and as the 51st

On March 14, 1899, a day of heavy action on Luzon, the firing line of the Washington Volunteer Infantry knew the disadvantage of not yet having been issued smokeless powder. Not all soldiers fired their rifles according to the training manuals; the fourth man from the right, lying on his back, has positioned his boot in the sling to steady his weapon.

National Archives

Iowa Regiment and the California Heavy Artillery advanced around the intense flames, the withdrawing Filipinos, armed with Mausers, thousands of which they had captured when the Spaniards surrendered, laid down a heavy defensive fire. On February 10, the Americans staged a general advance toward Caloocan, and the irresistible inertia of the recently liberated and their deliverers surging into bloody conflict became unstoppable. As the sound and the smoke and dust of battle reverberated through the tepid tropical air on February 11, Iloilo, set ablaze and abandoned by the insurgents, was taken over by the U.S. Army. That same day, two ships under Dewey's command, the *Charleston* and the *Monadnock*, shelled Malabon, as the opening exchanges of gunfire began at Caloocan. The 14th Infantry also found itself in a nasty firefight just 12 miles south of Manila.

The war then moved forward with savage intensity, including within Manila itself. By February 14, after a thousand Filipinos were driven out of Jaro, near Iloilo, in heavy fighting, a fierce engagement had been fought at Pateros, ten miles southeast of Manila, 500 insurgents were defeated near Santa Barbara. One of the high officials of the Philippine government, headquartered at Malolos, issued an order on February 15, that the secret "territorial militia" units and the "defenders of the

Philippines" who were scattered throughout metropolitan Manila should rise up that night to carry out a sudden campaign to liquidate the occupying Americans and all foreigners "without compassion." The order called for the extermination of "all other individuals (non-Filipinos), of whatever race they may be," including, it was supposed, the more than 40,000 ethnic Chinese — ingredients for an horrendous bloodbath! "...war without quarter (against) the false Americans who have deceived us," was of the first order. But the U.S. command caught wind of it, and the 13th Minnesota and the 1st Oregon Infantry quickly dispersed throughout the city, arresting 150 suspected conspirators, giving their leaders second thoughts and the plot fizzled out, only to resurface a week later.

This time the more fanatical elements among Filipino patriots had decided that the best way to rid Manila of foreigners was to simply burn down the entire city! On the night of February 22, several neighborhoods consisting largely of frame and thatch structures were simultaneously set alight, but foreign civilians and American soldiers brought most under control, except in the Tondo district, which was a native quarter, containing few homes or businesses owned by the enemies of the incendiaries. When American soldiers fought the flames, "... our men were received with a fusillade of rifle and revolver shots. The 'defenders of the Philippines' had to be shot or expelled before their houses could be saved," according to *Harper's*. Within three days, over 1,200 suspects were arrested in Manila, squelching plans to set fire to the walled sector of the city and the business district north of the Pasig River.

The Filipinos were far from united in opposition to American rule, as Major General Elwell S. Otis was pleasantly surprised to discover on that memorable George Washington's birthday, February 22, 1899. Even as the guns of Dewey's fleet and those on the Manila fortresses were firing salutes honoring the first American president, a commission of high-ranking native officials from one of the biggest islands, Negros, met with Otis in the capital. The four commissioners, speaking on behalf of the inhabitants of Negros, offered to accept any peace terms stipulated by the Americans, adding that Aguinaldo's sympathizers had already been forced to leave the island. General Otis promised them that a considerate government would be established, prompting the ranking commissioner and president of the Negros provisional government to propose the raising of an army of his citizens to fight as allies of the Americans against the insurrectionists on Luzon. This apparent combination of tribal animosity and shrewd realization that the United States would win the conflict enabled the leaders on Negros to ensure a most favorable position for their jurisdiction under American rule. A press report just five days later stated that "8,000 rebels were anxious to surrender" and that "Aguinaldo was inclined to accept pacific overtures." The same despatch reported that Otis had refused to meet with a delegation from the Aguinaldo government. It was reported in Washington, D.C. that "the only instructions sent to Otis were to refuse all overtures, but, if the natives continue in a hostile attitude, to pursue them to the death," which was exactly what the U.S. field commanders were doing.

In the first week of heavy fighting, the Americans claimed to have inflicted 4,000 casualties and captured 5,000 prisoners, nearly half of the insurgent forces surrounding Manila. As Brigadier General Arthur MacArthur (promoted to Major General during this campaign) advanced north of Manila beyond Malabon, his division was repeatedly attacked. U.S. reinforcements kept arriving, as President McKinley quickly responded to urgent calls for additional men by General Otis. Since Congress, still cautious and left behind by the rapidity of the military situation in the Philippines, had increased the authorized strength of the regular army from the paltry 25,000 of February 1898, to an anemic 65,000 a year later, the President was forced to call up ever increasing numbers of militia units, mostly infantry and artillery from western states, to fight in the Philippines. On March 10, 1899, Major General Henry Lawton, the bold officer who had courageously disregarded Shafter's order to withdraw at the peak of the battle for El Caney eight months previously, arrived at Manila with the 4th Infantry and a battalion of the 17th. There could be no doubt that the government of the United States was taking its new role as a colonial power deadly seriously, committing its entire military resources to the effort.

Through the month of March heavy fighting continued as the U.S. Army divisions advanced north, east and south of Manila. The battalion of Americans which landed at Negros early that month, at the behest of the provincial government, were "magnificently received and entertained" as they began their occupation duties, according to reports from Bacólod, the local capital. On March 31 the U.S. forces captured Malolos, the insurgent capital, and Aguinaldo's government fled. The McKinley administration had appointed the Philippine Commission, consisting of four civilian officials, plus Admiral Dewey and General Otis, to govern the islands and, on April 4, it issued a lengthy proclamation which analyzed the current military and political situations and declared 11 principles of democratic guarantees covering all of the issues of civil rights that would be found in a constitution governing a republic. The wordy preamble to the defined rights stated some interesting "democratic" policies: "The Commission emphatically asserts that the United States is not only willing, but anxious, to establish in the Philippine Islands an enlightened system of government under which the Philippine people may enjoy the largest measure of home rule and the amplest liberty consonant with the supreme ends of government and compatible with those obligations which the United States has assumed towards the civilized nations of the world.

"The United States striving earnestly for the welfare and advancement of the inhabitants of the Philippine Islands, *there can be no real conflict between American sovereignty and the rights and liberties of the Philippine people* (emphasis added). For just as the United States stands ready to furnish armies, navies, and all the infinite resources of a great and powerful nation to maintain and support *its rightful supremacy over the Philippine Islands* (emphasis added), so it is even more solicitous to spread peace and happiness among the Philippine people; *to guarantee them a rightful freedom* (emphasis added); to protect them in their just priveledges and immunities; to accustom them to free self-government in an ever-increasing measure; and to encourage them in those democratic aspirations, sentiments and ideals which are the promise and potency of a fruitful national development." As a statement of long-term democratic goals, it sounded noble; as blatantly imperialistic rhetoric for the immediate convenience and justification of U.S. policy, a German or Spanish propagandist could not have worded it in more strident and contorted verbiage!

The reply of the Filipino government to the American proclamation included the following statements which provided a serious intellectual challenge: ". . . the North American government undertakes to extend its sovereignty over the Philippine Islands, basing its claims upon a title null and void. This title is the treaty of Paris, agreed to by the Spanish-American Commission . . . This contract to cede the islands was concerted and concluded when the Spanish domination had already ceased in the Philippines . . . Moreover, in this act of cession *no voice whatever was allowed the representatives of the Philippine people* (emphasis added) to which belongs the sovereignty of the islands by natural right and international laws. What a spectacle it is to see at the end of the century of enlightenment and of civilization, a people jealous and proud of its own sovereignty employing all its great powers, the result of its own continued free existence, to wrest from another people, weak but worthy of a better fate, the very rights which in its own case it believes to be inherent by law natural and divine!"

As Lawton's and MacArthur's divisions made rapid advances in early May, more indications of dissension and collapse emanated from the Filipino side, as General Antonio Luna, the chief of staff of the insurgent commanding general, was crossing back and forth through the lines since the end of April, even meeting with General Otis in Manila, to effect a cease-fire to give the native congress time to consider ending the fighting. Since the three-month cessation of hostilities proposed by Luna would also give the Filipinos much-needed time to regroup and resupply, the instructions to the Philippine Commission from the State Department in Washington, D.C. were unequivocal and tough: "Promise liberally; promise autonomy

— to follow unconditional surrender." Aguinaldo reportedly disavowed the Luna mission, and on June 6th the self-appointed negotiator was assassinated as he waited to meet with Aguinaldo. The desperate Filipino leader then made his own intentions clear by unilaterally dissolving the Philippine congress and declaring himself "Dictator."

As early as May 11, General Otis reported: "Passage of (U.S. Army) gunboats through Macabebe country hailed with joyful demonstrations by the inhabitants . . . In country passed over by troops temporary civil administration inaugurated and protection to inhabitants against insurgent abuses given as far as possible. Signs of insurgent disintegration daily manifested." But among the fighting units, advancing through mud, fording rivers and engaged for long periods without respite in intense heat and humidity, it was a different

255

story, as reported by the Associated Press on May 12: "...the men (of the 1st Nebraska Regiment) are willing to fight, but are in no condition to do so, owing to the strain of long marching, continual fighting, and outpost duty in which they have been engaged... Since February 2 the regiment has lost 225 men in killed and wounded, and 59 since the battle of Malolos. Only about 300 members of the organization were fit for duty. They have been worked beyond endurance." It was becoming obvious that the 26,000 officers and enlisted men already in the Philippines were an inadequate number to pacify the country and that the pessimistic predictions of some military strategists that it would take as many as 100,000 to achieve that goal, might indeed by accurate. Ships with additional regiments and artillery batteries were arriving weekly in Manila harbor, but the worn-out units could not be rotated back home; every available man was needed.

As General Lawton advanced, Aguinaldo was forced to repeatedly move his government; from Malolos he went to San Isidro and then into rough mountain terrain 12 miles north. It was more than a year since the Battle of Manila Bay, yet vestiges of the Spanish-American War lingered, as armed Spanish garrisons sought to surrender only to American forces in remote parts of the country. The Spaniards were rightfully fearful of giving up to the bloodthirsty natives, and the peace treaty

had specified that the United States was responsible for the safety and return to their homeland of all Spanish *soldados* remaining after the cessation of hostilities between the two belligerents. Various American units were sent to contact the Spanish garrisons, disarm them and bring them to Manila to be processed and shipped home. On May 20, Rear Admiral John Crittendon Watson, who, as a commodore the previous year, was denied the opportunity of sailing his squadron to bombard Spanish coastal targets because the war ended, succeeded Admiral Dewey as commander of the fleet in Manila Bay. As each warship fired the admiral's salute and their bands played "Auld Lang Syne" and "Home, Sweet Home," the *Olympia* sailed majestically away on her four-month journey to a fervent and exultant welcome in New York. Watson did not actually arrive at Manila until June 20, when he raised his flag on the *USS Baltimore*. The next day, according to *Harper's:* "The transport *Centennial*, while on her way to Manila, struck a rock off Cape Engaño, the northeastern point of Luzon, and remained fast for several hours. During this time she was surrounded by swarms of natives in canoes, and her captain was obliged to throw overboard a hundred tons of supplies in order to lighten the ship sufficiently to get her afloat. The Filipinos thereupon abandoned the design of attacking the vessel, and fell to quarreling over the flotsam."

Advancing right into insurgent fire, American soldiers swim a river to assault a Filipino entrenchment.   Frederic Remington

By the end of June, with the approach of the rainy season and the great obstacles to military operations that it would bring, General Otis was able to report to the Adjutant General in Washington, D.C.: "During the rainy season little inland campaigning will be possible in Luzon . . . Insurgent armies have suffered great losses, and are scattered . . . The mass of the people, terrorized by insurgent soldiers, desire peace and American protection; no longer flee on approach of our troops, unless forced by insurgents, but gladly welcome them; no recent burning of towns . . . natives in southeast Luzon combining to drive out insurgents . . . Much contention prevails among (the insurgents) and no civil government remains. Affairs in other islands are comparatively quiet, awaiting results in Luzon; all are anxious for trade, and repeated calls for American troops are received. Our troops have worked to the limit of endurance. Sickness among troops has increased lately, due mostly to arduous service and climatic influences. Nothing alarming. Of the 12 percent of the command reported sick, nearly six percent are in the general hospital . . . Many officers and men who served in Cuba break under recurrence of Cuban fever, and regular regiments lately received are inadequately officered."

Although Otis's report told of serious problems, its more optimistic passages were countered by a press despatch from Manila just five days later: "The outlook at present is more gloomy for a speedy ending of the war than ever before. The method of making raids into the country and then withdrawing, leaving the friendly natives at the mercy of the returning insurgents, has tended to alienate the population and not materially to weaken the insurgents, whose organization is still good . . . More than twice the number of troops already here, including the volunteers, are necessary . . . The troops in the north are in bad condition . . ." It was the lack of enough manpower to occupy vast areas that caused the policy of search, engage and leave, that was so threatening to the natives, so Secretary of War Alger stated, on June 29, that the army in the Philippines would be enlarged to 40,000 — an increase of nearly 14,000 — to get the job done.

Even though a severe rainy season, with typhoons, raged through October and November, the American advance, although slowed by mud and flooding that made use of wheeled vehicles often impossible, was pressed forward, especially in central Luzon, where four of the most formidable and daring of the generals of the 8th Army Corps — Lawton, MacArthur, Wheaton and Young — advanced on San Fabian, Tarlac and Dagúpan. Although American casualties were not light, they were quite acceptable when compared to those of the insurgents; a typical engagement would result in three or four U.S. deaths and 20 to 40 wounded, with their enemies suffering a hundred killed, 200 wounded and scores of prisoners and defectors. Stealth and surprise were utilized in remarkably

good measure by the American commanders against an enemy which, by all the fates of warfare, should have been greatly superior in those categories, resulting in the capture of vast amounts of Filipino guns, ammunition and supplies — including Aguinaldo's personal baggage and some of his staff and close family members.

With the fading of the rainy season and the arrival almost daily of troopships from the United States, a final American offensive was launched, wreaking havoc on the insurgents. Advancing rapidly north and with the railroad and telegraph lines often suffering breaks at the hands of insurgents behind U.S. lines, Lawton and Wheaton were not heard from for days at a time. General Otis's despatch from Manila on November 25 was illustrative of the complexity and confusion: "Vessel from Lingayen Gulf, with despatches from Wheaton to 23 inst., brought in Buencamino, insurgent Secretary of State, captured 21st inst. He was with Aguinaldo, and party left Tarlac night of 13th to be escorted north by 2,000 troops from Bayambang and Dagúpan. These troops Wheaton struck at San Jacinto, and Young eastward. Aguinaldo, with part of family, escaped north with 200 men, passing between Young and Wheaton. Young was still in pursuit at last accounts. Aguinaldo, mother, and oldest child, with Buencamino, separated from rest of party; mother lost in woods, and child four years old, with Wheaton's troops. Two thousand dollars in gold, belonging to the mother, captured, and now in Manila treasury. Heavy storm in Lingayen has prevented loading of troops there for the north. MacArthur has captured insurgent director of railroads, who endeavored to destroy the railroad to Dagúpan; also Captain Lawrence, Englishman, who served in Aguinaldo's artillery . . . Our troops have liberated some three hundred Spanish prisoners recently."

While the insurgents in the Philippines often behaved in a barbaric fashion, at times American troops were no better, as reported by correspondent John T. McCutcheon in the *New York Herald*, concerning the actions of some men of the 33rd Volunteers, referred to as "a second edition of the Rough Riders" since many of them were hardriding and fast-shooting frontiersmen, commanded by officers from 23 states. The 33rd, assigned to Wheaton's command, was fighting hard in the mountains during the expedition to Lingayen Gulf on December 2, 1899: "The fight above the clouds at Tila Pass . . . was in many respects the crowning achievement of the war . . . The general entrusted with the (insurgent) command was Gregorio del Pilar, Aguinaldo's best friend . . ." The Filipinos were well entrenched in rock formations above a zigzag trail where the Americans had to advance with little cover and concealment. They came under sudden, intense Mauser fire and suffered heavy casualties, before another company was able to execute a difficult flanking movement, all the while climbing steep hills covered with jagged rock formations. Upon realizing that rein-

forcements were outflanking the insurgents, "... the troop sprang to its feet, oblivious of danger ... Then, mixed with the sounds of cheering, came the sounds of volleys, and then came the quick popping of Mausers from the rock. There were also smashing reports of Krag-Jorgensens and a blaze from the sharpshooters ... With a wild rush the men followed (Major) March up the winding trail, there was a confusion of rifle reports, in which the Krags and Mausers blended equally; then the Krags seemed louder and the Mausers fainter, and the men of Company E were scrambling over the huge barricade where the insurgents had been a moment before. The latter were endeavoring to escape up the trail to the second barricade half a mile beyond, but as they fled, they were targets for the sharpshooters across the valley, for the men of Company H above them, and for the throng of men behind them in pursuit ... General Gregorio del Pilar was the last man to fall. He was striving to escape up the trail and had already received a wound in the shoulder. A native was holding his horse for him, and just as he was preparing to mount, a Krag-Jorgensen bullet caught him in the neck, and passing through, came out just below his mouth."

Then, the men of the 33rd, who had fought so

One advantage held by U.S. Army forces was their modern breech-loading artillery pieces and the means to move them swiftly (except in the mud of the rainy season) between positions. With a rampart of sandbags and their tents alongside, these gunners are in place just before the battle of Caloocan.

bravely moments earlier, besmirched their own honor: "At that time no one knew who the dead man was, but from his uniform and insignia they judged that he was an officer of high rank. The souvenir fiend was at once at work, and the body was stripped of everything of value, from the diamond ring to the boots." Months later, on March 14, 1900, a letter in the *New York Evening Post* elaborated: "... when del Pilar's body was found, American soldiers stripped it of every bit of clothing, taking the rings from the fingers and a locket from the neck. Not a stitch of any kind was left on the body, everything being taken for souvenirs. For two days the body was left by the roadside unburied, until its odor was offensive, until some (natives) were ordered to cover it with dirt..."

"He towered above the landscape, giant that he was, with his yellow slicker trailing to his feet like a gown. The water streamed from his white helmet in the steady downpour of rain.

258

"Suddenly, when they were within twenty feet of him, he brushed his hand before his left breast, as if stung by an insect, turned his head slightly, and spat a clot of blood; the single exclamation 'God!' came from his lips.

"King, the man who idolized this brave soldier, sprang forward with a cry touched with agony, exclaiming, 'General, are you hurt?' He answered, in a natural voice, 'I'm hit.' King questioned back, 'Where?' and the general replied 'Through the lungs.' These were the last words this wonderful man uttered — a man who was the dominating spirit, though not the highest in rank, of the Army of the Philippines. He swayed backward and forward, clinching his nails into the palms of his hands in one mighty effort to stand on his feet, and fell into King's and Fuller's arms — into the arms of men who in their loyalty and devotion would have sacrificed their own lives gladly to save the other."

That was how William Dinwiddie, a correspondent and friend and confidant of Major-General Henry Ware Lawton, described the death of one of the finest, bravest and distinguished officers in the history of the U.S. Army, as he led his men in a skirmish at San Mateo on December 19, 1899. Lawton was the highest-ranking casualty suffered by America during her rocketing rise to world power in the final three years of the 19th century. When the fight was over, U.S. forces occupied the town at a cost of one dead and 13 wounded — but so expensive a death that one was! The two officers in whose arms the veteran of heavy fighting in the Civil War, the Indian campaigns, the liberation of Cuba and the Philippine Insurrection died, were joined by every soldier and sailor in the war zone, as well as the American nation, in mourning his death so soon before a peaceful retirement, in which he and his ever-devoted and supportive wife had invested their final thoughts together. One of the last utterances she had said, as he left their house in Manila the previous evening, was "...dear. You're going home with me to southern California to raise oranges. That is good enough for us." It was not to be; instead the winner of the Congressional Medal of Honor went back to America, to the resting place of many of her heroes — Arlington National Cemetery. The American troops on Luzon gave their beloved general the most elaborate and respectful of military funerals — a striking contrast to what had befallen another brave and honorable commander who had been their opponent, just 17 days earlier in that Christmas season of 1899!

As the last year of the 19th century began, operations in the north of Luzon pressed forward, while south around Laguna de Bay, the cavalry and infantry of General Theodore Schwan's force went on the offensive, inflicting heavy casualties on the insurgents and capturing many guns, rifles and much provisions and equipment. On February 6, 1900, as the battle for Luzon dragged into its second year, President McKinley appointed a political ally from his home state of Ohio, Judge William Howard Taft, as chairman of the Philippine Commission. Taft later was made Secretary of War in Theodore Roosevelt's administration and, in 1908, he was elected President of the United States, succeeding Roosevelt. Meanwhile, several thousand Spanish prisoners of war, still held by Filipinos, had been liberated, in groups ranging from half a dozen to more than 400. Others were murdered by the insurgents, including forty (as well as 68 Chinese) at Calabanga. As the insurgents suffered more defeats, their behavior became more atrocious, including the beheading of captured American soldiers. A few of the liberated Spaniards had other problems, as related in *Harper's:* "Spanish officers about to be returned to Spain were notified that they must take their Filipino wives with them. This caused consternation, as some of them had wives in Spain. A Spanish lieutenant about to leave for Madrid complained to the Manila Board of Health that his wife was insane. Examination proved otherwise and she was put on the steamer with him."

By April 1, 1900, 63,585 officers and enlisted men, including 15 generals, were engaged with the U.S. Army in the Philippines. Several thousand Navy and Marine Corps personnel were also deployed in suppressing the insurrection. General Otis reported the casualty figures on both sides for the first three months of 1900: "Our casualties were three officers and 78 enlisted men killed, 13 officers and 151 men wounded; insurgent . . . loss in killed and left on field, 1,426; captured, mostly wounded, 1,453; small arms secured, 3,051; pieces of artillery, 165; large captures of other insurgent property. A number of important insurgent officers are surrendering, and the situation is gradually becoming more pacific." The comparatively low figures for American casualties are suspect; these numbers seemed all too similar to the notorious "bodycounts" in Vietnam 70 years later!

Emilio Aguinaldo continued to avoid capture by the Americans and his army, thoroughly devastated by autumn 1900 when William McKinley, with Theodore Roosevelt as his vice presidential running mate, was re-elected President of the United States by a wide plurality, began to disintegrate, turning to hit-and-run guerilla tactics. The Filipino leader was captured at Palanan in 1901, but some of his diehard followers fought on until a peace was declared on July 4, 1902. As a statesman, Aguinaldo renounced violence and cooperated with the victors in developing the Philippines into a modern democratic nation. He lived to realize his lifelong cherished goal when his country achieved independence on July 4, 1946. In the three years of the insurrection he had led between his Spanish-American War alliance with the United States and the more than 40 years of cooperation which preceded independence, nearly 1,000 Americans and more than 10,000 Filipinos were killed; a stark example of the sacrifices endured in the development of the international order at the birth of the American Century.

Photographed in 1899, Filipino insurgent forces are seen in their rudimentary field positions, such as the small garrison guarding a road (opposite, bottom), and at an earthworks and bamboo firing position (above), as well as a hospital (below), constructed with adjoining tents. The group of Filipino soldiers at San Roque (opposite, top) could be prisoners, the man at left appears to be an American solider.

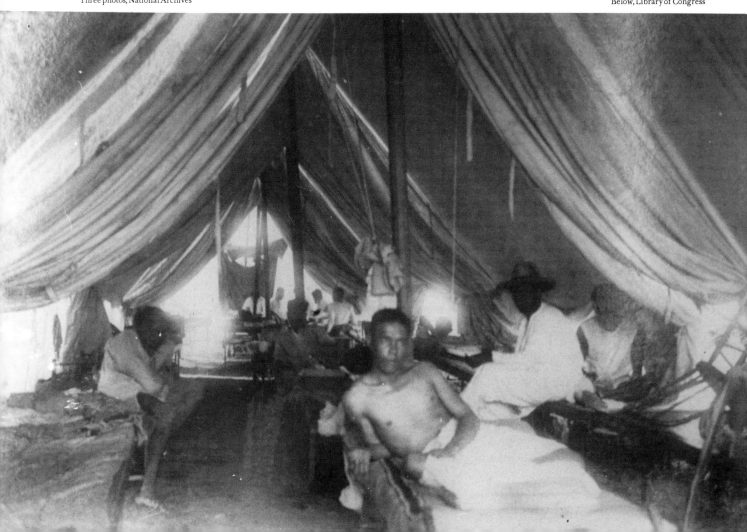

The Filipino insurgent leader (they were fighting the U.S., which called them "insurgents," while the Cubans in arms against Spanish rule were always referred to as "patriots") Emilio Aguinaldo is shown in similar poses (above) wearing civilian clothes as head of government and the uniform of commander of the Philippine Army. His chief of staff, General Antonio Luna (left) tried to negotiate peace with the Americans, but his ef-

forts were repudiated by Aguinaldo, and on June 6, 1899, he was killed by his own men. The general who was Aguinaldo's best friend and confidant was killed at the Battle of Tila Pass on December 2, 1899. Gregorio del Pilar (right) was a dashing young field commander who did not deserve the thievery and disrespect practiced by American soldiers within minutes of his death.

Two insurgent officers, one brandishing a knife, the other with his hand on the hilt of his sword, alongside the thatch headquarters structure, posed in their uniforms and bare feet. The ruggedness and adaptability of the Filipinos who, living off the land, could move more rapidly than the Americans with their heavy supplies, was not enough to impede the advance of the conquerors.

Two photos, Library of Congress

The Americans could be as tough as their Filipino adversaries, as these troops of Company I, Kansas Volunteers in a firing line at Caloocan, will attest. Chomping on a cigar, his .45 revolver at the ready, the squad leader in the foreground certainly appears able to handle anything the enemy may thrust at him and his men.

The battle near Caloocan was a major American victory on February 10, 1899. In a painting made from life by artist G.W. Peters, the battery of Utah artillery is in action and in the

background, on the wall behind the Chinese Church, General MacArthur and staff officers are watching; the 10th Pennsylvania Volunteers wait for the orders to move forward.

The original caption for the photo of troops writing messages and with rifles ready (above) reads: "Pasig. Telegraph station in charge of Corporal Ten Eyke, Signal Corps, near firing line. A short time before this, station was fired on from across the river. The station was then in the shack above. The candle was shot off the table and several shots came through the house. The corporal then moved his instrument below and piled up stones for its protection." Scenes of the action in Manila, after the Americans occupied the city, banning insurgent soldiers from entering: A rare night picture (below) was exposed late on February 22, 1899, as the fires ignited by insurrectionists in the Tondo district raged out of control.

Top photos, National Archives   Bottom, Library of Congress

The mascot of the Idaho Volunteers in the Philippines was an American eagle (above) named "Dewey." The U.S. Army used several small armor-plated gunboats of shallow draught to reinforce infantry attacks along the rivers, and they wreaked much havoc among the Philippine resistance fighters. Since most of the objectives of the American advances were located riverside, the boats, armed with small-calibre rapid-fires and Gatling guns, could move in close to shore, and if the insurgents had no artillery, the little craft could maneuver while pouring in murderous fire, their crews protected from rifle shot by the light armor plating. The four Army gunboats were *Laguna de Bay* (below), *Cavadonga, Napidan,* and *Oeste,* the most active being the one shown, which partook in many engagements against the native partisans with devastating results, as related in the book *The Story of the Spanish-American War and the Revolt in the Philippines,* written by U.S. Navy Lieutenant W. Nephew King and published in 1900: "The *Laguna de Bay* also ascended the Pasig, and did terrible execution at Santa Ana with her Gatlings . . . regiments (were) supported by the Army gunboat *Laguna de Bay* which operated from the Pasig River . . . On April 8, General Lawton, with a force of fifteen hundred men, started to make an attack upon Santa Cruz, about fifty miles from Manila. The expedition was towed up the Pasig River by seven tugs and convoyed by three Army gunboats, the *Laguna de Bay, Napidan,* and *Oeste.* By 1:30 the next day, the gunboats had reached Santa Cruz, and the *Napidan* opened fire on the enemy, four miles south of the town. The troops were then landed, while the *Laguna de Bay* attacked the entrenchments of the village . . . A few days later (in September 1899), Guagua, which had been occupied by two companies of the 9th Infantry, supported by the Army gunboat *Laguna de Bay,* was also attacked by the enemy, but with even more disastrous results than they suffered at Angeles." With their thin armor plating, the little river craft were not referred to as "ironclads," but were affectionately known as "tinclads."

Two photos, National Archives

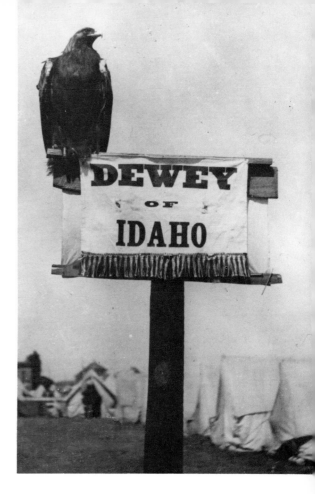

There was at least one photographer present at the battle for Chinese Church and Caloocan, on February 10, 1899. Men of the 10th Pennsylvania Volunteers (right) are ready to fire from the parapet of an old Spanish blockhouse near Chinese Church. Close by, the Utah Light Battery (below) prepare their guns moments before opening fire. From *Harper's* came the story of Captain O'Hara of the 3rd Artillery: "... the 3rd Artillery, acting as infantry ... (American guns) so demoralized the enemy that they deserted the Chinese Church, and flying up the hill, made their last stand on Cemetery Ridge, where is Binondo Church. Captain O'Hara, 3rd Artillery, who does not know when he is in danger, led his men up the hill in full view of everybody, as if they were marching up Broadway, and took the Chinese Church at 2:30 p.m." Generals MacArthur and Frederick Funston (opposite, above) on horseback as they issue orders during the Battle for Caloocan. The entrenchments of the Montana Volunteer Infantry were covered with corrugated metal (opposite, below) in this picture, made shortly before the regiment joined in the attack.

Opposite, above, Library of Congress   Three photos, National Archives

269

A dramatic painting by Frederic Remington (above) shows American troops storming a Filipino position in a bayonet charge, as viewed from the insurgent line. The Kansas Volunteers in action (opposite) in March 1899, firing at enemy entrenchments across the Bigoa River. Although somewhat blurred, the picture of U.S. troops running across a field (below) is of interest since the men were under heavy fire as they assaulted a Filipino stronghold.

The ruggedness of the terrain of rocky hills, swamps, and rivers, with poor or non-existent roads and few railways did little to slow the American advance on Aguinaldo and his Tagalog Army. A field gun (above) was ferried across a river on a raft of rough-hewn tree trunks and palm matting. A firing line and advance guard (below) were shooting at insurgent forces as they moved forward at Antipole on June 3, 1899. By this time Major General Wesley Merritt had been transferred from the Philippines, but his command of American forces besieging Manila added to his long and devoted service record. He was an impressive figure on horseback (opposite), and even his name — Wesley Merritt — sounded like the hero of a war novel. Born in New York in 1834, his family moved to Illinois in 1841, and he graduated from West Point in 1860. There followed a fast rise in rank as a result of his actions in the Civil War: captain, April 1862, and brigadier general of volunteers

a year later, his regular rank being breveted to major for his actions at Gettysburg. He was promoted to lieutenant colonel and colonel, both during the month of May 1864 and major general of volunteers in September. In March 1865, Merritt was breveted both brigadier general and then major general of regulars. Then, in the manner of his army peers, he fought in the last Indian campaigns. In the mid-1880s he was superintendent of West Point, then served as commander of various departments west of the Mississippi River. In May 1898, General Merritt was ordered to command the Army in the Philippines, his 8th Corps taking Manila the day after the war ended. Serving as military governor just two weeks, he was ordered to Paris for the negotiations of the peace treaty with Spain. He retired in June 1900 and died at Natural Bridge, Virginia, on December 3, 1910.

Two photos, National Archives   Opposite, T. de Thulstrup

Above, National Archives

Company M of the 20th Kansas Volunteer Regiment went into action on February 5, 1899, and just a moment after the unit's first combat fatality, a plate was exposed (opposite, top) of the next volley being fired. Just beyond the tenth man from the left, Private Pratt has fallen, shot through the head, several men on either side of him are holding their fire, apparently reacting to his death in the mud and water behind the cover of a rice paddy dike. Life in the field during the Luzon rainy season (opposite, bottom) was not very pleasant, as soggy soldiers spread over soggy ground ate their soggy meals. This illustration by Frederic Remington, showing details such as rain water flowing off hat brims, depicts the constant annoyance and frustration the troops had to live with as they were defeating hardened and well-acclimated foes. On March 31, Malolos, then the insurgent capital, was occupied by American forces (above, below), but Aguinaldo and his officials and military commanders fled further inland, establishing his headquarters in the mountains.

Two photos, Library of Congress

Terrain and conditions on Luzon were rough for the Americans who were fighting there in 1899. 14th Infantry troops manned a sandbag road-block (opposite, top) as they extended their control north from Manila. Fording rivers (opposite, bottom) was a common occurrence. The rugged, hilly terrain made difficult the movement of men, horses, artillery, and wagons as the scene (above) near Santa Cruz illustrates. In the right background, Brigadier General Lloyd Wheaton met with other officers, while in the center, an artillery gun is emplaced and ready. Colonel Emerson H. Liscum (left), one of three commanders of the 3rd Brigade who were casualties within 11 minutes at Bloody Ford during the Battle of San Juan Hill, recuperated from his near-fatal wound and was given command of the 9th U.S. Infantry. After three months in the Philippines, he and the 9th Infantry were detached to join the allied forces in suppressing the Boxer Rebellion in China, where, at Tientsin, on July 13, 1900, Colonel Liscum was killed in action.

Opposite and above, Library of Congress

The commanding general of the U.S. Army in the Philippines before and during the Insurrection was Major General Elwell S. Otis (above), seated in the center with five of his staff officers in Manila. His biography was also typical of his military generation, born in Frederick, Maryland, March 25, 1838, but he was one of the few high-ranking generals not to attend West Point, graduating from the University of Rochester in 1858 and receiving a Harvard Law School degree three years later. He left his law practice in Rochester, New York, to accept a captain's commission in the 14th New York Infantry. Otis saw much Civil War action with the 5th Corps, Army of the Potomac, and he was a lieutenant colonel by the end of 1863. In October 1864, while commanding the regiment, he was severely wounded near Petersburg, ending his service in the War Between the States. He joined the regular army in 1866 as lieutenant colonel of the 22nd Infantry, and for the next 14 years, he fought in the Plains Indian campaigns. Then, in 1881, he established the School of Application for Infantry and Calvary (which later became the Command and General Staff School). From 1885 to 1890 he commanded the 20th Infantry in Montana, then he was in charge of the recruiting service, and then, being promoted to brigadier general in 1893, he headed the Department of the Columbia and later the Department of Colorado. Appointed major general of Volunteers in May 1898, he sailed for the Philippines two months later, to reinforce General Merritt's forces on Luzon, succeeding to command of the Department of the Pacific, the 8th Corps and military governor of the Philippines a few weeks after his arrival, when Merritt was sent to Paris. In May 1900, General MacArthur replaced Otis, who returned to the United States to command the Department of the Lakes until his March 1902 retirement. Major General Otis died on October 21, 1909. Major Generals Lloyd Wheaton (lower left) and Wesley Merritt (lower right), wearing dress uniforms.

Three photos, National Archives

Arthur MacArthur was a prominent and accomplished general in the U.S. Army, but his reputation was to be eclipsed by that of his son, Douglas, who commanded the entire Pacific theatre of operations during World War II. The elder MacArthur (above) was born in Massachusetts in 1845, and in 1862, at the age of just 17 years, he was appointed a first lieutenant of the 24th Wisconsin Infantry. He was awarded the Medal of Honor for bravery at Missionary Ridge, when he was 19 and was severely wounded in Tennessee on November 20, 1864. When he received the regular rank of lieutenant colonel in May 1865 — a few weeks before his 20th birthday — MacArthur also gained fame at the "Boy Colonel of the West." Mustered out of the volunteers, he joined the regulars in 1866, spending more than 20 years on the frontier. Serving in other assignments in the 1890s, he was promoted to Brigadier General of Volunteers and left for the Philippines, where he led his brigade in the capture of Manila. Once again cited for his courage, MacArthur was promoted to major general in August 1898, later being in command of the largest force fighting the Insurrectionists. In 1900, he succeeded Otis and as military governor made many democratic reforms (a record matched by son Douglas when he ruled Japan following World War II). Back in the United States as a major general in July 1901, MacArthur had several departmental commands, then was sent as a special observer with the Japanese in their 1904-05 war with Russia. When Congress authorized the three-star rank of lieutenant general, he was promoted, becoming the Army's ranking officer. Retiring in June 1909, he

died in Milwaukee on September 5, 1912, at the age of 67. Standing with General Otis in front of headquarters in Manila (below), MacArthur posed with staff officers in 1899.

Below, Library of Congress

While attacking Filipino positions on the horizon (opposite), advancing American troops wound up in the path of a crazed herd of carabao, stampeded by the gunfire. One man has been injured by a beast, while his comrades come to his assistance. To these soldiers, the careening water buffalo are a greater threat than the insurgents, who have just shot a man in the background. The Philippine railways were utilized by American forces during the insurgency. A light rapid-fire naval gun and a Gatling (above) were mounted in a gondola car of the Manila-Dagupan line, on August 2, 1899, and a detachment of Signal Corps photographers, armed with huge 8 x 10-inch glass-plate cameras (center) were working at San Fernando on May 1 — the anniversary of the Battle of Manila Bay. American humor surfaces even in such debilitating situations as greeted them in the Philippines, as the graffiti (below) on a steam dummy locomotive shows. Since the Kansas Infantry and Utah artillery regiments had commandeered the engine for their own transportation needs, they lettered it "Kansas and Utah Short Line."

Above and center, National Archives

Below, Library Congress   Opposite, G.W. Peters

One reason that the U.S. Army won every engagement in both the Spanish-American War and the Philippine Insurrection was the impressive expertise and combat experience of all of the generals, that of Major General Henry Ware Lawton being typical. He was born near Toledo, Ohio, on March 17, 1843, leaving college in 1861 when he enlisted in the 9th Indiana Regiment. A few months later, he was commissioned at first lieutenant of the newly organized 30th Indiana and led his men in many hard fights, including Shiloh, Murfreesboro, and Chickamauga; he received the Medal of Honor for his gallantry in the advance on Atlanta on August 3, 1864. Having attained the rank of colonel, Lawton left the Army in November 1865, to attend Harvard Law School, but the military was his calling, so he accepted a lieutenancy in the 41st Infantry (colored), which in turn was merged into the just-activated 24th, which would gain fame in Cuba less than 20 years later. As an officer of the "Buffalo Soldiers," he had the experience of leading black troops, and in January 1871, Lawton was sent to fight the Indians with the 4th Cavalry in the southwest. In 1886, serving under General Nelson A. Miles, Lawton gained respect and renown for leading his men on a grueling 1,300-mile chase through the Sierra Madre Mountains, pursuing and finally capturing Geronimo. A lieutenant colonel in the regular Army when war was declared on Spain, he was made brigadier general of volunteers. After his decisive and courageous leadership in the struggle for El Caney, he was promoted to major general on July 8, 1898, then became the first military governor of Santiago province and city but was transferred to command the 4th Corps at Huntsville, Alabama. In March 1899, Lawton took command of the 1st Division of the 8th Corps on Luzon, capturing Santa Cruz and San Isidro, later forcing the insurgents out of Cavite, and by October, he led the right wing of the push into northern Luzon. Leading an expedition east of Manila, he was killed in action on December 19, 1899, being the highest-ranking American to die in the three-year period of combat operations against Spanish and Filipino forces. In his very basic headquarters tent at Angat, General Lawton (above) studied maps with other officers to his left and right. At the Battle of Baliuag, Lawton, dressed in white helmet and light jacket (opposite, upper left), studied the battlefield with binoculars, with General O. Sumner in the foreground. In the rain at San Mateo on December 19, Lawton clutches his breast where an enemy bullet has just torn through his lungs (opposite, upper right), as two junior officers rush to his assistance. He died almost instantly. General Lawton was wearing his characteristic white pith helmet and a bright yellow slicker that gray morning; it is still a mystery how so knowledgeable and experienced a combat veteran of four wars would purposely dress to stand out that conspicuously, making himself a prime target! The caisson bearing the body, with Lawton's horse with empty saddle behind (opposite, bottom), passes one of many honor guards as it arrives at the Manila docks for shipment home and a hero's burial at Arlington National Cemetery.

Three photos, Library of Congress

282

Various scenes of life (and death) in the Philippines during the insurgency. A group of American prisoners of war (opposite, top) was rescued by Colonel Hare and Lieutenant Colonel Houze, some barefoot and many wearing Filipino clothing. The gruesome scene of dead insurgent soldiers (opposite, bottom), lying just as they fell during an American attack, shows only a few of the bodies in an elaborate circular trench after the Battle for Santa Ana. An army doctor and a medical corpsman give first aid to a soldier (right) who was shot through the forearm just minutes before this picture was made. There were sufficient large buildings in the Philippine towns that in many instances enabled U.S. troops to be housed (below) in relative comfort and security. With rifles, ammunition belts, and canteens hanging along the wall, each man could quickly retrieve his gear if a timely emergency arose.

Opposite, National Archives
Above and below, Library of Congress

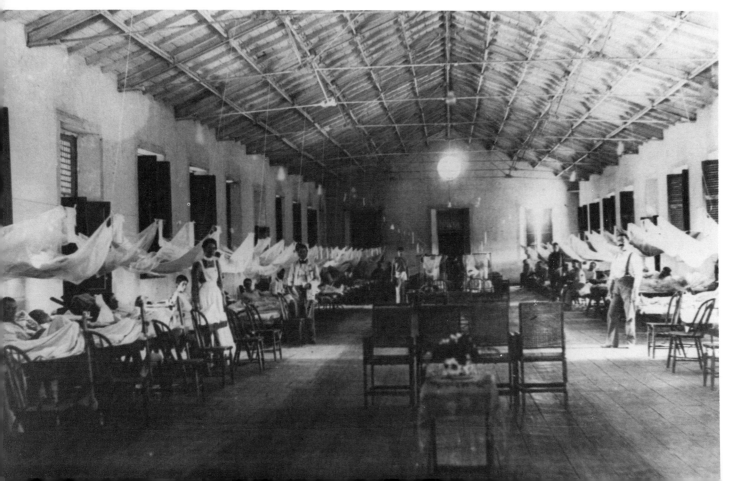

Rough terrain made the transport of severely wounded soldiers a difficult, painful, and sometimes fatal task. One of the methods used was to harness a pair of horses or mules in single file (upper left) with the casualty slung between, this method absorbing much of the shock effect of the movement. Ward No. 2 of the 2nd Division Hospital in Manila (lower left) was spacious with all beds equipped with a mosquito net that was lowered at night. His body covered with a blanket (right), a dead American is brought back from the front on a stretcher. Many U.S. soldiers were already buried in the Battery Knoll Cemetery (below), at Manila, where their graves were decorated with flags and flowers on Memorial Day, May 30, 1899. Over the following two years, hundreds more would join them.

Three photos, National Archives   Right, Library of Congress

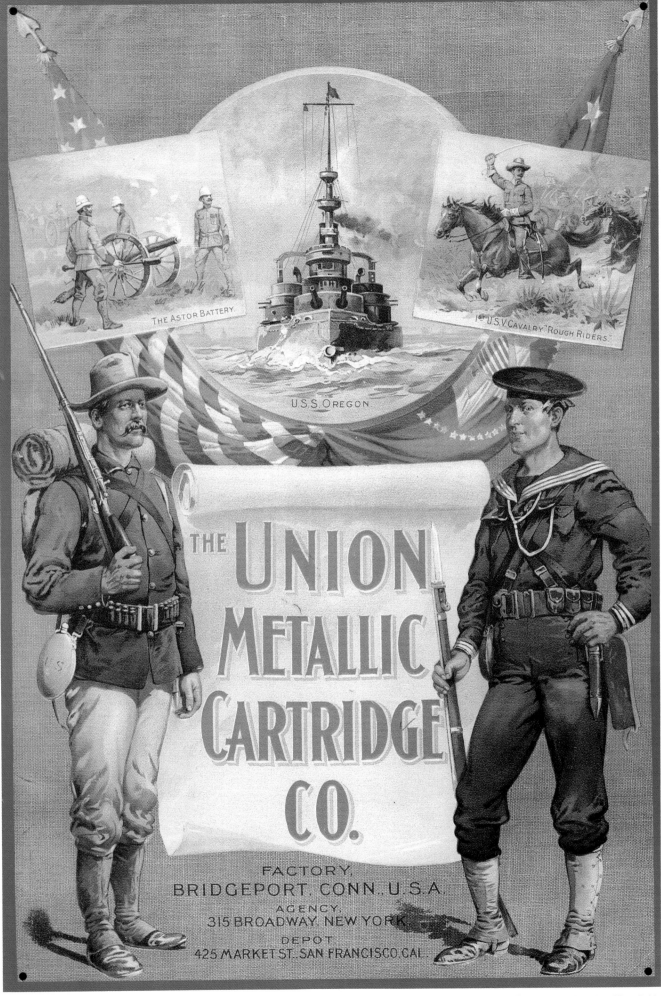

THE ASTOR BATTERY.

1st U.S.V. CAVALRY "ROUGH RIDERS."

U.S.S. OREGON

THE UNION METALLIC CARTRIDGE CO.

FACTORY,
BRIDGEPORT, CONN., U.S.A.
AGENCY,
315 BROADWAY, NEW YORK.
DEPOT,
425 MARKET ST., SAN FRANCISCO, CAL.

20th Century Legacy of the War

With the end of the war with Spain and the securing of the Philippines, the United States had found that events which had occurred so rapidly, unexpectedly and beyond its control, had propelled it into the forefront of the most powerful nations of the world. The American people and their government quickly emerged from their bemused fixation, as the newspapers and publishers began churning out vast amounts of reading material concerning the newly acquired possessions. The century-old slogan of "Manifest Destiny" — the irresistible force which would secure a continent-wide land mass for the American nation — was quickly transformed into a far more expansive interoceanic dimension. Although the United States had gone into the recent war largely unprepared and totally inexperienced, it had learned quickly and well, with grim realization of the expenditures — human and financial — that would be necessary to retain and expand on the gains of 1898. It would not do just to try to match Germany or Japan in warship construction — a parity might even eventually have to be reached with the grandest sea power of all, Great Britain. The celebrated 13,000-mile run of the *USS Oregon* around South America had been a stark awakening that even before the United States had graduated to major-power status, transferring warships from one seacoast to the other was a prohibitive exercise. With the huge expansion of the Navy planned, a canal across Central America had become an absolute national security as well as a commercial priority, and there was no question that it could and would be built immediately, and by Americans. Mahan's theories concerning sea power and the prosperity and security of modern nations had already been accepted as unconditional gospel; now they must be implemented!

The fact that, aside from the challenges emanating from the German fleet in Manila Bay, which were diplomatically and brusquely answered by Admiral Dewey, there was no serious disputing of American actions by the other powers, only reinforced the totality of the victories over Spain, as well as the seeming invincibility of the United States. The overwhelming formidability of American arms, built up after just a few weeks with little preparation, dumbfounded every general staff and admiralty around the world. Their intricate battle strategies, huge standing armies and navies, and cherished military doctrines were severely shaken by the accomplishments of the upstart, uncivilized and crude "mercenaries" who had steamed out of the frontier of North America to annihilate one of Europe's oldest colonial empires. The emerging international role of the United States was all the more disconcerting, since alliances were being forged, preparatory to World War I, which many already foresaw and which was to break out just 16 years later. Lest any European military authorities be lulled into thinking that the Spanish-American War had been merely an aberration and that isolationism and shortsightedness would turn the policies of Americans inward once again, the no-quarter-given campaign in the Philippines, plus the United States taking a leading role in suppressing the Boxer Rebellion in China in 1900, made it clear that not only would the new great power stay involved, but it surely intended to eventually dominate in world affairs.

Of course, isolationism was far from finished in the United States, but the American people were quick to realize at the turn of the 20th century that they had no choice but to become participants in international politics, now that their country had suddenly emerged as the dominant ascending power. This was to prove to be a troublesome conundrum over the ensuing half-century, as the United States went through the growing pains of the assumption of world leadership. Had not the first American president, George Washington, wisely advised against the pitfalls of "entangling foreign alliances" in his farewell address? Leaders of the young republic, during its first century, had rightfully avoided the complexities and dangers of European intrigues, relying on the surrounding oceans to isolate her during her vulnerable adolescence. But in 1898, America had matured in just four months and destiny beckoned her to control the vast expanses of sea that had protected her. Indeed, it was to be the issue of "Freedom of the Seas" that would be the principal cause of U.S. intervention in World War I. But once that conflict was won, many Americans cried "Enough!," and an isolationist mood took hold, resulting in rejection of the League of Nations, the imposition of high tariffs and other manifestations of a "fortress America" mentality. The prevalent attitude of the public and Congress during the 1920s and 30s was a cause of the unpreparedness that was to prove so disastrous for American armed forces in the early months of World War II. While isolationism surged again after the defeat of Germany and Japan in 1945 and following the demise of Communism by 1990, the bitter lessons had been learned, and the United States continued in its role as leader and protector.

While most governments had vacillated or had supported Spain, then seemed undecided as to how to handle the delicate business of the roaring ma-

The advertisement for the Union Metallic Cartridge Co. (left) was a good example of 1890's advertising art. Patriotic posters, illustrations and advertising in 1898 which showed both a representative soldier and sailor invariably presented the soldier as appearing older than the sailor and wearing a mustache. The younger salts were always clean-shaven, as seen here and on pages 1 and 10.

With the *USS Connecticut* in front, part of the 16-battleship Great White Fleet is seen at the beginning of its 14-month, 46,000- mile journey around the world in December, 1907. During the presidency of Theodore Roosevelt, the fleet had increased in size five-fold, eventually becoming the most formidable sea power in the World.

turing of the American lion cub, there was apparently not the slightest doubt in London, dating right back to the day that the U.S. Navy Asiatic Squadron sailed out of Hong Kong, bound for Manila Bay. For a century and a half, relations between the United Kingdom and the United States had fluctuated between cooperative loving trust and all-out warfare, with the American Revolution of 1776-1783 and the War of 1812, which ended in 1815, being the worst periods. With the passing of a half-century, at the end of the American Civil War, fading animosities caused by the early conflicts, the continuing strong bonds of language, culture and religion, plus immigration and increasing trade, all combined to juxtapose the destinies of the former mother country and her first breakaway colonies. British intervention in the *Virginius*

crisis in Cuba in 1873 had gained the appreciation of the Americans, and even disputes which could have grown into serious military confrontation as late as the mid-1890s could not hinder the drifting of the two nations toward an alliance. It was to be the Spanish-American conflict that sealed it, contributing greatly to the outcomes of the two world wars and numerous other crises over the next one hundred years and into the third millennium. Anglo-American cooperation in the Korean War,

British muting of criticizing the United States over Vietnam and American support of England in the Falklands War, plus U.S. support of the U.K. in touchy colonial issues, including Hong Kong in the 1990s, all helped decisively in maintaining the world order. The most serious breach was the Suez Crisis of 1956, when the United States sided with Egypt against the Anglo-French-Israeli attack. The arrogance of the Germans at Manila Bay toward the United States, coupled with British support turned the mood of American public opinion toward deep suspicion of Teutonic intentions, contributing to later decisions by Washington to side with America's British brothers against her German cousins.

An alliance with the United States was a natural extension of the British policy of joining with the weaker side in European disputes to maintain the balance of power, thereby diminishing threats to her own sovereignty. Germany, France, Spain, Russia, Japan — even little Belgium and Holland — could separately, or more menacingly, in concert, threaten English political and commercial interests, but with a closely allied powerful United States, a peaceful *status quo* would be of great benefit to London. Although unannounced publicly, this policy was apparent to British naval officers in 1898, for when Admiral von Diedrichs sought the support of the Royal Navy in his confrontations with Admiral Dewey in Manila Bay, Captain Chichester, with little subtlety, answered, "Ask Admiral Dewey." As the German officers left the English man-of-war, its band struck up *The Star-Spangled Banner!"*

Such pro-American acts, plus British government pronouncements and diplomatic moves, dampened a very serious threat that European powers would intervene, especially in the Philippines, on the side of Spain, enabling, according to Watterson: ". . . the President to express, under terms of courteous acknowledgment, the unalterable determination of the United States not to permit interference by the European concert in any of our differences with Spain, was as annoying to the concert as it was gratifying to the American people. At the opportune moment Great Britain had chosen between aliens in language and political ideals and a people possessing substantially those she possessed. And she chose her own."

Senior English officials continued to raise the pro-American rhetoric, culminating in a speech at Birmingham by Colonial Secretary John Chamberlain, on May 13, 1898, less than two weeks after the Battle of Manila Bay: "A new situation has arisen and it is right that the people of this country should have it under their consideration. All the powerful States of Europe have made alliances, and as long as we keep outside these alliances, as long as we are envied by all, and suspected by all, and as long as we have interests which at one time or another conflict with the interests of all, we are liable to be confronted at any moment with a combination of Great Powers so powerful that not even the most

extreme, the most hot-headed politician would be able to contemplate it without a certain sense of uneasiness. That is the situation which I want you to have in view, which you must always have in view, when you are considering the results of the foreign policy of any government in this country. We stand alone, and we may be confronted with such a combination as that I have indicated to you. What is the first duty of a government under these circumstances? I say, without hesitation, that it is to draw all parties of the empire closer together, to infuse into them a spirit of united and imperial patriotism. We have not neglected that primary duty. We have persued it steadfastly and with results that are patent to all the world. Never before in the history of the British Empire have the ties which connected us with our great colonies and dependencies been stronger; never before has sense of common interests in trade and in defense and in war — never before has the sense of these interests been more strongly felt or more cordially expressed.

"What is our next duty? It is to establish and to maintain bonds of permanent amity with our kinsmen across the Atlantic. They are a powerful and a generous nation. They speak our language, they are bred of our race. Their law, their literature, their standpoint upon every question are the same as ours: their feeling, their interest in the cause of humanity and the peaceful development of the world are identical with ours. I do not know what the future has in store for us. I do not know what arrangements may be possible with us, but this I know and feel — that the closer, the more cordial, the fuller and the more definite these arrangements are with the consent of both peoples, the better it will be for both and for the world. And I even go so far as to say that, terrible as war may be, even war itself would be cheaply purchased if in a great and noble cause the Stars and Stripes and the Union Jack should wave together over an Anglo-Saxon alliance. Now it is one of the most satisfactory results of Lord Salisbury's policy that at the present time these two great nations understand each other better than they have ever done since more than a century ago. They were separated by the blunders of the British Government."

This startling endorsement of an Anglo-American alliance, wherein Britain considered the United States to be her equal in power and prestige, came as a shock to all the European powers and an inflation of national pride to the Americans. It obviously had the full endorsement of Queen Victoria's Government, for no minister could have made so daring a commitment without prior consultation and approval. So impressive had been Dewey's victory at Manila Bay that the most powerful nation in the world did not even await the outcome of the conflict to pick the winner and join forces with the United States! So it was that the most powerful and lasting alliance through all of the 20th century and beyond was formed because of the virtually forgotten Spanish-American War; that "Special Relationship" between the United

A "BONE IN HIS TEETH."

The two most recognizable images of Theodore Roosevelt — the Rough Rider and the powerful Navy proponent — were combined in a popular political cartoon, with the face of Roosevelt on the bow of a battleship and naval guns protruding from the superstructure, which is his Spanish-American War campaign hat. The bow wave — the "bone in this teeth" — is his "Big Stick" foreign policy. At the Naval Academy on May 2, 1902, the President prognosticated his view of the importance of sea power in the new century: "We — all of us — earnestly hope that the occasion for war may not arise, but if it has to come, then this nation must win; and...in winning, the prime factor must of necessity be the U.S. Navy. If the Navy fails, then we are doomed to defeat. It should therefore be an object of prime importance for every patriotic American to see that the Navy is built up; and that it is kept to the highest point of efficiency, both in personnel and material."

Kingdom and the United States.

Following close on the Chamberlain speech was a revealing commentary in the Social Democratic publication in Germany, which must have reflected popular opinion, there being no objections from the Kaiser's regime: "Into the putrid swamp of European politics has been cast a stone, and the turbid, slimy waters spout up. The great Republic on yonder side of the ocean, without castles, nobles, or a standing army, has suddenly sprung out of her position of neutrality to Europe, and one European State which has slaughtered myriads of men wrestling for freedom is undone. Old Europe, in consequence, is shaken to her foundations. It is a new power — no militarism, no huge fleet, yet a mighty, an overwhelmingly mighty, elemental power.

"In Asia the same phenomenon has appeared. The new power has become the balance of the scales. Even if an alliance with England comes to nothing, the new American position in the Far East crosses every combination hitherto effected."

President William McKinley, aware of both the tides of history and the wishes of the American people, was to steer a prudent course ahead as he constructed a powerful foundation for the ascendancy of the United States to global dominance in the coming American century. His policies were cautious, but unwavering and effective, as he forged the means by which his successor in office, Theodore Roosevelt, of a much more volatile and aggressive temperament, was able to assure that the United States would profoundly influence — then dominate — international events and relationships. When McKinley was assassinated in September 1901 Vice President Roosevelt was not yet 43 years of age — the youngest President to take office. Many high government officials at home and abroad feared that Roosevelt was but a hip-shooting warmonger who would embroil the United States in conflicts with great and lesser powers all over the world, but his foreign policy credo of "Speak softly, but carry a big stick" proved — for all time — to be the only sure diplomatic guarantor of peace. In fact, President Roosevelt became the first American to win the Nobel Peace Prize, when he used his considerable persuasive talents to negotiate the end of the Russo-Japanese War in 1905.

Based on Roosevelt's experience as Assistant Secretary of the Navy and Cavalry Colonel in the Spanish-American War, he worked closely with trusted confidants such as Mahan and Senator Lodge, as well as General Wood and other intellectual imperialists, to construct for the United States the "Big Stick" needed to reinforce his soft-speaking diplomacy. Of the first order was the digging of the Panama Canal — the largest and most expensive public works project ever accomplished. Blatantly engineering the secession of the province of Panama from Colombia, he had a treaty to build the canal within days of Panamanian independence. Equal in importance was the creation of a vast armada of battleships, the President calling for a construction schedule of one ship quarterly. With the canal project progressing at a feverish pace (66 giant railroad steamshovels working at one time in Culebra Cut alone), the President combined his naval administrative experience with his executive powers to order an around-the-world cruise of the 16 largest and newest big-gun vessels in the fleet.

Many naval experts were of the opinion that it would be impossible to send a big fleet of capital ships on a sustained voyage around the world without long intervening delays for maintenance and even major overhauls, but the President, recalling the grand dash of the *USS Oregon*, had great faith in his ships and the crews which manned them, with two pressing political objectives overruling all caution. Roosevelt knew that the successful unprecedented daring voyage, which would span 14 months and 46,000 miles (the equivalent of nearly twice circumnavigating the globe) would focus the attention of the entire world on the sea power of the United States, and, with a major crisis looming in the Pacific with Japan, "showing the flag" in such an impressive and sobering manner would cool down the imbroglio. Critics feared that the Yankee armada sailing not only into the western Pacific, but right into Japanese waters, could be the ignition of a Nipponese-U.S. conflict. Although Roosevelt had brokered the end of the Russo-Japanese War the previous year, the victorious Japanese felt shortchanged and American opposition to Japanese workers coming to the United States was a major affront to their national honor. According to *The U.S. Navy, An Illustrated History*, by Nathan Miller: "With most of the U.S. Navy concentrated in the Atlantic, Roosevelt was anxious to avoid an open break with Japan. The United States was so ill-prepared for war in the Far East that the Orange Plan, drafted by a joint Army-Navy board for use in the event of such a conflict with Japan, required that the Philippines be abandoned and the Asiatic Fleet be withdrawn to the west coast until America had the strength to go on the offensive. Roosevelt hoped, therefore, through diplomatic negotiation, to freeze the *status quo* in the Far East before the balance of power tipped too far in Japan's favor." That was *Theodore* Roosevelt in 1906; it could have been the same scenario for *Franklin* Roosevelt in 1941!

Despite the racial tensions, epitomized by California officials barring Japanese pupils from attending classes with native Americans (which Roosevelt condemned as "foolish"), Anglo-Nipponese ties were strong, dating back a half-century, so both sides worked to cool the ardor. After sailing from Hampton Roads, Virginia, around South America and up the West Coast of the United States, the Great White Fleet headed west across the Pacific, the Japanese welcoming its visit to Yokohama, which defused the crisis and proved again the wisdom of Roosevelt's "Big Stick" policy. Continuing onward, the battleships went across the Indian Ocean, through the Suez Canal and the Mediterranean Sea, visiting many ports before returning home in February, 1909, just before President Roosevelt left office. The work he had begun as Assistant Secretary of the Navy in 1897 was completed a dozen years later; as the father of the modern U.S. Navy, Theodore Roosevelt had been primarily responsible for making American sea power eventually becoming the dominant force on the surface (and later, above and beneath the surface) of the

---

Admiral Dewey's flagship, *USS Olympia* (below), is the only surviving U.S. Navy warship from the Spanish-American War era and historically the most important vessel, for when she led the Asiatic Squadron into Manila Bay in the pre-dawn of May 1, 1898, she was unleashing the chain reaction that would profoundly alter the

entire world order and make the 1900s the American Century. She was still in Navy service as a training ship in the World War II era and very well preserved in much of her original configuration. The *Olympia* is open to the public at her retirement site, the Delaware River waterfront in Philadelphia, Pennsylvania.

Ron Ziel

world's oceans. It was all a direct result of the "Splendid Little War" of 1898 and the vision of its most influential personality.

The events and policies of William McKinley's presidency had made the United States into a great world power and those of Theodore Roosevelt's administration had provided the impetus to ensure the maintenance and expansion of American influence and might far into the future; each succeeding chief executive building on the McKinley-Roosevelt foundations. The Panama Canal, having become an absolute imperative because of the War with Spain, was to be the site of the greatest celebration the world had ever seen, when it opened the first week of August, 1914. But in one of the saddest ironies in all of human history, the very day that one of mankind's grandest, most noble accomplishments was celebrated, was also the beginning of the greatest self-inflicted calamity of nations up to that time — World War I! The great parade of the naval capital ships of 50 nations through the canal was cancelled and not one head of state of the great powers was in attendance — perhaps the ultimate triumph of evil over good. Not only was the opening of the canal an unprecedented boon to world commerce, but while open to ships of all nations, it was to be the U.S. Navy that would be the greatest beneficiary.

Power abhors a vacuum and overlapping concentrations of power can create mammoth explosions. With the recent possessions acquired by the westward race of American power across the Pacific Ocean during the Spanish-American War heading right into the teeth of the southerly and easterly expansion of the Japanese Empire, war between the two nations immediately became a possibility and, in less than a decade, a probability. The wisdom of having outmaneuvered the Japanese in the acquisition of Hawaii was quickly realized in the United States, and when war between the two greatest Pacific powers finally commenced on December 7, 1941 with the attack on Pearl Harbor, the value of the islands, more than 2,000 miles from the continental United States, was appreciated with relief. Had the Hawaiian Islands been the base of the Imperial Japanese Navy, rather than the American fleet, the World War II battle cry of "Remember Pearl Harbor!" would instead have been "Remember San Francisco!" True to the vision of the U.S. Army-Navy Orange Plan of 35 years earlier, the Philippines and all other colonial possessions in the Far East were quickly overrun by Japanese naval and ground might by the spring of 1942. Under the command of Admirals Spruance, Halsey and Nimitz and General Douglas MacArthur, the Japanese threat to American security, which arose because of the 1898 war, ended with the unconditional surrender and occupation of the Japanese home islands in 1945. MacArthur, whose father had been Military Governor of the Philippines in 1900-01, was chosen to rule Japan during six years of American occupation. Both generals are remembered for their democratic reforms and for laying the groundwork of turning defeated and devastated countries into strong economic and human-rights proponents.

Even through the second half of the 1900s the legacy of the Spanish-American War was strongly impressed upon the American population, with the Communist regimes of the Soviet Union and China, as well as North Korea and Vietnam, challenging U.S. interests, resulting in two major Far East conflicts during the 1950s to the 1970s. Even in 1996, American B-52 bombers based on Guam were attacking targets in Iraq. The strategic importance of the possessions wrested from Spain had increased over 100 years! The proximity of the bases established in those locations ensures the quick projection of American power wherever and whenever it is required in the Pacific Basin, be it the Taiwan Straits, Korea or Southeast Asia. The added combat and diplomatic factor of air power — never envisioned in 1898 — has become even more important in the utilization of the far-flung bases than their original purpose of servicing the battleship fleet. The capital ships are now 90,000-ton plus aircraft carriers — the mobile airbases of modern warfare. It was entirely appropriate that one of the biggest and most sophisticated warships in the world, the aircraft carrier USS Theodore Roosevelt (CVN-71) was commissioned in the 1980s as a flagship of U.S. Navy might to carry the memory of the man most responsible for her and a thousand preceding and succeeding men-of-war onto the high seas.

At the beginning of the third millennium, the United States stood astride the land masses, the sea lanes and the airways of the world as a great — although at times bumbling — keeper of the peace and missionary of democratic and free societies, as the only superpower that the world had ever known. (The now-vanquished Union of Soviet Socialist Republics never was entitled to be honored with the term superpower; a more accurate description being "third-world country with rockets." After World War II, Western Europe and Japan became economic superpowers, the Soviet Union a military superpower; only the United States, through the second half of the 20th century, was both.) Looking forward, beyond the year 2000, there appeared to be no compromising of the formidable Pax Americana. The roots of that singular accomplishment by the United States were planted in 1898 by the second most important conflict in its history, which in just four months had turned the Pacific Ocean into an American lake and the Caribbean Sea into an American pond. Yet the understanding of the Spanish-American War and its long-term ramifications is completely lost after just 100 years. Even prominent scholars of history appear to reside in a haze of ignorance concerning the importance of the awesome American onslaught of 1898. It transformed the United States into a great world power and was the midwife at the birth of the American Century.

Wars produce great military operations in the fields and oceans, and souvenirs and relics preservation on the homefront, and although the Spanish-American War was short, it left as a legacy much in the way of commemorative items and collectibles, including some fascinating advertising art. A Krag-Jorgensen rifle in good condition brings about $500.00 a century after its extensive use and the carbine is worth considerably more. Interesting bits of victorian *schmaltz* include the three items (above) of parlor decoration. In the foreground, the pair of glass ships, (*USS Oregon* at left and "Remember the *Maine*" at right) whose superstructures lift off, were candy jars. Behind them stands a weird kerosene lamp, the shell portion embossed with a likeness of the *Olympia* and the lettering "Admiral Dewey's Lamp" and "Remember the *Maine*"; the globe also shows the ship. All that remains of the most celebrated battleship of the era which saw the beginning of the modern U.S. Navy, are the two smokestacks and the mast (below) — a poor legacy of the *USS Oregon* displayed in the Battleship Oregon Memorial Marine Park, in Portland, Oregon. For many years, the historical vessel was displayed in Portland, on loan from the Navy, where she became a popular attraction. Then, in 1942, the Navy sought her return, so the superstructure and interior fittings could go to the World War II scrap drive, while the gutted hull would be used to transport a cargo of high explosives to Guam. A raucous public furor then commenced, with one side rightfully abhorred at the very idea of the destruction of the great man-of-war and the other sickly proclaiming that the grand ship would also be serving in the current war — by its scrap being used to build modern weapons! Sadly, the shortsighted scrap hounds won and just these relics and a few lesser ones remain. Wars are fought for national survival, one of the most important factors of which is the heritage of past struggles and accomplishments. For

a paltry 5,000 tons of scrap steel and using the hull of the *Oregon* as an explosives barge, the only surviving first-generation American battleship was sacrificed. The United States accomplished in World War II what its' enemies could not do, hard as they tried: the destruction of the American heritage!

Above, Ron Ziel *Maine*, lamp, Richard Keogh collection   Below, Eric Fellows

President Roosevelt's grand circumnavigation of the earth by the Great White Fleet was an expensive and hotly-debated exercise, but it achieved its two objectives: it impressed all of the nations that may have contemplated challenging American power and by making an extended visit to Japan, strained relations between the two Pacific powers were eased. Led by *USS Kansas* and *USS Vermont* (right), the fleet is shown at the start of its long voyage, leaving Hampton Roads, Virginia. Less than ten years previously, Dewey, Schley and Sampson would not have imagined that their Navy could grow so fast and to such a degree! The Japanese accorded the ships a warm welcome when they arrived at Yokohama, where the junior officers of His Imperial Japanese Majesty's Ship *HIJMS Nisshin* posed on board the first battleship *USS Missouri* (below), with her junior officers. When the Great White Fleet steamed back to Hampton Roads just a few weeks before Roosevelt left office, he boarded *USS Connecticut* along with other officials (lower right), to give a welcoming address on George Washington's birthday, February 22, 1909.

Three photos, U.S. Naval Historical Center.

Having become a great power so rapidly and unexpectedly in 1898, the United States moved quickly and overwhelmingly to consolidate its ascending dominance of the world order. As soon as he became President, Theodore Roosevelt launched the intrigues and political forces that would assure that the United States would build and operate an isthmian canal across Central America. Rather than pick up where the French left off after their disastrous canal construction attempt in Panama, many American experts favored the much-touted route across southern Nicaragua, the final decision favoring Panama not being made until shortly before digging commenced. Hindsight shows that the rejected route was preferable, for the canal would have been along the southern edge of Nicaragua, rather than running right through the center of the country, as in Panama, a major irritant to the Panamanians, being the prime motivation of their demands to take it over. The

strategic importance of the Panama Canal to the U.S. Navy is emphasized in the picture of three battleships (upper right), in transit through the locks on August 31, 1915, just a year after the opening of the canal. The *USS Missouri* (left) and *USS Ohio* (right) are in the locks while *USS Wisconsin* waits in the background. In a picture taken about fifteen years after the Spanish-American War, the Atlantic Fleet is shown at the base at Guantanomo Bay, Cuba (lower right), the facility having begun as a coaling station for Admiral Sampson's blockading squadron even before Cuba was liberated in 1898. Perhaps the most vital of all U.S. Navy bases was — and still is — Pearl Harbor, Hawaii (above), which also passed to U.S. sovereignty in 1898. This aerial view, taken just a year and half before the Japanese attack, gives a good idea of the peaceful scene that greeted the enemy bombers!

Three photos, U.S. Naval Historical Center

The legacy of the Spanish-American War a century later. The aircraft carrier *USS Theodore Roosevelt* (CVN-71), launched on October 27, 1984, is shown at sea (opposite), with about one-fourth of her aircraft on the flight deck. Originally slated for a different name, President Ronald Reagan ordered that the ship be named for the father of the modern U.S. Navy. It is one of the few Navy ships that has a museum aboard, honoring its namesake, as well as a civilian support organization: The Theodore Roosevelt Association, her captain having told the author that his peers commanding other ships are quite envious of what the T.R.A. has done for his ship and crew. Like the battleships they replaced as capital ships, the super carriers such as CVN-71 are the dreadnoughts at the birth of the 21st century. A popular illustration shows a bow view of *USS Theodore Roosevelt* with the thought-provoking slogan: "90,000 tons of Diplomacy." That she is, bringing to ultimate fulfillment the work and the vision of great men like Mahan, Dewey and Roosevelt, as well as many others in the armed forces and in government who seized the outcome of the Spanish-American War, realized its fateful ramifications, and showed the way for the United States to become the only superpower in the history of the world.

U.S. Department of Defense

Recommended Reading

Admiral George Dewey. John Barrett. Harper & Brothers, New York, 1899.

A Ship to Remember: The Maine and the Spanish-American War. Michael Blow. William Morrow and Company, New York, 1992.

*Colonel Roosevelt. Theodore Roosevelt goes to War, 1897-1898.** H. Paul Jeffers. John Wiley & Sons, Inc., New York, 1996.

Harper's Pictorial History of the War with Spain (in two volumes). Harper & Brothers Publishers, New York, 1899.

Harper's History of the War in the Philippines. Harper & Brothers, New York, 1900. (Published well before the war ended!).

History of the Spanish-American War. Henry Watterson. A. J. Holman & Co., Philadelphia, 1898.

The American Colonial Handbook. Thomas Campbell Copeland. Funk & Wagnalls Co., New York, 1899.

*Although *Colonel Roosevelt* contains some glaring errors, it is a lively read and informative.

The Influence of Sea Power Upon History. Alfred Thayer Mahan. Little, Brown, and Company, Boston, 1890.

The Little War of Private Post. Charles Johnson Post. Little, Brown, and Company, Boston, 1960.

The McKinley and Roosevelt Administrations, 1897-1909. James Ford Rhodes. The Macmillan Company, New York, 1922.

The Rise of Theodore Roosevelt. Edmund Morris. Coward, McCann and Geoghean, 1979.

The Rough Riders. Theodore Roosevelt. Corner House Publishers, Williamstown, Mass., 1979. (Reprint).

There are many other books, some dealing with the entire subject of the Spanish-American War and the Philippine Insurrection, others with individual facets, including naval operations, political and diplomatic venues, economics, Army operations and other topics. Those listed here are of the greatest interest for those who wish to acquire basic knowledge of the attainment of Great Power status by the United States. At publication time (Autumn, 1997) major cinematic and television shows were being produced to observe the centennial.

Larger, heavier and more deadly battleships were under construction before the War with Spain began and one month before hostilities actually commenced, the Newport News Shipbuilding Company in Virginia launched two big battleships on the same day — March 24, 1898 — in an impressive display of the industrial might of the United States. Not all American battleships were named for states, BB-5 being the *USS Kearsage*, christened to honor the memory of the famed Union wooden sloop-of-war, launched in 1861 and named for a mountain in New Hampshire. Her sister was the *USS Kentucky* (BB-6), both of which had a controversial turret arrangement that was not to be repeated. As the gun-plan top view of both ships shows, the problem of having the 8-inch turrets mounted on the sides, rather than the center-line, which limited their traverse range, was resolved by mounting an 8-inch turret on top of the 13-inch turret. While using just two turrets to replace four — as on the older ships — the problems in coordinating the piggyback arrangement were formidable. Since the 8-inch turrets were rigidly mounted, they could not be traversed independently, with just separate elevation of the guns being possible. The 8-inchers were mere satellites of their 13-inch turret foundations and could only fire at the same target. Weighing more than 11,500 tons, *Kearsage* and *Kentucky* had four 13-inch and four 8-inch turret guns; 14 5-inch broadside mounts and sixteen 6-pounders.

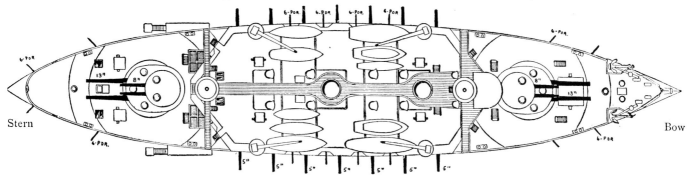

Stern   Bow

Index

*Artillery, Cavalry and Infantry operations are so prolific that they are omitted from this Index.

Transportation of U.S. Army supplies in the Philippines during the Insurrection.

Night maneuvers of the North Atlantic U.S. Navy squadron during patrolling operations in the Spanish-American War.

Artwork by R.F. Zogbaum